THE CAMBRIDGE COMPANION TO

H.D.

H.D. (Hilda Doolittle) was one of the central figures in literary modernism in the 1910s. She collaborated with Ezra Pound and others and played an important role in the early development of modernist poetry. The *Cambridge Companion* is a critical introduction to H.D.'s work containing essays on all her major works. The first part explores the author's initial exclusion from the canon and her subsequent reinstatement; her tendency to merge fact with fiction in her autobiographical texts; her contribution to the 'little magazines'; her relation to modernism; her representation of gender; and her influence on later generations of writers. The second part offers close and accessible critical analyses of H.D.'s style, her poems *Hymen* and *Trilogy*, her novels *HERmione* and *Majic Ring*, her understanding of translation as literary practice and of her notion of history in *Tribute to Freud* and *The Gift*.

NEPHIE J. CHRISTODOULIDES was a lecturer in English at the University of Cyprus.

POLINA MACKAY is Assistant Professor of English at the University of Nicosia.

A complete list of the books in the series is at the back of this book.

THE CAMBRIDGE COMPANION TO

H.D.

EDITED BY

NEPHIE J. CHRISTODOULIDES AND POLINA MACKAY

CAMBRIDGE
UNIVERSITY PRESS

CAMBRIDGE UNIVERSITY PRESS
Cambridge, New York, Melbourne, Madrid, Cape Town,
Singapore, São Paulo, Delhi, Tokyo, Mexico City

Cambridge University Press
The Edinburgh Building, Cambridge CB2 8RU, UK

Published in the United States of America by Cambridge University Press, New York

www.cambridge.org
Information on this title: www.cambridge.org/9780521187558

First published 2012

Printed in the United Kingdom at the University Press, Cambridge

A catalogue record for this publication is available from the British Library

Library of Congress Cataloging-in-Publication Data

The Cambridge companion to H.D. / edited by Nephie J. Christodoulides and Polina Mackay.
p. cm. – (Cambridge companions to literature)
Includes bibliographical references and index.
ISBN 978-0-521-76908-2 (Hardback) – ISBN 978-0-521-18755-8 (Paperback)
1. H.D. (Hilda Doolittle), 1886–1961–Criticism and interpretation. 2. Modernism (Literature)–United States. I. Christodoulides, Nephie II. Mackay, Polina, 1975–
PS3507.O726Z59 2011
811′.52–dc22
2011019453

ISBN 978-0-521-76908-2 Hardback
ISBN 978-0-521-18755-8 Paperback

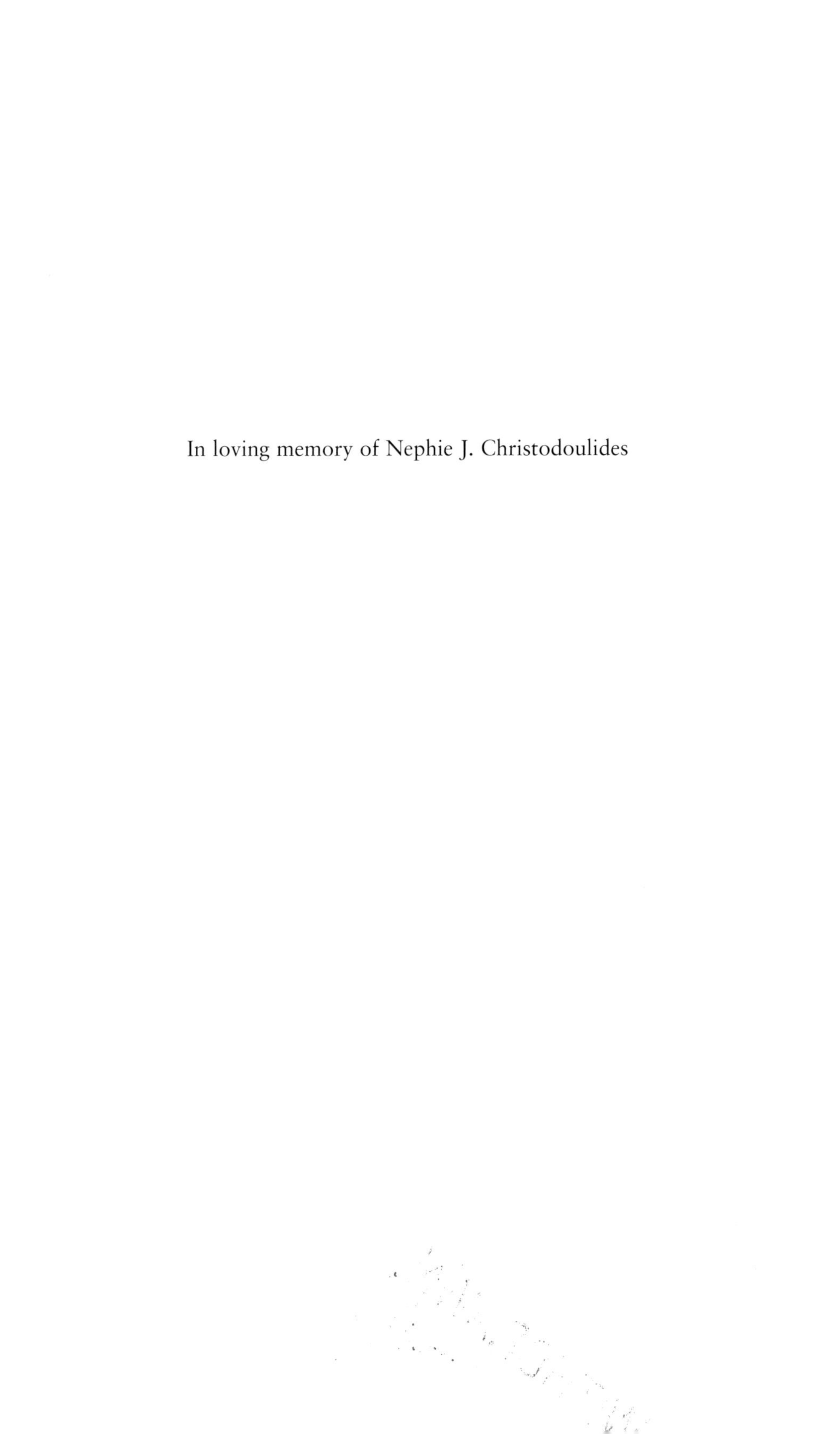

In loving memory of Nephie J. Christodoulides

CONTENTS

CONTRIBUTORS

NEPHIE J. CHRISTODOULIDES worked for the University of Cyprus from 1992 until her death in February 2011. She gained her BA in English and her MA in Creative Writing and Literature from Emerson College, Boston and a Ph.D. in English Literature from Stirling University, UK. She authored *Out of the Cradle Endlessly Rocking: Motherhood in Sylvia Plath's Work* (2005) and numerous articles on, among others, Virginia Woolf, H.D., Ted Hughes, Christina Rossetti, literature and psychoanalysis, life writing and alchemical studies.

DIANA COLLECOTT'S publications include essays on Bryher, Bunting, H.D., James, Lawrence, Levertov, Pound and Williams; her book, *H.D. and Sapphic Modernism, 1910–1950*, appeared from Cambridge University Press in 1999. She regularly broadcasts for the BBC.

MIRANDA B. HICKMAN is an Associate Professor of English at McGill University in Montréal, where she specialises in transatlantic modernism, modern poetry, textual criticism and gender studies. Her book on the Vorticist idiom, *The Geometry of Modernism*, appeared in 2006. Her most recent book is *One Must Not Go Altogether with the Tide: The Letters of Ezra Pound and Stanley Nott* (2011), and a volume of essays co-edited with John D. McIntyre, *Rereading the New Criticism*, is forthcoming (2012). Her essay on the minor works of James Joyce appeared in *Visions and Revisions: James Joyce* (2009); she has also contributed articles to *The Cambridge Companion to Modernist Women Writers* and *Ezra Pound in Context*. Current work includes a project on the construction of critical authority among women critics of the modernist period.

JO GILL is Senior Lecturer in Twentieth-century Literature at the University of Exeter, UK. She is the author of *Anne Sexton's Confessional Poetics* (2007), *Women's Poetry* (2007) and *The Cambridge Introduction to Sylvia Plath* (Cambridge University Press 2008) and the editor of *The Cambridge Companion to Sylvia Plath* (Cambridge University Press 2006), *Modern Confessional Writing: New Critical Essays* (2006) and, with Simon Barker, *Literature as History: Essays in Honour of Peter Widdowson* (2009). She is currently working on a new book on The Poetics of the American Suburbs.

SARAH GRAHAM'S research focuses on American texts from the modernist period to the contemporary, with a particular interest in gender and sexuality. Her main publications engage with the work of H.D. and J.D. Salinger, and she has an ongoing research interest in these writers and, more broadly, in twentieth-century American fiction, particularly representations of adolescence and of HIV/AIDS. She has published essays on trauma in H.D.'s poetry and on intersexuality in Jeffrey Eugenides' *Middlesex*. She is the author of *J.D. Salinger's The Catcher in the Rye* (2007), author of *Salinger's The Catcher in the Rye* (2007), and is currently writing a study of Salinger's short fiction. She is the Series Editor of 'Studies in Contemporary North American Fiction' and a founding member of the 'Studies in Youth' Network.

EILEEN GREGORY is Professor of English at the University of Dallas. She is the author of *H.D. and Hellenism: Classic Lines* (Cambridge University Press, 1997). Her work has appeared in *Contemporary Literature*, *Agenda*, and *Sagetrieb*, as well as in Susan Friedman and Rachel Blau DuPlessis (eds.), *Signets: Reading H.D.* (1990); Marina Camboni (ed.), *H.D.'s Poetry: 'the meanings that words hide'* (2003); Donna Hollenberg (ed.), *H.D. and Poets After* (2001); and Cynthia Hogue and Laura Hinton (eds.), *We Who Love to Be Astonished: Experimental Women's Writing and Performance Poetics* (2001).

BRENDA S. HELT received her Ph.D. in English and Feminist Studies from the University of Minnesota in 2008. She is currently adjunct faculty member in the Department of Literature and Language at Metropolitan State University in St Paul, Minnesota. She has published essays on Virginia Woolf, bisexual theory and feminist theory in *Twentieth-century Literature*, *Women in Higher Education* and elsewhere, and is currently researching a book project on spirituality and sexuality in H.D.'s late novels.

GEORGIA JOHNSTON, Professor of English at Saint Louis University, has particular interests in modernist autobiography in terms of sexual theories of the period. In her recent book, *The Formation of 20th-century Queer Autobiography* (2007), she shows how autobiographical forms intersect with theories of desire. She is currently working on concepts of deviancy in the modernist period.

POLINA MACKAY is Assistant Professor of English Literature at the University of Nicosia. Her research focuses on modern literature and gender with specific interest in work by women. She is the author of *The Aesthetics, Gender and Feminism of the Beat Women* (forthcoming) and the co-editor of *Authorship in Context: From the Theoretical to the Material* (2007) and *Kathy Acker and Transnationalism* (2009). Her latest essay on the Beat Generation appeared in

Naked Lunch @ 50: Anniversary Essays (2009); and her work on Diane Glancy is included in *The Salt Companion to Diane Glancy* (2010). She is also the co-founder and current Secretary of the European Beat Studies Network.

CYRENA N. PONDROM is English Board of Visitors Professor of English and Professor of Women's Studies at the University of Wisconsin-Madison. She has been an Honorary Member of the Advisory Board of the H.D. Society since 1994 and Secretary and Member of the Board of Directors of the T.S. Eliot Society since 2006. She received the Regents' Wisconsin Career Excellence in Teaching Award in 1991, and has held fellowships from NEH, ACLS, Fulbright and the Wisconsin Institute for Research in the Humanities. Her volume, *The Road from Paris: French Influence on English Poetry, 1900–1920*, was returned to print by Cambridge University Press in 2010. Her most recent scholarship has included an essay on *Helen in Egypt* in the forthcoming *Approaches to Teaching H.D.*, essays on T.S. Eliot in the *Blackwell Companion to T.S. Eliot and Modernism/Modernity* and a forthcoming essay on Eliot and Gertrude Stein entitled 'Constructing the Meaning in the Modernist Text'. She is at work on a book on 'T.S. Eliot and the Performance of Identity in Modernism' and an essay on 'Gertrude Stein and Minimalism' for a collection to be entitled *Modernism and Opera*.

MATTE ROBINSON is Assistant Professor of English and the Aquinas Programme, and Coordinator of ESL at St Thomas University in Fredericton, Canada. He is working on a book and several papers on H.D.

DEMETRIOS P. TRYPHONOPOULOS, University Research Professor of English and A/Dean, School of Graduate Studies at the University of New Brunswick in Canada, is the author or editor of ten books, including *The Ezra Pound Encyclopedia* (2005) and H.D.'s *Majic Ring* (2009). His current projects include *The Correspondence of H.L. Mencken and Ezra Pound* (forthcoming, 2011); *Ezra Pound's and H.D.'s Hellenistic Prosodies*; and *Approaches to Teaching Ezra Pound's Poetry and Prose* (2011).

ACKNOWLEDGEMENTS

We would first like to thank Ray Ryan at Cambridge University Press for believing in this project while it was still in its nascent state and for giving us the opportunity to produce this volume. We would like to thank the University of Cyprus for generous grants for library visits; the University of Nicosia for research time release; the staff at Beinecke Library, Yale University, for their help; and the H.D. International Society for their encouragement. Our sincerest thanks are also extended to Jane Augustine for her invaluable advice and friendship. We would like to express our gratitude to all the contributors whose hard work and unwavering support made this book possible. Finally, thanks to our families: to Zenon and Rafaella-Mariam, and to James and Sophia for their love and support.

CHRONOLOGY

1886	10 September: Birth of Hilda Doolittle in Bethlehem, Pennsylvania, daughter of Charles Leander Doolittle (1843–1919) and Helen Wolle (1853–1927).
1895	Moves with her family to Upper Darby, outside Philadelphia where her father becomes Professor of Astronomy and Director of the Flower Observatory.
1901	Meets Ezra Pound at a Halloween dress ball at the Burd School in Philadelphia.
1905	Is introduced by Pound to Yogi Books, Balzac's *Seraphita*, Swinburne, Ibsen, Maeterlinck, William Morris. Pound writes and dedicates to her 'Hilda's Book'.
1905	Meets William Carlos Williams.
1905–6	Attends Bryn Mawr College for three semesters but has to withdraw, perhaps because of a breakdown, and failure in Algebra.
1905 or 1906	Becomes engaged to Pound.
1909	First publications in New York syndicated papers.
1910	Meets Frances Josepha Gregg who becomes her first homosexual passion. Pound becomes involved with them; the first *ménage à trois* is formed as Frances has a brief affair with Pound. H.D. moves to Greenwich Village to be able to 'develop her artistic talents [away from] her conservative, unappreciative family'. Returns home after five months.
1911	Sails to Europe with Frances and her mother. Pound has already settled in London.

1911–13 When Frances and mother return to America, she stays behind. Becomes part of the London literary and cultural circles. Among others, she gets acquainted with May Sinclair, Ford Madox Ford, Violet Hunt, F.S. Flint and Richard Aldington with whom she falls in love.

1912 In one of the meetings with Pound and Aldington at the British Museum tea shop, Pound discovers her imagist traits and edits three of her poems. Travels to Genoa to meet her parents and accompanies them to Florence.

1913 'Hermes of the Ways', 'Priapus' and 'Epigram' are published in Harriet Monroe's *Poetry: A Magazine of Verse.* Marries Aldington in London.

1913–16 Resides in Kensington and Hampstead. Writes and translates.

1914 *Des Imagistes: An Anthology* published. Includes poems by Pound, H.D., Aldington, Amy Lowell, William Carlos Williams, James Joyce, Ezra Pound, John Cornos and others. Meets and forms cerebral friendship with D.H. Lawrence. H.D. becomes pregnant.

1914 First World War declared.

1915 Receives prize from *Poetry.* Birth of stillborn daughter. Forms close friendship and collaboration with Marianne Moore. *Choruses from Iphigeneia in Aulis* published in The Poets' Translation Series.

1916–17 Editor for *Egoist.*

1916 *Sea Garden* accepted for publication.

1917 Receives prize for *Sea Garden.*

1918 Goes to live with music composer Cecil Gray in Cornwall; mutual agreement with Aldington to live free erotic life. Becomes pregnant by Gray. Meets Bryher (Annie Winifred Ellerman). Relationship develops into a passionate erotic bond which turns into a lifelong companionship.

1919 Almost dies of double pneumonia. Saved by Bryher. Death of her father. Gives birth to Frances Perdita. Has 'jelly fish' and 'bell-jar' experiences in Cornwall. Writes *Notes on Thought and Vision.*

1920 Travels to Greece with Bryher and Havelock Ellis. Meets Peter Rodeck on board, has a visionary experience which she describes in *Tribute to Freud* and *Majic Ring*. Has 'Writing on the Wall' experience in Corfu.

1920–1 Travels to America with Bryher and Perdita.

1921–6 Lives in London and Switzerland.

1921–2 Writes *Asphodel*.

1921 *Hymen* published. Writes *Paint it Today*.

1922 Second trip to Greece with mother and Bryher. Visits Asia Minor.

1923 Trip to Egypt. Sees Tutankhamun's tomb.

1924 *Heliodora and Other Poems* published.

1925 *Collected Poems of H.D.* published.

1925–32 Develops interests in psychoanalysis, the occult, astrology, numerology and the tarot.

1926 *Palimpsest* published in Paris. Frances Gregg sends Kenneth Macpherson to meet her.

1927 *Hippolytus Temporizes: A Play in Three Acts* published. Writes *HERmione*.

1928 *Hedylus* published in Boston.

1929 First draft of 'Pilates's Wife'. *Red Roses for Bronze* published in New York.

1930 *Kora and Ka* written in Vaud. Stars with Paul Robeson in *Borderline*. Collaborates with Bryher on the editing and montage of the film. Publishes the *Borderline* pamphlet.

1931 *Red Roses for Bronze* published in London. Psychoanalytic sessions with Mary Chadwick in London. Writes *Nights*.

1931–2 Psychoanalysis with Hanns Sachs.

1932 Trip to Greece with Perdita. Visits Delphi.

1933 Psychoanalytic sessions with Freud in Vienna (1 March–12 June). Sessions terminated abruptly because of bomb scare.

1934	*Kora and Ka* and the *Usual Star* published. Nervous breakdown in August because of J.J. Van der Leeuw's aircrash accident. Returns to Vienna and resumes psychoanalysis with Freud (November to December).
1935	*Nights* published.
1935–8	Psychoanalysis with Walter Schmideberg.
1936	*The Hedgehog* published.
1937	*Euripides' Ion* published in London. Aldington asks for divorce.
1937–8	Trip to America with Bryher. Meets Norman Holmes Pearson who will become a close friend, editor and literary executor.
1931–9	Hermetic interest becomes stronger. Authors she reads include Robert Ambelain, Denis de Rougemont and Jean Chaboseau.
1939	3 September. Louis Silverstein mentions this as the date H.D. believed was the outbreak of the Second World War.
1940–1	'Within the Walls' written.
1941–3	*The Gift* written.
1941–6	Interest in spiritualism; joins the Society for Psychical Research; participates in séances. Meets Lord Hugh Dowding, who refutes her claims that she has been receiving messages from dead Royal Air Force soldiers.
1942	Writes 'The Walls Do Not Fall'.
1943–4	*Majic Ring* written.
1943	Participates in 'A Reading by Famous Poets'; the event is attended by the Queen and the two princesses. Visions continue.
1944	*The Walls Do Not Fall* and *What Do I Love* published.
1945	*Tribute to Angels* published.
1945	Moves to hotels in Lausanne and Lugano.

1946	*The Flowering of the Rod* published. Suffers breakdown triggered by ill health, war strain and rejection by Lord Dowding. Taken to Seehof, Privat Klinik Brunner Küsnacht.
1947	'The Sword Went Out to Sea' finished. 'Bid Me to Live (A Madrigal)' finished.
1947–8	Writes her Pre-Raphaelite novel *White Rose and the Red.*
1949	*By Avon River* published in New York. Starts correspon-ding with Robert Duncan, who will eventually write *The H.D. Book.*
1949–50	Writes 'H.D. by Delia Alton'.
1949–51	Writes *The Mystery.*
1951	Travels to New York to see her first grandchild, Valentine.
1953	Operation for abdominal intestinal occlusions at the Clinique Cecil in Lausanne. Later moves to the Klinik Brunner in Küsnacht. Book I of *Helen in Egypt* completed. Meets existential psychoanalyst Erich Heydt, who becomes a friend and one of her initiators. Begins Book II of *Helen in Egypt.*
1954	Begins Book III of *Helen in Egypt.*
1955	Records *Helen in Egypt.* Writes *Compassionate Friendship.*
1955–6	Writes *Magic Mirror.*
1956	*Tribute to Freud* published in New York. Travels with Bryher to America; is honoured for her seventieth birthday. Back in Switzerland, falls and breaks her hip; taken to Klinik Hirslanden. Writes the Hirslanden Notebooks (1957–1959).
1957	*Selected Poems of H.D.* published in New York. Writes 'Sagesse' (included in *Hermetic Definition*).
1958	Receives the Harriet Monroe Memorial Prize for three of her poems. *End to Torment* written.
1959	'Winter Love' written. Receives the Brandeis University Creative Arts Award for Poetry.
1960	*Bid Me To Live* (*A Madrigal*) published. Meets Lionel Durand, who will be one of the inspiring figures for *Hermetic*

	Definition. Travels to New York to receive her Award of Merit Medal for Poetry of the American Academy of Arts and Letters. Meets St John Perse, another inspiring figure for *Hermetic Definition*. Writes *Thorn Thicket*.
1960–1	Writes *Hermetic Definition*.
1961	*Helen in Egypt* published. Suffers stroke, taken to Roten Kreuz Spital in Zurich and then transferred to Klinik Hirslanden. Dies on 27 September. Cremated on 2 October, her ashes buried in Nisky Hill Cemetery, 28 October.
1972	'Sagesse' and 'Winter Love' published in *Hermetic Definition*.
1972	*Hermetic Definition* published.
1979	*End to Torment* published.
1978	*Kora Ka* published
1981	*HERmione* published.
1982	*Notes on Thought and Vision* published. *Vale Ave* published (whole).
1986	*H.D. by Delia Alton* published (whole).
1990	*Within the Walls* published.
2007	*The Sword Went out to Sea* published.
2009	*The Mystery*, *White Rose and the Red*, *Majic Ring* published.

NEPHIE J. CHRISTODOULIDES AND POLINA MACKAY

Introduction

The Cambridge Companion to H.D. is a critical overview of the author's work, featuring analyses of her major poetry, prose, translations and non-fiction, as well as arguments of how the author fits in the literary culture of the first half of the twentieth century. The essays we have specially commissioned for this volume were written by leading or emerging scholars in the field. In our choices we attempt to give a sense of the diverse viewpoints through which H.D. has been read.

The book is divided into two parts. The first examines the literary context of H.D.'s work. The essays focus on specific issues and debates, such as the author's initial displacement from and reinstatement in the modernist canon, her tendency to use biography in her work, her active contribution to 'little magazines', her work's affinities with modernism, her utilisation of gendered perspectives, and the lasting influence of her aesthetics on later generations of writers. These readings intend both to concisely map the field of H.D. and to help familiarise the reader with the contexts through which her work is read. These discourses are wide-ranging, taking in the history of canon formation, biographical approaches to literature, modernist culture and literature, gender theory/feminism and the writer's legacy.

The second part of the book explores a wide range of H.D.'s major texts, including her most well-known poetry and prose, translations and memoirs. The chapters are organised mainly in chronological terms, starting with her early poetry in *Sea Garden* (1916) and finishing with her 1940s works, *The Gift* and *Tribute to Freud*. We hope that this structural arrangement will help to locate H.D. both within the social and cultural context of modernity and also within the context of the dialectic between the Romantic, Victorian and modernist aesthetics.

This Companion, like others in this series, builds on the existing scholarship on H.D. The first essay by Miranda B. Hickman provides a critical overview of H.D. scholarship and deals head on with the negative critiques the author's work has received, such as Lawrence Rainey's 'Canon, Gender, and Text: The Case of H.D.' (1991). Hickman goes beyond the individual criticisms to discuss the author in light of the history of canon formation in modern literature. Nephie J. Christodoulides' piece is a detailed overview of the field with emphasis on the biographical readings of H.D., which, as shown here, are justified by the author's consistent use of her own experiences in her work. Cyrena N. Pondrom explores H.D.'s contribution to modernist little magazines, and provides detailed analyses of primary sources of, among others, periodical writings and collated letters such as *H.D.: A Bibliography, 1905–1990* (Boughn 1993) and *Between History and Poetry: The Letters of H.D. and Norman Holmes Pearson* (Hollenberg 1997). Polina Mackay's chapter draws on the readings of H.D. that have placed her at the centre of modernism, including Cassandra Laity's *H.D. and the Victorian Fin de Siècle: Gender, Modernism, Decadence* (Laity 1996) and Susan Stanford Friedman's *Penelope's Web: Gender, Modernity, H.D.'s Fiction* (Friedman 1990). Many ground-breaking works of criticism on H.D., such as Friedman's *Psyche Reborn: The Emergence of H.D.* (Friedman 1981) and Diana Collecott's *H.D. and Sapphic Modernism 1910–1950* (Collecott 1999), focus on her constructions of female subjectivity and, more generally, on how her work contributes to gender studies. These are summarised and expanded on in Georgia Johnston's chapter on H.D. and gender. Another mapping of sorts occurs in Jo Gill's essay: it offers an overview of H.D.'s long-lasting influence on later generations of poets, among them, Adrienne Rich, Diane di Prima, Denise Levertov, Margaret Atwood, Lorine Niedecker, Anne Sexton and Carol Anne Duffy.

The second part of the Companion, which concentrates on individual works by H.D., also makes extensive use of existing scholarship. Diana Collecott's essay on H.D.'s poetics builds on previous readings of her poems, ranging from Eileen Gregory's iconic piece 'Rose Cut in Rock: Sappho and H.D.'s *Sea Garden*' (Gregory 1986) and Adalaide Morris' fairly recent book *How to Live/What to Do: H.D.'s Cultural Poetics* (Morris 2003). Sarah Graham and the jointly written chapter by Demetrios P. Tryphonopoulos and Matte Robinson provide detailed analyses of individual works, while Eileen Gregory's examination of the notion of translation in H.D. goes beyond her own *H.D. and Hellenism: Classic Lines* (1997) to engage with the wider field of modernism and translation as it is shaped by recent work, such as S.G. Yao's *Translation and the Languages of Modernism: Gender, Politics, Language* (2002), which is the first to situate H.D. within the field of modernism and translation, and the edited volume *Translation and the Classic: Identity and Change in the History of Culture* (2008). Finally, Brenda S. Helt's essay on *The Gift* and *Tribute to Freud* makes use of the significant body of work on H.D. and psychoanalysis, including Friedman's *Analyzing Freud: Letters of H.D., Bryher, and Their Circle* (Friedman 2002) and Dianne Chisholm's *H.D.'s Freudian Poetics: Psychoanalysis in Translation* (Chisholm 1992).

The extensive engagement with H.D. scholarship, which the essays in the Companion offer and enhance, is the reason we did not feel the need to provide a critical overview of the field in this Introduction. The Companion, moreover, contains a bibliography of selected works, a comprehensive index and a chronology. Below we give a detailed overview of the chapters' contents. We hope that the summaries, just as the rest of this Introduction, will briefly map H.D. as writer and the contexts through which one might read her.

The book's opening chapter by Miranda B. Hickman discusses the turbulent history of H.D.'s canonisation. H.D. was not included in the modernist canon before her 'resurrection' by critics focusing on her gender, such as Friedman and Rachel Blau DuPlessis. Hickman reads H.D.'s initial placement outside the canon and her subsequent reinstatement, whereby her work is found in major anthologies, against the larger history of canonicity and literary production in the twentieth century, taking in the influence of the critical establishment (e.g. the New Critics) and the fact that H.D. insisted on not publishing her work widely. Hickman's aim, however, is to answer the simple question of what makes H.D. a significant writer, for as Hickman sensibly puts it 'our apologias must be very specific about what we think earns [women writers] a place in our modern canons'.

The second essay in this part illuminates the dialogic nature which H.D. consciously introduced and capitalised on, between her life and fiction. Nephie J. Christodoulides gives an overview of H.D.'s autobiographical work, and focuses on the social, cultural, geographical and literary intersections that affected her writing career. Her relationships with Ezra Pound, D.H. Lawrence, Havelock Ellis and Freud point to the direct engagement with the London modernist circles, her transnationalism and her bisexuality. Christodoulides' assumptions in discussing H.D.'s autobiographical modus are that she does not promise revelation, nor do her texts uncover a miraculously intact female subject. Instead, the autobiographical subject finds herself on multiple stages simultaneously, while her work is partly a process of fabrication and replenishment, a rewriting of life to generate a new textual identity by appropriating myths and revisiting personal history.

The third chapter in the book analyses the ways in which H.D. contributes to the culture of the 'little magazines' which are increasingly recognised as an important aspect of modernism. Cyrena N. Pondrom points out that much of H.D.'s early work published in the first two decades of the twentieth century first appeared in magazines, including *Poetry*, *The Egoist* and

The Little Review. Pondrom charts H.D.'s contributions and literary editing (for instance, her work in *The Egoist*) against the increasing activity of female authorship, editing and publishing at the time. By reading letters between H.D. and Marianne Moore, for instance, Pondrom shows how much H.D. valued her role as editor, publisher and promoter of avant-garde work.

Polina Mackay's essay examines H.D.'s relation to modernism. It maps the ways in which H.D. was influenced by discourses of modernity, such as the language of psychoanalysis, the focus on spirituality as a cultural phenomenon (as opposed to one of religion) and the interest in sexuality. The chapter then analyses H.D.'s modernist aesthetic, touching upon her imagism, her utilisation of Hellenic themes and, with specific reference to *Sea Garden*, her sense of modernity as it comes across through the poems' language. Mackay also discusses H.D.'s extensive focus on gender, which is more evident in her prose and later poetry (*Palimpsest*, *Helen in Egypt*), as indicative of her interest in writing the modern woman.

In her chapter on H.D.'s understanding of gender, Georgia Johnston argues that for the author 'gender is a text to be read', and goes on to explore H.D.'s strategies of writing against patriarchal scripts. Johnston focuses on the early autobiographical novel *HERmione* (1927), where H.D. suggests that the process of naming women is a foundation of patriarchy. H.D.'s protagonist, Her, fails to conform to any of patriarchy's gendered scripts and instead sets up her own texts which draw on various sources, one of which is Sappho. This Sapphic discourse enables H.D. to claim the queer writer for modernity/modernism.

The final essay of the book's first part charts H.D.'s influence on later generations of writers which in itself testifies to the increasing importance of her legacy and continuing relevance of her work to recent/contemporary literature. Jo Gill first establishes H.D.'s significance to the development of modernism and then focuses on the central role she plays in the emergence and eventual maturity of queer poetics, using Robert Duncan's drawing on H.D. as an example in point. Gill also shows that H.D. influenced a wide range of individual poets, including Adrienne Rich, Denise Levertov and Anne Sexton.

The second section of the book provides in-depth analyses of significant concepts and practices, together with readings of individual works. The section covers the main features of H.D.'s poetics, her sustained concern with translation as literary practice and her interest in the notion of history. Moreover, it offers extended examinations of *Hymen*, *Trilogy*, *HERmione*, *Majic Ring*, *The Gift* and *Tribute to Freud*.

Part II of the book starts with Diana Collecott's piece, which explores H.D.'s poetics in a trajectory that takes in her major collections of poems, including *Sea Garden*, *The God* and *Trilogy*. The chapter explores the poet's form in light of the intellectual, cultural and literary development of imagism. Collecott's examination finds a 'transitional quality' and many instances of 'betweeness' in H.D.'s poems. Through close critical readings of individual poems, the chapter shows how much care H.D. took in choosing her words, images, allusions and literary contexts. In Collecott's analysis H.D. is a craftswoman who builds significantly on literary heritage (Sappho, ancient Greek myth) without ever losing sight of her own modernity.

Sarah Graham's essay closely focuses on the literary form and theme of two of H.D.'s collections of poetry, *Hymen* and *Trilogy*. These exemplify two of the most important concerns of H.D.'s poetry: constructions of woman and the effect of war on humanity. Graham's reading of *Hymen* pays attention to the ways in which it differs from *Sea Garden*. While the earlier work is centrally concerned with imagery with a focus on flowers and landscape, *Hymen* for the first time in H.D.'s oeuvre brings to fruition the woman-centred poetry with which the poet has been associated, as it is centrally preoccupied with writing against patriarchal images of women. *Trilogy*, a work that has received much more critical attention than *Hymen*, is explored here as an epic which exemplifies H.D.'s spiritual response to war and destruction.

The piece by Matte Robinson and Demetrios P. Tryphonopoulos discusses H.D.'s prose and argues that, although she initially became known through her poetry, her prose writings should be analysed in their own right. The chapter suggests that these texts, which make extensive use of biography, 'exist on the borderline between fiction and memoir' and reveal the literary strategies the author implements in order to write the woman author into literary history. The essay concentrates on two books which are about the act of writing, *HERmione* and *Majic Ring*. These are placed both within the context of H.D.'s prose works as well as analysed as individual narratives with specific concerns of their own.

The penultimate essay in the book is Eileen Gregory's piece on the notion of translation, which she reads as central to H.D.'s work throughout her career. Although unlike many of her contemporaries (Ezra Pound, Richard Aldington) H.D. did not translate very much, she saw translation as paramount to her literary practice. As Gregory shows, H.D. understood translation as interpretation. The chapter explores examples from H.D.'s entire oeuvre, ranging from poems in *Sea Garden* and the translations of Euripides in *Hippolytus Temporizes* and *Ion*, finishing with *Helen in Egypt*. This latter text contains a third layer of translation-interpretation, beyond Euripides' *Helen* and H.D.'s own version, in the insertion of a commentator in the head notes of each section of the epic poem. Gregory's analysis demonstrates that for H.D., translation is not simply important as a literary/poetic practice but 'as a guiding trope' which, at the hands of a diverse writer like H.D., raises issues of translatability/untranslatability and to what degree one might be able to decode that which at points seems untranslatable.

The book ends with a discussion of H.D.'s understanding of history in her later memoirs, *The Gift* and *Tribute to Freud*. Brenda S. Helt shows that these two narratives use psychoanalysis as a way of interpreting history. She shows how H.D. reads history as personal story by disguising historical facts as self traumas. Helt's analysis shows that H.D.'s work cannot be disassociated from its historical circumstances, especially since the author tries to imagine history in her books as a kind of malleable narrative.

We hope that *The Cambridge Companion to H.D.* will complement the H.D. field. The study's wide range, containing chapters on her un/canonisation, biography, journalism, modernism, gender, influence, poetics, poetry, prose, translation, sense of history and individual works, brings together in one book the elements that make H.D. the significant, widely taught and influential writer that she is today.

PART I

Contexts and issues

I

MIRANDA B. HICKMAN

'Uncanonically seated': H.D. and literary canons

In *Tribute to Freud* (1956), her memoir of work with the founder of psychoanalysis, H.D. at one point describes herself as 'uncanonically seated', placing herself outside the circle of those around Freud who, she suggests, were 'richly intellectually and materially endowed'.[1] As she often does in her work, here H.D. constructs her 'uncanonical' status as an important source of alternative knowledge and ability. Surprisingly, she even allies herself with Freud on this basis, going on to note that he himself is 'uncanonical enough'. Her 'enough' here frames 'uncanonicity' as a quality one possesses to a greater or lesser extent (rather than as a lack of something) 'enough' of which can yield desirable effects. Here as elsewhere, H.D. places value on what lies outside the boundaries of that which is culturally sanctioned.

In her work more generally, however, in addition to featuring the position of the 'outcast', H.D. often also features compelling liminal zones, neither 'here' nor 'there',[2] raising questions about the costs of inhabiting the stable locations assumed by discourse about canons, which decides between inside and outside. When addressing H.D.'s place in our literary canons, it is important to bear in mind what H.D.'s work often implies both about the benefits of 'uncanonicity', as well as of inhabiting in-between conditions that problematise both the legitimacy of the borderline between inside and outside, and the value of being definitely positioned as one or the other.

Today, H.D. appears regularly in the canons of modern poetry and modernist literature, twentieth-century American literature and twentieth-century literature by women. Collections featuring her work include the *Norton* anthologies of *Poetry*, *Modern Poetry*, *American Poetry* and *Literature By Women*; *The Oxford Book of American Poetry* and *The Oxford Anthology of Modern American Poetry*; and *The Heath Anthology of American Literature*, attesting to her place in what Rachel Hadas calls 'the hefty tomes ... books in uniform ... designed ... to accommodate as much of the rapidly expanding canon as possible'[3] – volumes both reflecting and fostering canonical status. For many years, however, H.D. was 'uncanonically seated', considered chiefly a minor lyric poet who had achieved prominence through the short-lived early twentieth-century movement of imagism. H.D.'s rise in stature stems from the active work of feminist recuperative criticism of the last thirty-five years, which has often sought to uncouple H.D. from the 'Imagist' label that clung tenaciously to her for so long and restricted awareness of her range. Later in her career, H.D. herself wished to shed her reputation as an Imagist: writing in 1943 to Norman Holmes Pearson while composing her epic poem, *Trilogy*, she suggested that she had superseded the 'early H.D.' manner.[4]

The mid twentieth-century critical establishment, however, associated with the New Critics and their contemporaries, generally recognised neither the evolution nor the importance of H.D.'s work.[5] If mentioned, she was usually invoked as the erstwhile Imagist poet – notable for 'crystalline' lyric poems of the heroic early days of modernism but limited in talent and scope. After 1930, critical attention to H.D. waned, although during the 1910s and early 1920s, she had been acclaimed among a new generation of rising poets – not only by compatriots such as Amy Lowell and Marianne Moore, but also by such commentators as influential critic and anthologist Louis Untermeyer (he called her 'the only true Imagist'),[6] who reached a wider, more mainstream audience than did her avant-gardist advocates of the time. Contributing to this later neglect was not only that mid twentieth-century literary criticism favoured male poets, but also that after the mid 1920s, when *Collected Poems* (1925) appeared, H.D. did not publish widely. During the 1920s and 1930s, though she wrote an abundance of prose fiction, much of it autobiographical, she often chose not to publish. Exactly why remains opaque, though Friedman and Blau DuPlessis persuasively suggest that the frequent accent in this fiction on the 'culturally forbidden love of woman for woman' might have kept H.D. from publishing autobiographical *romans à clef* such as *HERmione*, *Asphodel*, and *Paint it Today*, which she wrote during the 1920s, the decade of 'the storm of abuse' directed at Radclyffe Hall for *The Well of Loneliness*.[7] Some experimental fiction that H.D. did submit to publishers was refused (Friedman 1990, pp. 361–6). When she published, she usually did so in limited editions, often through small presses such as Robert McAlmon's Contact Press – funded by H.D.'s lesbian partner Bryher – which brought out *Palimpsest* in 1926; or in the late 1920s and 1930s, in tiny editions, privately printed, intended only for friends: this was true, for instance, of novellas such as *Kora and Ka* (1934) and *Nights* (1935). Encouraged by her supporter at Yale, Norman Holmes Pearson, H.D. engaged in a wave of publication in the five years before her death (*Tribute to Freud*, 1956; *Selected Poems*, 1957; *Bid Me to Live*, 1960; *Helen in Egypt*, 1961), in some cases in trade editions,[8] but these late-career appearances could not overcome the many forces through which H.D. had come to be, as Susan Stanford Friedman puts it, 'buried' during the intervening years. In 1944, Babette Deutsch suggested that H.D. had been 'utterly silent' for two decades; when H.D. died in 1961, some critics thought she had passed away long before.[9]

The critical narrative of turnaround since then has become familiar: groundbreaking feminist recuperative work since the mid 1970s – inaugurated by such articles as Friedman's 'Who Buried H.D.?' – has gained H.D. a place as a major modernist writer and dramatically revised her canon. Thanks to scholarship and criticism since the 1980s by critics such as Friedman herself, Rachel Blau DuPlessis, Diana Collecott, Eileen Gregory, Donna Hollenberg, Cassandra Laity, Adalaide Morris, Alicia Ostriker, Cyrena Pondrom and Caroline Zilboorg, H.D. is now widely recognised for a repertoire including not only Imagist but a diversity of other lyric poetry; longer epic poetry (such as *Trilogy* and *Helen in Egypt*); involvement in cinema (four films with the collective *POOL*); film criticism (in the journal *Close Up*)[10] and a wealth of prose fiction, much of it based in autobiography.

Since the 1980s, the expansion and diversification of the H.D. canon has formed part of and benefited from rapid changes underway in modernist studies more broadly. During the last two decades especially, work on H.D. has exemplified the archive fever prominent in modernist studies over the past twenty years that fuelled the rise of the 'New Modernist Studies' in the 1990s. Much of H.D.'s current canon was published posthumously, drawn from the archive she developed at Yale with the support of Norman Pearson. Her Blakean meditation, *Notes on Thought and Vision*, appeared in 1982; the 1980s and early 1990s saw publication of three autobiographical *romans à clef* from the 1920s, *HERmione*, *Paint it Today* and *Asphodel*; Jane Augustine published a complete edition of H.D.'s memoir *The Gift* in 1998; in 2000, Joan Burke brought out the novel *Pilate's Wife*; and most recently, three novels of H.D.'s late period, written during and after the Second World War, have appeared: *White Rose and the Red* (Halsall 2009), a biography of Elizabeth Siddall, wife of D.G. Rossetti; and two novels registering H.D.'s spiritualist experiences during the Second World War, *The Sword Went Out to Sea* (Hogue and Vandivere 2007) and *Majic Ring* (Tryphonopoulos 2009).

As we enjoy the copia of an enhanced H.D. canon, critical narratives about H.D. will need modification, and we will need to justify her position in literary canons with care, since, to borrow diction from H.D.'s

'Sea Violet', H.D.'s newfound 'grasp' on canonical placement is still somewhat 'frail'. As difficult as it is to decipher the multiplex process of aggregate judgement yielding a canon, H.D.'s status is still haunted by the cultural belief that some writers make it in for the right reasons, others on suspect grounds. In the early 1990s, on the traces of the 'decade of the canon debate', Lawrence Rainey famously quarrelled with the bases on which H.D. had reached the modernist canon, suggesting that it was because she had the right credentials for politically corrective times (she was a woman, feminist, bisexual, pacifist, advocate of civil rights). He then sought to expose H.D.'s lack of literary 'greatness', comparing her 'Leda' unfavourably to Yeats' 'Leda and the Swan', asking H.D.'s poem to meet criteria derived from Yeats' poem and, in a hasty generalisation, positioning this one poem as representing H.D.'s work in its entirety (Rainey 1991, pp. 99–123; 'canon debate', p. 99).

Rainey's logical fallacies in this essay aside, his article raised important questions about how writers newly admitted to literary canons come to be recognised as deserving a lasting place therein. Rainey rightly suggests that writers often gain entrance to canons on winds of change that favour certain categories; he is right to ask whether they deserve to stay, and if so, on what grounds. Standards for admission to canons evolve over the decades, as they should: accordingly, for H.D., we need answers for our times – times of ongoing feminist work in the academy, newly enriched by feminist and post-feminist critiques of the perspectival limitations of first- and second-wave feminism; of growing awareness of diverse forms of queerness; of public debate about same-sex partnership and marriage; of interest in spirituality; and within literary studies, of renewed attention to formal technique. To prevent women writers such as H.D. (e.g. in modern poetry, Amy Lowell, Mina Loy, Edna St Vincent Millay, Marianne Moore, P.K. Page, Muriel Rukeyser) from being covered over again by the weeds of cultural inertia, our apologias must be very specific about what we think earns them a place in our modern canons.

In a lecture from the year of H.D.'s death, Lionel Trilling famously lauded modern literature's capacity to ask hard questions of its readers: 'It asks if we are content with our marriages, with our family lives, with our professional lives, with our friends ... It asks us if we are content with ourselves.'[11] Typically for his critical generation, Trilling's modern canon included only men, but his statement captures the H.D. we know today: H.D.'s writing provokes questions not only about relationships, but also about gender identities and sexualities, love and desire, the condition of women in our society. She seeks, as

Carolyn Heilbrun once said, to reinvent womanhood. For me, the importance of H.D.'s work lies in her distinctive isovist; demonstrated techniques for self-inquiry and cultural interrogation; strategies for ideological dissidence; and the new perspectives she helps readers to imagine. What her work displays, as it models forms of inquiry and Adrienne Rich's kind of 'revision',[12] is what Ostriker calls 'a mind working' on an array of problems.[13]

However, as Dianne Chisholm and Eileen Gregory argue,[14] at this juncture, we should remain wary both of the ways in which H.D. has been brought into the canonical fold, sometimes at the expense of robust understanding of her work, and of how the process of legitimating H.D.'s work in the academy may sometimes lead to misrepresentations of what Gregory calls 'H.D.'s heterodoxy'. Vital forms of dissidence essential to her work risk neglect when she is ushered into the canon in the ways in which she often has been in recent years.

One danger is that, in the forcefield of canonisation, critical lines of thought on H.D. may harden into a kind of critical 'orthodoxy'[15] that runs athwart what H.D.'s work suggests. The persistent questioning and uncertainty characterising the rhetorical strategies of H.D.'s late epic poem *Helen in Egypt*, for instance, which features a Helen figure vague about who she is and what has happened ('I wonder and ask / numberless questions')[16] but nonetheless resolved to recover her past towards clearer vision – all of this figures a mode of movement that forms a signature of H.D.'s work at different scales. This kind of motion, characterised by repetitions, revisions, candid admissions of ambiguity and indecision, yet consistent commitment to discovering ways towards better conditions ('possibly we will reach haven / heaven'),[17] signals in H.D., as it does in the work of Virginia Woolf, principled distrust of dogmatic certainties – and models a mode of thought resistant to facile truths and complacent orthodoxies.

Critical lines of thought that have surfaced about H.D. over the last thirty years also sometimes overlook important aspects of H.D.'s heterodoxy. As Meryl Altman, Dianne Chisholm and I have suggested,[18] the 'H.D.' often constructed within the recuperative climate is one whose writing is read as 'gynocentric' and whose sexuality is construed as 'maternal'; and these understandings of H.D. contribute to visions of her work often unable to accommodate its mutability and diversity. There are certainly vectors of H.D.'s cultural work that encourage such readings. H.D.'s *Notes on Thought and Vision*, for instance, summons the possibility of a woman-centred perspective by invoking the 'vision of the womb' affording females distinctive access to visionary consciousness.[19] When H.D. unveils the radiant 'Lady' in *Trilogy*, she presents a gynocentric religious vision, especially given her rhetorical deflections of readings of the 'Lady' as a Virgin Mary figure framed by patriarchal narrative.[20] H.D.'s imaginary theatre also features maternally coded erotic scenarios: *Helen in Egypt*, for instance, suggests that it is the force of the sea-goddess Thetis, Achilles' mother, that enables Helen and Achilles to reunite and Achilles to supersede his bellicose masculinist heroism.[21]

But if such elements appear in H.D.'s work, they are complicated by others quite different from these. For instance, H.D. leaves the tantalising rhetorical question in *Notes* – 'Is it easier for a woman to attain this state of consciousness than for a man?' (1982, p. 20) – notably unanswered, deliberately refraining from privileging a woman-centred vision. Her work also destabilises a gynocentric vision in other ways, though the degree of intentionality with which it does often remains ambiguous. In 'The Dancer', if the goddess figure of 'Rhodocleia' is sometimes elevated, at other moments she is positioned as subordinate to a higher 'sun-lover' god-figure, a 'Father' (H.D., *CP*, p. 445). If H.D. sometimes features maternally coded erotic moments, these jostle against erotic scenes that are conspicuously androgynous, like those conjured in *Sea Garden* (1916); still others recall the heterosexual 'romantic thralldom' Blau DuPlessis famously named as a major theme of H.D.'s work.[22] Indeed, H.D. often writes for and on behalf of women, but her work is too various in this regard to justify general constructions of her writing as 'gynocentric' or her erotic as 'maternal'.

More generally, H.D.'s oeuvre often displays a violent idiom that, while mentioned in criticism, usually remains under-acknowledged by constructions of her as woman-centred and maternally focused.[23] Violence is conspicuously on display, for instance, in H.D.'s inaugural volume, *Sea Garden*, whose imaginary garden, inspired by Sappho's Lesbos and Swinburne's wild seascapes, features a collection of shore-side flowers, buffeted by rough weather. When her speakers apostrophise individual flowers, the frequent passive voice used calls attention to the violence inflicted upon the flowers and emphasises the qualities they gain through subjection to the elements: the 'harsh rose' is 'caught in the drift' and 'flung on the sand'; the 'Reed', 'slashed and torn', is 'shattered / in the wind'. The wind 'furrows' the sea lily with a 'hard edge'.

Moreover, H.D.'s speakers suggest that the value of these flowers, greater than that of ordinary flowers, derives from subjection to wind and storm (H.D., *CP*, pp. 5, 14): in this world, what is 'frail' and 'marred' becomes 'doubly rich'. At first, the violence of *Sea Garden* comes across as that which allows the flowers to demonstrate admirable tenacity and survival under trial; and because flowers are markedly linked with women in the cultural imagination; because a poem featured in the volume, 'Sheltered Garden', suggests a call for release from the fetters of conventional post-Victorian femininity; and because the volume was published at a suffragist moment, also suggests the violence as figuring forms of cultural violence affecting women. Moreover, as 1916 occurs during the Great War, as H.D.'s spouse, Richard Aldington, is fighting at the front, the lexis of poems such as 'Sea Violet', whose 'white violet' 'lies fronting all the wind' 'among the torn shells', cannot but suggest the 'front' and the 'shells' of battle (H.D., *CP*, pp. 25–6).

If violence here signals damaging forces, however, it also sometimes suggests forces necessary for regenerative transformation. H.D.'s speaker seeking emancipation from the 'sheltered garden' calls for violence to 'break' the chains of a world of 'beauty without strength' (H.D., *CP*, p. 20); the trapped speaker of 'Garden' likewise implores the wind to 'rend' the 'heat' to 'tatters' (H.D., *CP*, pp. 24–5). Wished-for liberatory gestures here repeat the violence done to the flowers. Moreover, the poems increasingly imply that the flowers gain value through contact with violent forces that bring strength and emancipation: in aggregate, the volume's poems valorise the very stormy elements that impart to the flowers a 'hard edge'.

The celebration of such forces in 'Storm' – 'You crash over the trees, / you crack the live branch' (H.D., *CP*, p. 36) – exemplifies the poetics of the Romantic sublime in which H.D. clearly engaged, early and late. As Cassandra Laity notes, H.D. participates in a Burkean discourse of the sublime, which venerates power and terror as avenues to transformation of perspective and consciousness.[24] Accordingly, H.D. attributes to venerated deities in her work the capacity to affect mortals with terrifying force. In 'Amaranth', the supplicant of the formidable Aphrodite figure must 'stumble toward / her altar step' with 'flesh ... scorched and rent, / shattered, cut apart, / and slashed open' (H.D., *CP*, p. 311). In H.D.'s lexicon, it is the word 'shattered' especially that comes to be coded as indicating a sublime transformative experience. The 'sea lily' from *Sea Garden* is 'shattered'; the supplicant's flesh in 'Amaranth' is 'shattered'; and in 'Eros', the speaker observes that 'to sing love / love must first shatter us' (H.D., *CP*, p. 319).

As this last example suggests, sublime force is often eroticised in H.D.'s work, and erotic force is often presented as sublime. As Charles LaChance observes, H.D.'s work unites a Burkean natural sublime with a sexual sublime. Chisholm even reads the sublime forces of *Sea Garden* as suggesting elemental erotic frenzy (Chisholm 1996, p. 73). This is where H.D.'s violence can lead to critical trouble. Claire Buck comments, for instance, on *Sea Garden*'s valorisation of violence in a way that surfaces the uneasiness that H.D.'s sublime can occasion among commentators: '*Sea Garden* is uncomfortably caught up with a perverse eroticisation of violence that is central to H.D.'s rejection of heterosexual norms, yet is also at odds with her critique of militarism and masculinity.'[25]

While H.D.'s imagery of violence certainly figures crucially in her rejection of heteronormativity, I am not convinced that her 'eroticisation of violence' – if that is what these poems display – stands 'at odds' with H.D.'s 'critique of militarism and masculinity'. I do think that we need to reckon with this apparent aporia in H.D.'s work in order to take full measure of her achievement and to canonise her work on bases that accord with what it actually does.

Here, I think of how *Trilogy* invokes the word 'shattered' in Part I, Poem 21, which begins: 'Splintered the crystal of identity, / shattered the vessel of integrity' (H.D., *CP*, p. 526). By this point in H.D.'s widely praised epic poem, we are primed to note how acts of violence and shattering, if excruciating, also foster regeneration. The bombed landscape of London, featured at the beginning of Part I, yields opportunities for 'inspiration'. In this context, the body, like the buildings, has undergone 'shock':

> the flesh? It was melted away,
> the heart burnt out, dead ember,
> tendons, muscles shattered, outer husk dismembered. (H.D., *CP*, p. 510)

H.D. imagines a comparable strategy for cultural renewal at the opening of Part II of *Trilogy*, which imagines religious and cultural alchemy – transmutation of what has been 'shattered'.

However, critical disquiet arises when the vehicles of H.D.'s endorsed metaphorical violence cut too close to bone and flesh. One clue about the perceived difference between the transformative violence displayed in *Trilogy* and that which engenders trouble is suggested by Buck's diction. She claims that *Sea Garden* is 'caught up' with a 'perverse eroticisation of violence'. The former phrase cannot but invoke Yeats' 'Leda and the Swan':

> Being so caught up
> So mastered by the brute blood of the air,
> Did she put on his knowledge with his power
> Before the indifferent beak could let her drop?[26]

In light of feminist critiques directed over time at Yeats' use of a scene of rape to figure conditions of possibility for momentous historical change, this poem illuminates the critical anxiety about the prominence of violence in H.D.'s work: the concern is that, rather than just evoke violence to figure conditions necessary for historical and cultural transformation, H.D.

sometimes constructs speakers who celebrate the erotic thralldom of being 'mastered'. Contrary to what Rainey implies, H.D.'s oeuvre often does suggest the alignment Yeats employs: between a sublime ravishment akin to sexual ravishment (and thus effectively figured by way of an erotic encounter), involving aggression and even violence, and preconditions for crucial transformation – individual, cultural and historical. What can occasion unease is that this alignment, often suggested through H.D.'s 'sexual sublime', reads as implicitly endorsing a psychological and sexual dynamic too close to the very erotic 'thralldom' between unequals whom H.D. devoted so much of her work to critiquing and resisting.

Like Audre Lorde, H.D. reads the erotic as a vital resource for creativity and even visionary consciousness. As H.D. observes in *Notes on Thought and Vision*, the Blakean visionary meditation written during a period when she was exchanging frequently with both D.H. Lawrence and sexologist Havelock Ellis:

> All reasoning, normal, sane and balanced men and women need and seek at certain times of their lives, certain definite physical relationships ... Not to desire and make every effort to develop along these natural physical lines, cripples and dwarfs the being. (H.D., *Notes*, p. 17)

Given this, does H.D.'s work sometimes suggest that inspirational erotic experiences arise from situations in which one individual is temporarily 'mastered' by another? Does it sometimes suggest that such a condition of generative enthralment, often signalled in her lexicon by the figures of Eros and Aphrodite, involves a kind of 'self-shattering'? It does both of these things – through language suggesting breakage, rending, agony and shattering. Yet H.D. also alternates in her work between coding 'shattering' as signalling forms of breakdown and indicating a desirable process.

A crucial example of such oscillation, indicating self-ironisation, appears in *Nights*, a novella from what H.D. called her 'lost, sad period' (Hollenberg, *H.D. and Pearson*, p. 29) of the mid 1930s – an example marked by the word 'shattering'. In this narrative, H.D.'s alter ego Natalia engages in sexual 'experiments' aimed to assuage her grief at the loss of her husband, Neil, who has left her for amatory adventures with young men. At one point, Natalia drops a tray of cocktail glasses. Enlisting this as metaphor, H.D.'s narrator notes that 'Nat was in shattered pieces.' Natalia then reveals that these were the glasses Neil loved; accordingly, the tenor of the metaphor quickly shifts twice: 'she had shattered that love'; and 'Neil was being swept up, bits of him under the carpet.' Then we learn of what Natalia desires sexually from David, her lover: 'She wanted to fall, be alabaster, let herself be shattered.'[27]

Here, through the proximity of multiple uses of 'shattered', H.D. alerts readers to a current of masochistic desire for surrender to a power that might obliterate, of the kind she stages in her early poem 'Envy'. This passage also reveals how violent acts of 'shattering' are used ambivalently in her imaginative lexicon – sometimes to figure devastation and at other times to suggest a desired sublime experience. Moreover, although such moments in H.D.'s work occasionally signal the effects of traumatic loss, other instances of erotic 'shattering' indicate H.D.'s interest in what Leo Bersani calls 'self-shattering' through an erotic sublime, a rite of passage to extraordinary consciousness.[28]

Charles LaChance's commentary on H.D.'s 'sexual sublime' discerns this important heterodox dimension of H.D.'s work – but misreads it in significant ways. LaChance rightly notes that through her sexual sublime, H.D. invokes a discourse dating from antiquity: one suggesting that a - female's 'ravishment' by a male god 'expands the female victim's consciousness' (LaChance 2004, p. 31). LaChance also rightly notes that H.D.'s sexual sublime displays, and sometimes implicitly endorses, an erotic not easily accommodated by feminist readings of her work that have become dominant in criticism. He importantly emphasises that this trend in H.D.'s thought may well have been guided by her upbringing in the Moravian Church, which affirmed mystical insight gained through erotic experience and connected *jouissance* to pain by eroticising the wounds of Christ and encouraging meditation on his suffering.[29] However, LaChance claims that H.D.'s sexual sublime is 'masculinist' (p. 33) and 'phallocentric' (p. 38), comparable to that of Lawrence and Yeats (p. 40), that it shows a 'conservative' (p. 37) strand of her sexual politics and that it displays a 'heterosexual' (p. 43) vector of her desire. Accordingly, he maintains, it undermines claims that H.D.'s work registers commitments that are feminist, lesbian and sexually progressive.

What LaChance overlooks is the way in which H.D. significantly reappropriates and redirects this discourse of the sublime (admittedly phallocentric in the forms he cites from Greek antiquity), which in her poetry comes to be transmuted into one that involves a gender-unspecific dynamic that I would no longer read as necessarily masculinist or phallocentric.[30] H.D.'s sexual sublime, in other words, can be operative whether imagined participants are male or female; it does not consistently involve, as LaChance suggests, 'phallic worship'. As he notes, H.D.'s poetry sometimes suggests reverence for enthralling male figures, but it is the Aphrodite figure in 'Amaranth' who holds the female speaker in thrall; and despite what LaChance suggests, in 'The Shrine', it is an Artemisian goddess who 'strike[s]' the genderless speakers with 'terror' (H.D., *CP*, pp. 311, 9).

H.D. often imagined herself as both man and woman;[31] she sometimes read male lovers, such as Richard Aldington, as 'sister-loves' (Laity in Friedman and DuPlessis 1990, pp. 120–1); and imagined Bryher as a 'lad'.[32] Figures in her writing reflect this gender fluidity: Natalia loves 'the tall girl in Neil' (H.D., *Nights*, p. 69) in *Nights*, and the speaker observes in 'Envy' that a male lover's 'glance' was akin to a 'girl's' (H.D., *CP*, p. 321). *Bid Me to Live* celebrates the androgynous condition of the 'gloire' as Julia's way beyond the 'man-is-man, woman-is-woman' cry of Rico, the character based on D.H. Lawrence.[33] In general, H.D. presents gender and gender dynamics as mercurial and independent of biological sex. Accordingly, her scenes of sublime erotic transport, even when implicitly endorsed as sources of inspiration, do not depend upon a heterosexual dynamic whereby a male masters a female; and problematise the assumption that such a dynamic either involves 'masculine' figures dominating 'feminine' ones or privileges masculinity. They do, however, often imply a surrender on the part of one figure involving an intermingling of passivity and self-command of the kind Sword suggests in describing H.D.'s imagined route to visionary consciousness – a willed effort to abandon control (Sword 1995, pp. 126, 140).

'The Helmsman', one of the early poems LaChance showcases, offers an example. Even if we accept LaChance's reading of the poem as suggesting erotic play, and the 'we' as calling to a powerful male god, we do not know the gender of the collective speaker. LaChance maintains that the poem's implied dynamic signifies the 'roughness, risk, pain, and breathless push and pull of heterosexuality' (LaChance 2004, p. 43). But here again, H.D. leaves sex and gender unclear or fluid, signalling that her imagined dynamics do not entail specific stable combinations or configurations of sex and gender (Sword 1995, pp. 137–8).

Is H.D.'s sexual sublime, which, indeed, constitutes a major element in her repertoire, anti-feminist? Indeed, it sometimes involves, and sometimes implicitly valorises, dynamics resembling heterosexual 'thralldom', which can read as falling short of the feminist destinations that H.D.'s work articulates elsewhere. The desire she conjures also, at times, carries the baggage of her influences – Swinburne's sadistic eroticism, for instance, sometimes peopled with misogynistic femmes fatales. Through her sexual sublime, H.D. also sometimes imagines important feminist ways beyond the straitjackets of gender roles under a heteronormative order. Is this aspect of H.D.'s erotic 'at odds' with her anti-militarism and critiques of masculinity, as Buck suggests? I would say, not necessarily, and suggest that thinking carefully about how this erotic direction of her work might be compatible with such critiques might deepen readings of H.D.'s cultural politics. It might, especially, bring us closer to discerning what, today, we might think of as H.D.'s queerness.

When H.D.'s sublime violence becomes erotic, it sometimes signals interest in sexual self-shattering as what Bersani calls *ascesis*; and in so far as it aims to imagine new modes of consciousness transcending the logic of what H.D. calls '*you* are woman, *he* is man' (*Nights*, p. 46), it forms an important dimension of H.D.'s feminist and queer work. That H.D. often notably bypasses whether participants in transformative passion are male or female; homosexual, heterosexual or otherwise; focuses chiefly on 'intensities' of desire as an active force rather than the lack implied by the word 'eros';[34] and sometimes evokes masochistic modes of ecstasy – all this figures importantly in H.D.'s challenges to heteronormativity and homonormativity.

Replying to Susan McCabe's recent comments about queer historicism and the need to continue rethinking current queer theory in response to the 'embodied' queer lives in history, I would suggest that H.D.'s non-normative sexual-identity-in process, which evolved throughout her career; along with her related imaginative fictions, have been difficult to read through what McCabe calls 'conventional understanding(s) of the lesbian';[35] and even difficult to read through prevalent understandings of the bisexual woman. In 1934, H.D. reports being delighted by Freud's assessment of her as the perfect 'bi' (Friedman, *Analyzing*, p. 197). However, despite efforts in many quarters during the 1990s to theorise it and raise its visibility, bisexuality remains a fraught concept: some read it as reinscribing a heterosexist binary; some as indicating unfortunate 'fence-sitting'.[36] Perhaps in these times of shift to the term 'queer' to encompass a range of non-normative sexualities understood as fluid, we are in a position to try another lexicon.

As we continue to debate how to construct H.D. as initiate into modern literary canons, we should recognise her work's queer feminism and feminist queerness, its investment in a sexual sublime – all serving a larger commitment to what I would call 'thinking transformation', spiritual and cultural. We should also remember the distrust that her work consistently displays of the insides, outsides and forms of stability that discourse about canons often entails. As Lee Morrissey suggests, the best thought about canons demonstrates awareness of the ongoing controversy, revision, making and breaking inherent to the work of canonisation.[37] H.D.'s work can help us to maintain such an approach to canons – one 'uncanonical enough' to remain supple and productive.

NOTES

1 H.D., *Tribute to Freud* (New York: *New Directions*, 1972), pp. 15, 6.

2 See quotations from H.D. about the 'outcast' featured at the beginning of Susan Stanford Friedman, *Penelope's Web: Gender, Modernity, H.D.'s Fiction*

(Cambridge and New York: Cambridge University Press, 1990), Ch. 4, 'Borderlines'. For H.D.'s use of 'here' and 'there', see L.L. Martz (ed.) H.D., *Collected Poems 1912–1944* (henceforth *CP*), (New York: New Directions, 1983), p. 509, N.H. Pearson (ed.) *Trilogy*, Manchester, Carcanet, I.1.

3 R. Hadas, 'On Poetry Anthologies', *New England Review*, 19.4 (1998), 126.

4 D.K. Hollenberg (ed.), *Between History and Poetry: The Letters of H.D. and Norman Holmes Pearson* (University of Iowa Press, 1997), p. 31.

5 Reviewing *Red Roses for Bronze* in 1931 (*Poetry*, 41 (1932), 94–100), for instance, R.P. Blackmur suggested that H.D. still deserved her reputation as Imagist; he read her as having begun to grow beyond her initial mode in the early 1920s but never having fully made the transition.

6 L. Untermeyer, *American Poetry Since 1900* (New York: Henry Holt, 1923), p. 309.

7 See S.S. Friedman and R.B. DuPlessis, '"I Had Two Loves Separate": The Sexualities of H.D.'s *HER*' in S.S. Friedman and R.B. DuPlessis (eds.), *Signets: Reading H.D.* (Madison: University of Wisconsin Press, 1990), pp. 206–8.

8 See M. Boughn, *H.D.: A Bibliography, 1905–1990* (Charlottesville: University Press of Virginia, 1993).

9 'buried': Friedman, 'Who Buried H.D.?', *College English*, 36 (1975), 801–14; 'silent': B. Deutsch, 'The Last of the Imagists', *New York Herald Tribune Weekly Book Review*, 1 October 1944, 18; 'long before': L. Rainey in G. Bornstein (ed.), 'Canon, Gender, and Text: The Case of H.D.', *Representing Modernist Texts: Editing as Interpretation* (Ann Arbor: University of Michigan Press, 1991), p. 102.

10 For information on H.D.'s contributions to *Close Up* and on the journal more generally, see J. Donald, A. Friedberg, and L. Marcus (eds.) *Close Up 1927–33* (London: Cassell, 1998).

11 L. Trilling, 'On the Teaching of Modern Literature' in L. Wieseltier (ed.), *The Moral Obligation to Be Intelligent* (New York: Farrar, Straus & Giroux, 2000), p. 385.

12 A. Rich, *On Lies, Secrets and Silence* (New York: Norton, 1979), p. 35.

13 A. Ostriker, 'No Rule of Procedure: The Open Poetics of H.D.' in Friedman and Blau DuPlessis, *Signets*, p. 349.

14 D. Chisholm, 'Pornopoeia, the Modernist Canon, and the Cultural Capital of Sexual Literacy: The Case of H.D.' in M. Dickie and T. Travisano (eds.), *Gendered Modernisms: American Women Poets and Their Readers* (Philadelphia: University of Pennsylvania Press, 1996), pp. 69–94; E. Gregory, 'H.D.'s Heterodoxy: The Lyric as Site of Resistance', in M. Camboni (ed.), *H.D.'s Poetry: The Meanings that Words Hide* (New York: AMS Press, 2003), pp. 21–33.

15 C. LaChance, 'The Sexual Sublime and Hilda Doolittle', *English*, 53 (2004), 32.

16 H.D., *Helen in Egypt* (New York: New Directions, 1961), p. 85.

17 H.D., *Trilogy*, I.43, *CP*, p. 543.

18 M. Altman, 'A Prisoner of Biography', *Women's Review of Books*, 9 (1992), 39; Chisholm, 'Pornopoeia', p. 85; M. Hickman, *The Geometry of Modernism: The Vorticist Idiom in Lewis, Pound, H.D., and Yeats* (Austin: University of Texas Press, 2005), pp. 40–1.

19 H.D., *Notes on Thought and Vision* (San Francisco: City Lights Books, 1982), p. 20.
20 H.D., *Trilogy*, II.31, *CP*, p. 566.
21 H.D., *Helen in Egypt*, I.4, IV.4.
22 R.B. DuPlessis, 'Romantic Thralldom in H.D.', *Contemporary Literature*, 20 (1979), 178–203.
23 For the phrase 'violent idiom,' I am indebted to Hannah Harris-Sutro, unpublished Honours Essay, McGill University (2010).
24 LaChance, p. 35; C. Laity, 'H.D.'s Romantic Landscapes: The Sexual Politics of the Garden' in *Signets*, p. 114.
25 C. Buck, '"This Other Eden": Homoeroticism and the Great War in the Early Poetry of H.D. and Radclyffe Hall' in A. Ardis and L. Lewis (eds.), *Women's Experience of Modernity 1875–1945* (Baltimore: Johns Hopkins University Press, 2002), p. 76.
26 W.B. Yeats, *The Collected Poems of Yeats* (London: Wordsworth Editions, 2000, p. 182).
27 H.D., *Nights by H.D. [John Helforth]* with an introduction by Perdita Schaffner (New York: New Directions, 1986), pp. 68–9.
28 Bersani's concept, drawn from LaPlanche and Bataille, of a masochistic *jouissance*, reads sex and art as enabling a shattering of the ego. L. Bersani, *The Freudian Body* (Columbia University Press, 1986), pp. 38–9; 'Is the Rectum a Grave?' *October*, 43 (1987), 217, 222.
29 See J. Augustine, 'Introduction to H.D.' in *The Gift* (Gainesville: University Press of Florida, 1998).
30 For commentary on this gender unspecific dynamic, see H. Sword, *Engendering Inspiration: Visionary Strategies in Rilke, Lawrence, and H.D.* (Ann Arbor: University of Michigan Press, 1995), p. 152.
31 S.S. Friedman (ed.), *Analyzing Freud: The Letters of H.D., Bryher, and Their Circle* (New York: New Directions, 2002), p. 503.
32 G. Johnston, *The Formation of 20th-century Queer Autobiography. Reading Vita Sackville-West, Virginia Woolf, Hilda Doolittle, and Gertrude Stein.* (London and New York: Palgrave Macmillan, 2007), pp. 97–8.
33 H.D., *Bid Me to Live (A Madrigal)* (New York: Grove Press, 1960), pp. 176, 62.
34 See A. Carson, *Eros the Bittersweet* (Princeton University Press, 1986), pp. 10–12, 18; Chisholm, 'Pornopoeia', p. 89, quoting G. Deleuze and F. Guattari, *Kafka: Toward a Minor Literature* (Minneapolis: University of Minnesota Press, 1986), p. 19.
35 S. McCabe, 'Whither Sexuality and Gender?', *Pacific Coast Philology*, 41 (2006), 30.
36 See M. Pramaggiore, 'BI-Introduction I: Epistemologies of the Fence' in D. Hall and M. Pramaggiore (eds.), *Representing BiSexualities: Subjects and Cultures of Fluid Desire* (New York University Press, 1996), pp. 1–7.
37 L. Morrissey, 'Introduction' in Morrissey (ed.), *Debating the Canon* (New York: Palgrave Macmillan, 2005), pp. 1–2.

2

NEPHIE J. CHRISTODOULIDES

Facts and fictions

In her 1949–50 essay 'H.D. by Delia Alton', H.D. exemplified the dialogic nature between her life and work, an understanding of autobiography she had consciously introduced as early as 1920 in her first extant novel, *Paint It Today.* Delia Alton, her nom de plume, authors H.D.; though only a textual self, she 'writes' H.D. the woman, thus conjoining life and work. The dialogic nature between H.D.'s life and her 'highly autobiographical' work casts into sharp relief the way she, much like Sylvia Plath, manipulates life 'with an informed and intelligent mind': while writing, she is being written.[1]

H.D.'s autobiographical method does not promise revelation, nor do her texts uncover a miraculously intact female subject. Instead, the autobiographical subject finds herself on multiple stages simultaneously; thus, her work is partly a process of fabrication and replenishment, a rewriting of life to generate a new textual identity by appropriating myths and revisiting personal history. H.D.'s work represents the self as produced not by experience, but by autobiography itself,[2] '[t]he story must write [her]. The story must create [her]'[3] and, as if in accordance with Olney, she 'creates a self in the very act of seeking it'.[4] Her quest is bi-focal: she needs to determine her poetic vocation in a patriarchally dominated world, and second, to come to terms with her sexuality, which is amorphous and ambivalent, vacillating between homo-eroticism and a heterosexuality related to her quest for the eternal lover.

For H.D., autobiography also has therapeutic potential and can be seen as a lay self-analysis, a sort of talking cure, in which she becomes an analyst, being at the same time her own analysand. Her introduction to psychoanalytic circles through Bryher, her collaboration and friendships with Sigmund Freud, Mary Chadwick, Havelock Ellis, Walter Schmideberg, Hans Sachs and Erich Heydt not only assisted her in her own predicaments, but taught her that she could assume the role of the analyst. She was extremely grateful that Freud considered her a disciple and she enjoyed assisting Heydt in his handling of the Küsnacht case histories.[5] Putting her life on paper was like writing her own case history. As Norman Holmes Pearson saw it, 'the moment on paper for a kind of catharsis, the ordering and getting it down' freed her; it was 'the ordering, not the data which [was] important' (Friedman and Blau DuPlessis 1990, p. 232, n37). In her revisionary process 'one work relates back' to another.[6] Julia in *Bid Me to Live* becomes Hipparchia in *Palimpsest*, Delia in *The Sword* is Elizabeth in *The Mystery*, and Hermione in *HER* becomes Hermione in *Asphodel*. As Georgia Johnston has noted, the repetitions 'create a textual memory that folds over and recreates the event textually'. Repetitions, however, involve additions, 'becoming detailed with each recurrence',[7] the additions reflecting the author's wish for perfection, which involves stability, the crystallisation of 'the ego or centre of [her] amorphous, scattered personality' by manipulating the textual self.[8]

The 1920s: *Paint It Today, Asphodel, Palimpsest*

H.D.'s first extant novel, *Paint It Today* must have been written between 1920 and 1921 in California after H.D.'s and Bryher's trip to Greece in 1920. The typescript of the novel bears the *nom de plume* 'Helga Dart', a pseudonym that H.D. will later shift to 'Helga Doorn' in *Borderline* (1930). Ostensibly another effort to maintain the H.D. initials, a closer consideration of the choice of name reveals H.D.'s effort to repudiate the patriarchal notions of the author's singular and unified self. Deriving from Old Norse, 'Helga' means 'holy', while the surname 'Dart' denotes 'a pointed weapon, intended to be thrown by the hand; a short lance, a javelin or an arrow'. Much like Plath's persona in 'Ariel', who identifies herself with the phallic arrow ('Am the arrow'),[9] H.D.'s pseudonym suggests a sacred phallicised female figure who is ready to dart towards forbidden discourse.

For Susan Stanford Friedman, 'to paint a portrait' in time is 'to create a narrative'[10] and to take it a step further, as Anna Freud sees it in her Foreword to Marion Milner's (Joanna Field) *On Not Being Able to Paint*, the creative process in art 'remains within the realm in which unknown affects and impulses find their outlet, through the way in which the artist arranges [her] medium to form harmonies of shapes, colours or sounds'. Such a wish entails a 'joining of that split between mind and body that can so easily result from trying to limit thinking to thinking only in words'.[11] Helga/H.D. claims:

> All things become beautiful if we, through the creative use of the intellect, transform them by a process of resetting them or reconsidering them in relation to what they have been or, more important still, to what they may have become. Nothing is static. All things change.[12]

Things cannot change on their own; it is therefore up to the artist/writer to intervene and rearrange them accordingly. Hence, Helga Dart's pen undertakes the authorial role and imposes an order on events and people on the page, thus producing art.

Unpolished and not as revisited as her other manuscripts, *Paint It Today* revolves around issues such as H.D.'s poetic vocation and visionary experiences, but most importantly on the sisterly love between Midget/H.D. and Josepha/Frances Gregg at first and subsequently on Midget and Althea/Bryher.[13] For Midget 'the visible world exists as poignantly, as eternally as the invisible'. She feels that there is another world joining the two which she likens to the differentiation between the past and the future, linked by the present, 'at least a poignant and ethereal present which I call the visible world' (*Paint It Today*, p. 80). Thus, the present visible world is the 'today', which she tries to recapture by recording it as a work of art.

In *Paint It Today* and *HER*, H.D. presented what she had suppressed in her other novels as well as in her poetry: her lesbianism. The writing of the novel coincides with the newly formed friendship with psychologist Havelock Ellis.[14] For Ellis, lesbianism is a congenital inversion that traps a man in a woman's body,[15] but Midget of *Paint It Today* does not follow Ellis' trajectory; her model is closer to Freud's discussion of the homosexual girl in his article 'The Psychogenesis of a Case of Homosexuality'. The case was published in German in 1920 and in English in 1920 in *The International Journal of Psycho-Analysis* (translated by B. Low and R. Gabler). Whether H.D. read the case is unclear, but she was certainly familiar with psychoanalytic issues. In his discussion of the homosexual girl, Freud attributes her homosexuality and her 'homosexual libido' to a 'continuation of an infantile fixation on her mother'. He sees the girl's homosexual tendencies as her attempt to change into a man and take the mother in place of her father as the object of her love.[16] If homosexuality entails maternal fixation for Midget, it also entails a semiotic fixation that leads to a poetic discourse that unites Midget and Josepha: in *Paint It Today*, it is not George/Pound that initiates Midget/H.D. into poetry, but Josepha, who can reactivate the lost semiotic maternal bond: 'Poetry and the beat and drop of poetry, the swerve up and the swallow wing beating back' (H.D., *Paint It Today*, p. 10).[17]

What Freud would term maternal fixation manifests in *Paint It Today* as Midget's/Helga's/H.D.'s quest for the lost maternal figure ('Will I ever find my mother') and her attempt to find a soul-mate: she wanted 'most passionately a girl child of her own age, a twin sister', following her disappointment in heterosexual lovers in the 'erstwhile fiancé' who '[h]ad shown Midget what love might be or become if one, in desperation, should accept the shadow of an understanding for an understanding itself'. What he could not give her, Josepha (and later 'white Althea') could: 'Josepha had shown her or she had shown Josepha what love was or could be or become' (H.D., *Paint It Today*, pp. 56, 6, 33, 22).

Much like in Freud's discussion of the homosexuality of the 'no-name' girl, maternal hatred stemming from disappointment or rivalry is a feeling that Midget experienced: 'How did Orestes feel when he held the knife to slay his mother? What did Orestes see? What did Orestes think?' (*Paint*, p. 42). For Kristeva, maternal hatred stems from the girl's ambivalent desire both to detach from and join with the mother. One of Kristeva's analysands confesses: '"I have her within me", the frigid woman seemed to say, "she doesn't leave me but no one else can take her place, I am impenetrable, my vagina is dead."'[18] Following Helen Deutsch, Kristeva observes that frigidity 'betrays an imaginary capture by the frigid woman of a maternal figure anally imprisoned and transferred to the cloaca-vagina'.[19] Midget is experiencing the same sort of frigidity in her sexual relations with Basil (Aldington): 'She knew that she did not feel as [Basil] wanted her to feel, with warmth and depth and warm intensity. She knew that if she felt at all it was not with warm but with cold intensity' (H.D., *Paint It Today*, p. 59).

For Robert Spoo, *Asphodel* and *Paint It Today* constitute one of the earliest surviving examples of the sustained experiments in autobiographical fiction that H.D. began in an effort to free herself from 'an old tangle' of the troubled thinking about the events of her past – in particular those of World War I – and to move beyond the 'H.D. Imagiste' role which seemed to tighten about her after the publication of her first volume of poetry, *Sea Garden* in 1916.[20]

For H.D., *Asphodel* is a continuation of *HER* (H.D. to Bryher, 18 April 1949) and an 'early edition' of Madrigal.[21] Thus, the three novels along with *Paint It Today* constitute important works, but they cannot be considered exclusive sources of information for H.D.'s life or as manifestations of her mere intention 'to tell the story of her life' as Guest sees them.[22] For Friedman, the events in the novels cannot be identified with facticity, but since Hermione is a persona for H.D., they can be seen as a trajectory 'through concepts of womanhood, work, and love that probably characterize H.D. of the twenties' (Friedman 1981, p. 44). Further, they can be seen as important texts which 'paved the way for the mother/muse and poet/mother figures of H.D.'s later poetry' (Friedman 1990, p. 190).

Like *Paint It Today*, *Asphodel* delves into Hermione's homoerotic love for Fayne Rabb (Frances Gregg) and Beryl (Bryher), 'I Hermione, tell you I love you Fayne Rabb.' She does not 'want to be . . . a boy. Nor [does she] want [Fayne] to so be. I don't feel a girl' (H.D., *Asphodel*, pp. 52, 53). Interestingly enough, Hermione's homo-eroticism is associated with the woman's visionary power: Fayne and Hermione are 'wee witches' who in George Lowndes' (Pound's) fury deserved to be burnt in Salem. His fury is not directed at their bond, but at their visionary power which his patriarchal self could not accept. Hermione is Morgan Le Fay, a seer and a priestess with regenerative power, 'I am a witch. I have made this thing.' She knows that she will cause men's fury: 'For God has told you some of his little secrets but you are in a world of men and men can blight you, men can ruin you' (H.D., *Asphodel*, pp. 50, 158, 160–1).

Further, in *Asphodel*, Hermione's motherhood experience becomes one of the most lyric hymns to the experience of pregnancy, unprecedented in any other works of H.D. Her strong feelings in gestation pre-evoke the Kristevian experience of motherhood in 'Stabat Mater'.[23] She is a subject in process; she is a cocoon, a receptacle, and there is a sort of fluidity as boundaries are blurred blending subject and object, mother and child; 'I feel no difference between in and out' (H.D., *Asphodel*, pp. 170, 179, 87–8). The blurring of boundaries entails not only primary narcissism but also the strong bond between mother and child. Highlighting H.D.'s maternal feelings, her daughter, Perdita Schaffner confesses that she 'was intensely maternal – on an esoteric plane' and 'venerated the concept of motherhood'.[24]

Further, *Asphodel* exemplifies women's productivity, a notion that preoccupies H.D. It is first seen in George Lowndes' remark: 'Did you like the opus . . . Why this petulance, Dryad? Jealous, I suppose?' Much like H.D., who wants to step out of the imposed imagist gown, Hermione exclaims: 'I should like to be – somebody . . . I am something like a magic lantern sheet and on it the most horrible and dreary pictures.' George 'wants . . . to somehow suppress' her. 'When the woman is clever (brilliantly clever) the husband takes quick action.' '. . . George would write for them both' (H.D., *Asphodel*, pp. 57, 62, 74).

Talking about the nature of the title of her other important biographical work of the 1920s, *Palimpsest*, Deborah Kelly Kloepfer, observes its anagrammatic version, i.e. 'simple past', and notes that

> it creates both an augmented or extended text and a reduced or narrowed one; it accommodates multiplicity and yet, in the privacy of its intersections, creates a cryptic and distorted space, as well.[25]

Going further than this, I can note that the palimpsest becomes an important tool for H.D. to 'mend a break in time',[26] or as Kloepfer notes, to make 'some sense of her past' (p. 186). The novel consists of three, on a surface level unrelated, stories: 'Hipparchia: War Rome (*c.* 75 BC)'; 'Murex: War and Postwar London (*c.* 1916–1926)'; and 'Secret Name: Excavator's Egypt (*c.* 1925)'. All three heroines, Hipparchia, Ray(monde) and Helen, are engaged in a self-tracing quest and become survivors, like H.D., through writing.

As H.D. mentions in 'H.D. by Delia Alton', the story of *Bid Me to Live*, a war story, 'was roughed out, summer 1939', was 'left simmering or fermenting . . . run through a vinter's sieve, the dregs . . . thrown out' and in winter 1949 she tasted 'the 1939 gathering' as 'at last, the War I story had "written itself"'.[27] The book recreates the literary and social scene of London between 1916 and 1919, 'the times and the customs' (H.D., *Bid Me To Live*, p. 7). As Friedman sees it, without 'frills' as per Freud's admonitions.[28] It looks like a textual montage of scenes and incidents, taken from H.D.'s autobiographical novels such as *Palimpsest*, *HER*, *Asphodel* and *Paint It Today*, but names are different, certain events are suppressed (homo-eroticism), and some new characters appear for the first time: D.H. Lawrence – Rico, Frieda Lawrence – Elsa, Cecil Gray – Cyril Vane. For H.D., it is 'a novel in historical time . . . the eternal story of the search' of the 'Eternal Lover' whom Julia/H.D. seeks 'in contemporary time, among her own associates of England and America' (H.D., *Bid Me To Live*, pp. 1, 3).

The First World War becomes an agent under whose hand Rafe Ashton (Aldington) has changed from the romantic poet, the lover-companion into an insensitive over-sexed authoritarian Roman soldier, 'the stranger became singularly strange' (H.D., *Bid Me To Live*, p. 45). As Friedman observes, Julia is married to war and her name stresses her connection to it, she is of the ash: 'She is Mrs. Ash-ton in a "city of ashes"' (p. 144). This connection is one that governs her pro-creativity and love-life. She gives birth to a stillborn child and, significantly enough, it is not the insensitive husband who causes this because of the way he breaks the news of *The Lusitania*, but the war itself. The matron advises Julia not to have another child while the war is being waged (p. 25). This causes frigidity; Julia avoids her over-sexed husband, who is estranged and promotes the double sexual politics: the woman as a passionate lover or the frigid intellectual dilettante. This double bind is seen not only in her estrangement from Rafe, who loves her 'but desire[s] l'autre' (p. 56), but also in the way she is perceived by Rico (Lawrence). Her bond with him is 'cerebral' (p. 57) and alien to his notion 'man-is-man-woman-is-woman'. He seems to be promoting the cultural stereotype of the intellectual woman as asexual, unfeminine and frigid and his distinction of the two women, Julia and Elsa, as the two complementing parts of the ideal feminine figure clearly manifests this.[29] However, a lurking sisterly complementary bond seems to be binding Bella and Julia. Looking at Bella (Dorothy Yorke), Julia feels that 'she was looking at herself in a mirror, another self, another dimension but nevertheless herself' (p. 103). The antithesis between the two brings them together (a sense of desired duality), since the 'frozen altar' meets the passionate 'autre' (pp. 163, 56).

The 1940s and after: *White Rose and the Red*, *The Mystery* and *Helen in Egypt*

For Alison Halsall, *White Rose and the Red*, H.D.'s 1948 Pre-Raphaelite novel, expounds upon her wish to foreground 'heterosexual power relations that span the two centuries', and 'to draw attention to issues of ownership and possession of the female figure that mimetic art affords the artist – issues that H.D. was also addressing at this time in *Trilogy* and *Helen in Egypt*'. Further, she attempts to recover the figure of Elizabeth Siddall, Dante Gabriel Rossetti's muse, unfortunate wife and suppressed artist, as a 'marginalized art sister'.[30]

Cassandra Laity sees the novel as a *roman-à-clef*, a 'fictional autobiography' in which H.D. recasts modernist contemporaries as Pre-Raphaelite personae. Elizabeth Siddall is H.D., whereas Rossetti stands for Richard Aldington; William Morris is a 'composite' figure of Freud and D.H. Lawrence.[31] The novel constitutes a supplementary jigsaw part to add to H.D.'s effort to solve subjectivity predicaments either by mythologising the self or recasting events as catalysts. As she puts it in 'H.D. by Delia Alton', in the Pre-Raphaelites, whom she had studied extensively, she senses a sort of continuity:

> But something of my early search, my first expression or urge toward expression in art, finds a parallel in the life of Rossetti and Elizabeth Siddall. So, as a very subtle emotional exercise, I go over the ground, find relationships or parallels between my own emotional starvation and hers, between a swift flowering soon to be cut down, in her case, by death, in mine, by a complete break after War I, with the group of artist's described in *Madrigal*. ('H.D. by Delia Alton', p. 25)

The affinity she perceives does not stop here, but her strong sense of the intricacies of language, that 'similar sounding words by the fact of their sound alone establish a connection between their referents'[32] leads her to a discovery: first, that her grandmother's 'submerged terror in *The Gift* is not unlike that of Elizabeth Siddall' and, second most importantly, that she comes upon the following:

> Oddly, as things happen, *The Secret*, the key-chapter of *The Gift*, deals with the family history of the Seidels. The grandmother's first husband was a

> connection of a certain Henri, Chevalier de Seidel, who had been at the Russian court. Though the name is commonly accepted as German, *seidel*, a cup or mug is originally a *fremdword* according to Grimm's dictionary, as from the Latin *situlus* or *situla*. *Situlus* is a small pail, measure, hence cup – a box or ballot-box. Was it a mere accident that drew me to Elizabeth Siddall? My grandmother's first married name was Elizabeth Seidel. ('H.D. by Delia Alton', pp. 27, 28)

The semantic affinity of Siddall's surname with the cup strongly recalls the quest for the Holy Grail which, in H.D., however, becomes the quest to find the Eternal Lover, but also to retrieve the forsaken self, the marginalised and denigrated artist, the used muse she was, especially at the beginning of her career, much like Elizabeth Siddall, whose creative power, like hers, emerges in dreams and trances.[33]

While it is true that *The Mystery*, written between 1949 and 1951 and published in 2009, is regarded as 'historical fiction', it is, at the same time, seen as deeply 'rooted in [H.D.'s] childhood life and wartime experience' (H.D., *The Mystery*, pp. xxiii, xxiv) and, along with *The White Rose and the Red* and her children's book *The Hedgehog*, can be read as 'psychological autobiography' (Friedman 1990, p. 72).

The novel is situated in Prague a little before the French Revolution. Two cousins, Elizabeth and Henry Dohna, have visited Prague in an effort to collect 'evidence of their grandfather's [Count Nicholas Louis Zindendorf, founder of the Moravian Church in Bethlehem, Pennsylvania] spiritual inheritance', which H.D. associated with the 'earlier di-established or "lost" Church of Provence [sic]' and which has to do with a plan for 'peace on earth' ('H.D. by Delia Alton', p. 15). Elizabeth, bearing the name of H.D.'s maternal grandmother, can be a mask for H.D. and her task for the establishment of universal peace resembles hers. She shares with her the quest for the lost plan, what H.D. is trying to retrieve through the seances (see *The Sword Went Out to Sea* and *Majic Ring*); like her, Elizabeth is a little 'sister', tending the sick Saint Germain, strongly recalling H.D.'s reminiscences about tending the wounded father in *The Gift*.[34] Henry Dohna, who bears H.D.'s initials, is the masculine part who complements Elizabeth's femininity and who recasts the two as Isis and Osiris, thus enabling H.D. 'to understand her own incorporation of both the mother and the father' (H.D., *The Mystery*, p. xxi).

The figure of Saint Germain is a composite figure based on Count Louis Zinzendorf (they have the same first name), but he also bears resemblances to H.D: he suffers a physical and mental breakdown like her; he is blessed with the gift of being accessible to visitations, a gift she also had; in Elizabeth he seeks the ideal and eternal love that H.D. strives throughout her life to access.[35]

The Mystery is the locus where H.D. will terminate her quest successfully, as she claims in a 1951 letter to Norman Holmes Pearson, 'I wanted you to tell me if you feel it is finished? I do. And FINIS too, to a whole processus [sic] or life-time of experience' (Hollenberg, 'Between', pp. 107–8). Yet this does not seem to be the case, as the self-analysis is carried on with *Helen in Egypt*. For Philippe Lejeune, 'autobiography is not an act of analysis but a lived activity of synthesis'.[36] With *Helen in Egypt*, H.D. in a way reverses this and shows that by marrying myth and reality, ficticity and facticity – and she does so by using the mythical figure of Helen as a hypothetical construction – she engages in an act of synthesis, and she can achieve a successful *analysis*, which in her case turns out to be a lay self-analysis. I see this task as important for the creation of a new kind of autobiography, a hybrid one, composed of myth, reality, fictions, all constituting a self-written case history.[37] An important part of the autobiographical tint of the poem focuses on the characters, the 'cavalier' group who sealed H.D.'s life indelibly: Theseus is Sigmund Freud (psychoanalytic sessions May–June 1933; October–December 1934); Paris is Erich Heydt, her doctor at Küsnacht sanatorium; Achilles is Lord Hugh Dowding, the hero of the battle of Britain. By creating her own plot in the encounter between Helen and Paris, H.D. finds the chance to revisit and reverse Freud's Oedipal theory, thus disagreeing with him in her own special way and proving that the 'Professor was not always right' (H.D., *Tribute*, p. 18). In *Helen in Egypt*, H.D. seems to be discreetly, slightly ironically, casting into sharper relief his Oedipal theory: Helen comes to Theseus with injured feet ('your feet are wounded').[38] She thus becomes both Oedipus with the swollen feet and Achilles with his arrow-pierced heel. She delicately pokes fun at Freud's diagnosis about her own Oedipal complex and the way in which he is trying to account for her symptoms: 'F. says mine [maternal fixation] is absolutely FIRST [sic] layer, I got stuck at the earliest pre-OE stage, and "back to the womb" seems to be my only solution. Hence islands, sea, Greek primitives and so on. It's all too wonder-making' (H.D., *Analyzing Freud*, p. 142). Freud's use of the Oedipus myth to denote a child's individuation/subjectivity path takes two different routes, depending on the sex of the child: for boys, the Oedipal complex leads to castration fear, which is triggered by the fear of being punished for having the mother as a love object. For the girl, the procedure is modified, since it is the castration complex, experienced at the sight of the boy's penis, that triggers the Oedipal complex. Rather than sharing the boy's fear, the girl experiences envy for not having a penis, blames the mother for this lack, becomes hostile to her and directs her love to her father.[39] By donning Oedipus' identity, H.D. alludes to Freud's theory, but at the same time she indicates the way

Helen's/her trajectory deviates from the normal route as she becomes male (Oedipus), thus authenticating her bisexuality.

One of H.D.'s 'heros fatals', men with whom she was infatuated, was Lord Dowding, who repudiated the validity of the seance messages she was getting from the dead RAF boys, merely dismissing them as coming from 'beings of a lower order' (H.D., *The Sword*, p. 34). In *Helen in Egypt*, he as Achilles and Helen are reconciled and the fruit of this reconciliation is the child, Euphorion. The child is what H.D. aspired to be getting from her own spiritual union with Lord Dowding: not only would his dead pilots become her boys as well – they had actually chosen her to disseminate their message – their own child would be the outcome of their joined spiritualist efforts to establish universal peace, thus bringing euphoria (hence Euphorion) to the world; but Lord Dowding would dismiss her plan.

Helen in Egypt as autobiography is also imbued with the figure of Paris palimpsestically formulated on Erich Heydt. Paris wants the earlier Helen; he wants to obliterate any time barriers and be able to recover her as she used to be. Heydt wants H.D. to retrieve 'the fiery moment',[40] her budding sexuality experienced in Philadelphia with Pound, memories she was repressing. Remembrance would bring healing, but H.D. has her doubts: Heydt will be the mirror to reflect the fiery moment; she will be the one to substantiate it, to recall it, but catching it through Heydt, the speculum, she may burn herself, like the burnt paper under the magnifying glass she and her brother were playing with, thus arousing the anger of the father (*Tribute*, pp. 26–7).

Autobiographical poetry of the late 1950s: *Hermetic Definition*

Friedman points out that H.D.'s early poetry is very impersonal, with few exceptions – she names the three purely autobiographical poems, 'Envy', 'Eros' and 'Amaranth' – concomitantly becoming 'more narrative, more secretly personal, more centered in culture, more directly female', examples being *Hymen* and *Heliodora* (Friedman 1990, p. 66). Her 1961 poem, *Hermetic Definition*, is essentially autobiographical. In it feature Haitian journalist Lionel Durand, the poet St John Perse and, to a lesser extent, Rafer Johnson, the decathlon star, three figures who will help H.D. to 'keep [her] identity' while at the same time 'walk unfalteringly toward a Lover, / the *hachish supérieur* of dream'.[41]

Throughout the poem, but most importantly in 'Red Rose and a Beggar', preoccupation with sexuality symbolised with the *motif* of the rose is seen as strongly associated with spirituality, a notion she develops in *Notes on Thought and Vision*: 'we must be "in love" before we can understand the mysteries of vision'.[42] The text of *Hermetic Definition* is, indeed, Hermetic but at the same time alchemical, since Hermes is patron of alchemy. As such, he guides her towards the definition she seeks this time; she is seventy-three years old and the reawakened sexuality falls heavily on her, but since Hermes, her guide, maintains that 'sexuality does not exclude spirituality nor spirituality sexuality, for in God all opposites are abolished',[43] she rests complacent. She knows that she and her new 'cavaliers' 'meet in antitheses' (H.D., *Hermetic*, p. 31) and the reddest rose that was 'so slow [. . .] to open' finally opened:

> the reddest rose unfolds,
> (which is ridiculous
> in this time, this place,
>
> unseemly, impossible,
> even slightly scandalous),
> the reddest rose unfolds;
> (nobody can stop that. . . .). (p. 3)

Her reawakened sexuality is tightly linked to her productivity. She sees new light in her contact with St John Perse: 'my hand worn with endeavour, / one curious, pre-occupation with stylus and pencil / was re-born at your touch'. When the rose unfolded, 'the Red-Roses-for Bronze' – the reference is to her 1932 collection *Red Roses for Bronze* – proved that they 'were for an abstraction'. The roses she evokes in *Hermetic Definition* are offered to 'a reality; / the ecstasy comes through [him] / but goes on' (pp. 26, 14).

In which way has he affected her poetic perfection? What was it that was resurfaced? Talking about H.D., one recalls the incident at the British Museum tea room where 'H.D. Imagiste' emerged through the foams pounded by Pound's caduceus. It took H.D. years to abandon the crystalline poems[44] and assume her own voice. Now, she thinks 'perhaps humility is more becoming / in a woman' (H.D., *Hermetic*, p. 13). She intersperses her work with Perse's and claims: 'your words free me, / I am alive in your recognition' (p. 33). Despite the textual blending, they are finally separated. Lionel Durand dies and St John Perse must be brushed aside, '[i]f she were to resolve this curious "condition"' (p. 49). The paradox remains unresolved, but what matters is writing:

> I did know that I must keep faith
> with something, I called it writing,
> *write, write, or die.*
>
> . . . I had to go on
> the writing was the un-born,
> the conception. (pp. 49, 54)

Much like her mask Her, H.D. is cognisant of her 'nebulous'[45] self and is aware that '[w]hen the ego or centre of our amorphous, scattered personality crystallizes out, then and only then, are we of use to our selves and to other people' (H.D., *The Sword*, p. 140). Thus, she attempts to do so via her text: 'She herself is the writing' (H.D., *Helen in Egypt*, p. 22), and 'performs a female presence via textuality'.[46] In this way, any time gaps are obliterated, 'Past, present, future: it only becomes clear when I wrote of it' (*Helen in Egypt*, p. 55) and in her quest she assumes various identities. She knows that 'Isis takes many forms as does Osiris' ('H.D.', p. 63); she does this to test the self against each mask and beget a unified entity: 'I am for a moment . . . Egyptian; a little cell of my brain responds to a cell of someone's brain who died thousands of years ago.'[47] As her daughter Perdita Schaffner sees it, 'she offers an image of autobiography as open-ended, never finished yet strongly present' (Vanacker 1997, p. 194) and, whether Midget, Delia, Julia, Hermione, Raymonde, Helga, Rhoda, E/Rica, Margaret, John Hellforth, H.D. always remains a subject in process.

NOTES

1 S.S. Friedman and R.B. DuPlessis, '"I had Two Loves Separate": The Sexualities of H.D.'s HER', in S.S. Friedman and R.B. DuPlessis (eds.), *Signets: Reading H.D.* (Madison: The University of Wisconsin Press, 1990) p. 206. 'Interview' in Peter Orr (ed.), *The Poet Speaks: Interviews with Contemporary Poets* (London: Routledge, 1966).

2 L. Gilmore, *Autobiographics: A Feminist Theory of Women's Self-representation* (Ithaca and London: Cornell University Press, 1994), p. 25.

3 H.D., *Bid Me to Live (A Madrigal)* (New York: Grove Press, 1960), p. 181.

4 S.S. Friedman, 'Women's Autobiographical Selves: Theory and Practice', in S. Smith and J. Watson (eds.), *Women, Autobiography, Theory: A Reader* (Madison: The University of Wisconsin Press, 1998), p. 73.

5 H.D., *Tribute to Freud* (New York: New Directions, 1972), p. 44; 'Compassionate Friendship' (Yale Collection of American Literature, Beinecke Rare Book Room and Manuscript Library, Yale University), Box 38, p. 106.

6 'H.D. by Delia Alton' (Yale Collection of American Literature, Beinecke Rare Book Room and Manuscript Library, Yale University), Box 44, folders 1121–5, p. 6.

7 G. Johnston, *Queer Autobiographies* (New York: Palgrave Macmillan, 2007), p. 123.

8 Delia Alton in C. Hogue and J. Vandivere (eds.), *The Sword Went Out to Sea (Synthesis of a Dream)* (Gainesville: University Press of Florida, 2007), p. 140.

9 S. Plath, *Collected Poems* (London: Faber & Faber, 1989), p. 239.

10 S.S. Friedman, *Penelope's Web: Gender, Modernity, H.D.'s Fiction* (Cambridge and New York: Cambridge University Press, 1990), p. 196.

11 A. Freud, 'Foreword', in M. Milner, *On Not Being Able to Paint* (Los Angeles: J.P. Tarcher, Inc., 1957), p. xiv.

12 H.D., *Paint It Today* (New York and London: New York University Press, 1992), p. 84.

13 In 'Compassionate Friendship', she mentions that she plans to revisit the 'sister motive' in *Helen in Egypt* with the figure of Clytaemnestra, p. 140. In the 1950s, she established a sisterly relation with the author, E.M. Butler, 'the "Astarte" of [her] *Helen* sequence, the sister of Helen, Clytaemnestra' (pp. 139–40). Butler's *Fortunes of Faust* gave H.D. the motive to write *Helen in Egypt* (Yale Collection of American Literature, Beinecke Rare Book Room and Manuscript Library), Box 38, folder 1013. In *Paint It Today*, the reference to the First World War is only fleetingly done, much like a device marking the quick passage of time. Midget comments on Basil's return from the front: 'with the smell of gas in his breath, with the stench of death in his clothes' (p. 46).

14 H.D. and Bryher met Ellis in 1919. After the stillbirth of her child and her separation from Aldington, H.D. 'found solace in Ellis' quiet understanding'. See P. Grosskurth, *Havelock Ellis: A Biography* (New York: Alfred A. Knopf, 1980), p. 295.

15 H. Ellis, *Sexual Inversion: Studies in the Psychology of Sex*, 3rd edn (Philadelphia: F.A. Davis, 1915).

16 S. Freud, 'The Psychogenesis of a Case of Homosexuality', in J. Strachey (ed.), *Case Histories II*, vol. 9, *Penguin Freud Library* (London: Penguin Books, 1979), pp. 145–72.

17 In *Revolution in Poetic Language*, Julia Kristeva notes that there are two kinds of signifying process in the creation of meaning: these are the Symbolic, which is paternal, patriarchal and subject to systematisation, and the Semiotic, which is maternal, resists meaning and hence systematisation. The Semiotic is identified with a child's developing language which is characterised by sound, rhythm and babble, manifested in both poetic language and psychosis. See *Revolution in Poetic Language*, (trans.) M. Waller (New York: Columbia University Press, 1984), pp. 25–30.

18 J. Kristeva, *Black Sun*, (trans.) L. Roudiez (New York: Columbia University Press, 1987), p. 77.

19 H. Deutsch, *Psychology of Women* 2 vols. (New York: Grune & Stratton, 1944), vol. 1, p. 218; *Black Sun*, p. 77.

20 R. Spoo, 'Introduction' in *Asphodel* (New York: New Directions), p. ix.

21 S.S. Friedman, *Psyche Reborn: The Emergence of H.D.* (Bloomington: Indiana University Press, 1981), p. 39.

22 B. Guest, *Herself Defined: The Poet H.D. and Her World* (New World: Doubleday, 1984), p. 34.

23 J. Kristeva, 'Stabat Mater', in *Tales of Love*, (trans.) L. Roudiez (New York: Columbia University Press, 1983), pp. 234–63.

24 P. Schaffner, 'A Sketch of H.D.: The Egyptian Cat', in *Signets*, p. 4.

25 D.K. Kloepfer, 'Fishing the Murex Up: Sense and Resonance in H.D.'s *Palimpsest*', in *Signets*, p. 185.

26 See 'May 1943', in L.L. Martz (ed.) H.D. *Collected Poems 1912–1944* (New York: New Directions, 1983), pp. 492–501.

27 'H.D. by Delia Alton', pp. 1, 50a.

28 S.S. Friedman (ed.), *Analyzing Freud: The Letters of H.D., Bryher, and Their Circle* (New York: New Directions, 2002), p. 307.

29 H.D. adapts Lawrence's prose techniques and embeds parts of his poetic work in *Madrigal*. Her intertextual embedding has nothing to do with her 'cerebral fire' that 'ignites' her own (p. 55), but is triggered by her anger at his double bind. She manipulates his phallic patriarchal language only to show the creative power of the woman who is empowered by the semiotic force of the patriarchal language to resist the double bind promoted by patriarchy.

30 A. Halsall (ed.), *White Rose and the Red* (Gainesville: University Press of Florida, 2009), pp. xxii, xxxv.

31 C. Laity, *H.D. and the Victorian Fin de Siècle: Gender, Modernism, Decadence* (Cambridge and New York: Cambridge University Press, 1996), p. 155.

32 H.D., in J. Augustine (ed.), *The Mystery* (Gainesville: University Press of Florida, 2009), p. 204.

33 H.D.'s fascination with the Holy Grail and the quest motif is seen in many of her works, including *Helen in Egypt*. See pp. 149, 181, 191.

34 *The Gift*, 'What It Was' (Gainesville: University Press of Florida, 1998), pp. 185–206.

35 St Germain is also associated with Erich Heydt. See H.D. 'Sagesse' in *Hermetic Definition* (New York: New Directions, 1969), pp. 57–84.

36 P. Lejeune in J.P. Eakin (trans.), *On Autobiography* (Minneapolis: University of Minnesota Press, 1989), p. 104.

37 In *Helen in Egypt*, H.D. unearths and recycles the myth of Helen of Troy as this is used by Stesichorus and Euripides. For both Stesichorus and Euripides, it was the phantom of Helen ('eidolon') that was actually present on the ramparts of Troy. The real Helen was transported by her father Zeus to Egypt, where she was joined by her husband Menelaus on his way back to Sparta.

38 *Helen in Egypt* (New York: New Directions, 1974), p. 151.

39 S. Freud, in J. Strachey (ed.), An *Outline of Psychoanalysis*, new edn (London: Penguin Books, 2003).

40 H.D., *End to Torment: A Memoir of Ezra Pound* (New York: New Directions, 1979), p. 17.

41 H.D., *Hermetic Definition* (New York: New Directions, 1972), p. 21.

42 H.D., *Notes on Thought and Vision* (San Francisco: City Lights Books, 1982), p. 22.

43 C.G. Jung, *Psychology and Alchemy*, trans. R.F.C Hull, 2nd edn (London: Routledge, 1993), p. 124.

44 In her autobiographical account of her work 'H.D. by Delia Alton', she feels displeased with the label 'crystalline' attached to her earlier poems, but realises after all that it is the pent-up energy, 'the concentrated essence of the rough matrix' that matters, the 'energy itself and the matrix itself [that] have not yet been assessed' (p. 8).

45 *HERmione* (New York: New Directions, 1981), p. 3.

46 S. Vanacker, 'Autobiography and Orality: The Work of Modernist Women Writers' in T.L. Broughton and L. Anderson (eds.), *Women's Lives/Women's Times: New Essays on Autobiography* (Albany: State University of New York, 1997), p. 188.

47 H.D., 'Dark Room', in *The Gift*, p. 51.

3

CYRENA N. PONDROM

H.D. and the 'little magazines'

Like most modernist poets, H.D. found her first chance to publish her avant-garde work in 'little magazines': 'Priapus' (later renamed 'Orchard'), 'Hermes of the Ways' and 'Epigram, After the Greek' appeared in 1913 in the third issue of Harriet Monroe's new *Poetry* magazine. Until after the Second World War, some of H.D.'s most important poetry and crucial critical essays continued to appear first in such magazines. During the teens and twenties, her poems could be found in all of the most daring and innovative journals of the time – including (in addition to *Poetry*), *The New Freewoman*, *The Egoist*, *Glebe*, *The Little Review*, *Contact*, *Sphere*, *The Dial*, *Coterie*, *Gargoyle*, *Rhythmus*, *Double Dealer*, *Transatlantic Review*, *This Quarter*, *The Chapbook*, *Close Up*, *transition*, *Agenda*, *Pagany*, *Seed* and *Life and Letters Today*.[1]

This was the era of the great women editors and publishers, including Harriet Monroe of *Poetry*, Dora Marsden and Harriet Shaw Weaver of *The New Freewoman* and *The Egoist*, Margaret Anderson and Jane Heap of *The Little Review* and Sylvia Beach and Adrienne Monnier of Shakespeare & Company. H.D. knew them all, but like Marianne Moore, who for a few years edited *The Dial*, she was deeply committed to her own writing career and never wished to make editing and publishing the work of others her dominant literary contribution. Despite this, she was thrust into the role of literary editor on *The Egoist* during the teens, when she also undertook a stabilising editorial role in the compilation of *Some Imagist Poets 1915*, *1916* and *1917*. In those roles, she exercised formative influence in the shaping and achievements of the imagist movement. She also provided models for the practice of imagism through her development, with Richard Aldington, of two sequences of volumes in The Poets' Translation Series. Moreover, her association with Bryher, which began in 1918, led her to major contributions to two other avant-garde journals which Bryher supported during the period from 1927 until the end of the 1940s – *Close Up, first journal on experimental film in English*, and *Life and Letters Today*, one of the few ventures to continue to provide opportunities for publication during the Second World War.

The Egoist was founded as *The Freewoman* in November 1911 by Dora Marsden as a means of advocacy for Marsden's philosophical and feminist ideas. Soon after it was retitled *The New Freewoman* in June 1913, Ezra Pound became its literary editor,[2] and the journal became a forum for the exhibition of the imagists. H.D.'s poem 'Sitalkas' appeared in September 1913. Pound handed over the job of assistant editor to Richard Aldington in December 1913,[3] and on 1 January 1914, the magazine reappeared as *The Egoist*, under which it continued to publish until December 1919. Aldington was listed as assistant editor from January 1914 until May 1917, but H.D.'s editorial role was not formally recognised until June 1916, when Aldington enlisted in the army and H.D.'s name was added as another assistant editor. She executed the duties of both until after the issue for May 1917, when T.S. Eliot took over the job. Although front-page editorial matter was normally taken up with feminist cultural analyses and philosophical discussions, principally by Dora Marsden, the remainder of the journal, usually twelve to fifteen closely printed double-columned pages, was devoted to discussions of developments in poetry, literature, music and the arts, in England, France, America and, to some extent, Germany and Russia, and to the publication of some of the finest current examples of both poetry and fiction in English. It was easily the single most important English language journal devoted to the avant-garde arts at that time. Thus, H.D.'s editorial position with the journal places her among the significant women editors of the day, notwithstanding her own diffidence in asserting such credit.

In fact, it is clear that H.D. had a significant connection with the literary editing of *The Egoist* from the beginning of the imagists' association with it. An indicator of this early role is suggested in part by the important place *The Egoist* had in bringing Marianne Moore's poetry to the widespread attention of the poetic avant-garde. Moore was first published in *The Egoist* on 1 April 1915, with 'To the Soul of "Progress"' (later 'To Military Progress') and 'To a Man Working His Way Through a Crowd'. She reappeared the next month, in the extremely important special 'Imagist' issue with 'To William Butler Yeats on Tagore', and contributed two more poems in August 1915. Although Aldington was the sole assistant editor listed, and H.D. at this time was deeply involved in two other publishing ventures in which she would have major editorial responsibility (The Poets' Translation Series and *Some Imagist Poets 1915, 1916* and *1917*), H.D. nonetheless played a key role in assessing Moore's significance and in assuring her publication in *The Egoist*.

H.D. did not respond immediately, for she was far into pregnancy which led to the stillbirth of a child on 21 May 1915,[4] but her involvement is explicit in her first letter to Moore on 21 August 1915:

> I remember you at Bryn Mawr May Fête, in a green dress. I imagine that this *you*, which sends poetry to the 'Egoist' is the same . . .! – I am H.D. – also Mrs. R. Aldington, and R. has spoken often of your work! We both think you have achieved a remarkable technical ability![5]

Some years later, responding to inquiries about the imagist period from Norman Holmes Pearson, the friend and professor who established the H.D. Archive at Yale University, H.D. recalled an incident concerning Pound and continued:

> that must have been 1907, about. Marianne did not come into it till later. It was I who met her at Bryn Mawr. She sent some poems when R[ichard] A [ldington] and I were Egoist, 1913 or 1914 [sic]. I jumped in, said yes, yes, E.P. liked them, a few were published. E. and the others, I think then, met her in New York.[6]

In the same initial letter to Moore, H.D. further demonstrates her role as editor and publisher, particularly of imagists and other women poets, by encouraging Moore to continue the battle to gain publication: 'I hope you are going on writing your works. I know, more or less, what you are up against, though I escaped some time years ago . . . I wonder if you ever feel like coming here for a time!'[7] H.D. and Richard Aldington had already begun to plan a series of small volumes publishing translations from the classics, and in this letter H.D. attempted to recruit Moore's participation in The Poets' Translation Series. She continued: 'I am sending you prospectus [*sic*] of our latest . . . venture. We will go on with it if these numbers prove a success. – Perhaps, if the other six are attempted you would like to try your hand translating some obscure Greek or Latin! – I will get R. to send you some suggestions if you would be interested.'

H.D. sent a separate envelope, which included an advertisement of the forthcoming 'Poets' Translation Series, published by *The Egoist*, (six pamphlets)'. This series was established to publish in pamphlet form translations from the Greek and Latin, chiefly by contemporary poets associated with the imagist group, and all of the volumes of the first series contained poems which initially appeared in *The Egoist*. Poems from the first number, Aldington's *The Poems of Anyte of Tegea*, appeared in *The Egoist* in September 1915, and poems included in the second, Edward Storer's translation of the 'Poems and Fragments of Sappho', appeared the following month (pp. 153–5). It was in this issue that the six-volume series of translations of the classics was formally announced, together with the advertisement that the next month's selection in *The Egoist* would be the 'Choruses from the "Iphigeneia in Aulis" of Euripides', translated by H.D. These poems appeared in November 1915, and comprised the nine-part first and brief second 'Choruses of the Women of Calkis' (pp. 171–2). They amounted to slightly more than a third of the eighteen pages published by *The Egoist* as a separate volume early in 1916.

Some poems from Aldington's translations of 'Latin Poems of the Renaissance', which made up the fourth volume of the series, appeared in *The Egoist* in December 1915. At this juncture, H.D. and Aldington's editorial duties for *The Egoist* and the Poets' Translation Series appear to have been completely intertwined. The first issue for 1916 announces a second series of translations which were to include H.D.'s translations from Euripides' *Ion*, and contains poems which would be issued as the fifth number of the current series, the 'Poems of Leonidas of Tarentum'. The translation of Leonidas is ascribed to James Whitall, but apparently the reality was more complicated, for Caroline Zilboorg claims that 'both Whitall and H.D. helped . . . [Aldington] translate "The Poems of Leonidas of Tarentum", which became Number 5 in the first series'.[8] The sequence was completed the next month with the publication of poems from F.S. Flint's translation of 'The Mosella of Decimus Magnus Ausonius' in February 1916. When the complete first Poets' Translation Series was reviewed in the *Times Literary Supplement* that spring, it was H.D.'s work that was singled out from the six for special praise. The reviewer judged H.D.'s volume 'the most notable . . . a rendering, of surprising novelty and interest, and in a method hardly hitherto attempted'.[9]

Although Aldington bore the responsibility of frequently writing a major article or review for each issue until he actually enlisted in the Eleventh Battalion of the Devonshire Regiment in late May 1916 (Zilboorg 1992, p. 21), his frenzy and depression at the prospect of being called up appear to have left an increasing amount of the management and mediation for all three of their joint editorial projects to H.D. In this stressful eventuality, H.D. kept *Some Imagist Poets* and *The Egoist* moving forward. One of the first ways in which her increasing responsibility was probably felt was a return of Pound to its pages. Although he was a frequent essay contributor in 1914, he contributed nothing from 1 February 1915 to 1 March 1916 – a period in which conflict between many of the imagists and Pound over control of the movement was particularly acute. As H.D. quietly took greater control over the collection of poems for *Some Imagist Poets* and the fortunes of *The Egoist*, Pound reappeared, first in the essay 'Meditatio' in March, and then in the long-running translations of the

'Dialogues of Fontenelle', which ran almost continuously until June 1917, when H.D.'s literary editorship ended.

H.D. told Flint on 17 May 1916, 'Miss Weaver writes that I can take R.'s place on *Egoist* when he goes (do not speak of this please). We will try to keep the rag going . . .'[10] Her literary editorship finally was acknowledged in a terse 'Notice to Readers' on 1 June 1916: 'Mr Aldington will shortly be called up for military service and during his absence the assistant editorship of *The Egoist* will be taken over by 'H.D.' (Mrs Richard Aldington)' (p. 85). But the masthead still listed Richard Aldington and H.D. as joint assistant editors. This status continued until the end of H.D.'s editorship, even when it was patently clear that Richard had no hand in the editing, since he was at the front in France. H.D. felt the additional burden immediately. She wrote to Flint in mid July 'I am going to Corfe Castle in a few days to be near R . . . I don't know what to write you – I am so tired typing for *Egoist* – but you must keep up your heart & keep out of the war' ('H.D. to Flint', p. 575).

When she formally began to substitute for Richard, H.D. initially wrote a major essay or review for nearly every issue. Her increased influence was apparent even before the official acknowledgement, in an immediate increase in the attention given to Marianne Moore, followed swiftly by greater attention assigned to William Carlos Williams. In May 1916 *The Egoist* included Moore's '"He Wrote the History Book" It Said' and an untitled poem later known as 'The Chameleon'. In the June issue this was followed by Moore's 'Pedantic Literalist'. It was in the August issue that H.D. weighed in with a full review of Moore's work, announcing: 'I have before me a collection of poems. They have appeared for the most part in various American periodicals. And readers of *The Egoist* are familiar with certain of these curiously wrought patterns, these quaint turns of thought and concealed, half-playful ironies' (p. 118).

The 'collection of poems' H.D. held (and from which she had apparently printed poems in May and June) must have been sent in response to her request to Moore in a letter of 15 April 1916. In it she wrote 'your work has a sort of eternal quality . . . I feel your work stands quite apart. Have you made up a volume? . . . I feel we might place it here for you some time if you cared to make it up!'[11] H.D.'s appreciative essay 'Marianne Moore' in August incorporated publication of the poems 'Feed Me, Also, River God', 'He Made this Screen' and 'Talisman', and identified Moore as 'the perfect technician', . . . 'the perfect artist', . . . 'the perfect craftsman' who 'turns her perfect craft . . . to some direct presentation of beauty, clear . . . – frail, yet . . . absolutely hard – and destined to endure . . .' (p. 118). H.D.'s praise and publication of her poems was extremely important to Moore, who responded in a letter of 9 August 1916, 'Why, when you have written

"Shrine" and "The Wind Sleepers", should you be willing to find worth in that which the ordinary reader finds worthless!'[12] She continued to send things to H.D., who responded on 3 September [1916], 'Miss Weaver . . . liked your article very much';[13] Moore's very substantial essay, 'The Accented Syllable' appeared in October. H. D. sought to place Moore's collection of poems for publication during the next two years, assuring her in the same letter 'I am quite confident that we will find some intelligent publisher in time'. We can reasonably presume that it is, slightly augmented, the volume that became Moore's first book, *Poems* (1920), published by The Egoist Press with financial assistance from Bryher.

H.D.'s reference to Miss Weaver is a useful reminder that the literary editing of *The Egoist* was not conducted without editorial oversight. During 1916, H.D. and Aldington were living first at Woodland Cottage in North Devon and, after Aldington's assignment for training to a military base in Dorset, in the town of Corfe Castle, on the English Channel. H.D. engaged in voluminous correspondence, and depended upon friends such as Flint and John Cournos to bring or send books that she needed. Neither H.D. nor Pound nor Aldington could simply do as they pleased with the journal – a fact attested to by H.D.'s efforts to placate Amy Lowell during preparation of the Imagist issue of May 1915: 'R has done his best for that blooming old *Egoist* – though I know how disappointed you & Fletcher will be to see Miss. M. on the first page. I assure you we both fought hard enough – But Miss Weaver runs the paper for Dora Marsden – swears by her, and R. is after all only sub-editor.'[14]

H.D. followed her essay on Moore with a substantial review essay on Charlotte Mew's *The Farmer's Bride* in the September 1916 issue (p. 135) and an extended review of John Gould Fletcher's *Goblins and Pagodas* in December (pp. 183–4). At least equally important, she published William Carlos Williams' account of *Others* and the avant-garde scene of 1915, in his essay 'The Great Opportunity' (p. 137) and his five-part poem 'March' in October 1916. Williams' expostulations surrounding the publishing of this poem demonstrate that H.D. was anything but a passive editor. She wrote to him in a letter of 14 August 1916:

> I trust you will not hate me for wanting to delete from your poem all the flippancies. The reason I want to do this is that the beautiful lines are so very beautiful – so in the tone and spirit of your *Postlude* – (which to me stands, a Nike, supreme among your poems) . . .
>
> I don't know what you think but I consider this business of writing a very sacred thing! – I think you have the 'spark' – am sure of it, and when you speak *direct* you are a poet. I feel in the hey-ding-ding touch running through your poem a derivative tendency which to me is not *you* – not your very self.[15]

Despite declaring in the 'Prologue' that he would 'write whatever I damn please', according to his editors, Walton Litz and Christopher McGowan, Williams preserved H.D.'s cuts from the much longer poem, not only in the publication in *The Egoist*, but also in his book *Sour Grapes* (1921) and thereafter, making only 'minor changes in spacing and punctuation'.[16]

Also important are the poems H.D. herself published in *The Egoist* during her tenure. During the first half of 1916, H.D. contributed some of the major poems from *Sea Garden*, for which the war had delayed publication until autumn. During that delay, H.D. published some of the lengthiest poems of that collection: 'The Cliff Temple', 'The Helmsman', 'Sea Gods', 'Cities' and 'The Contest'. After *Sea Garden* was published, she began a sequence of poems that was to become the section which she entitled 'The God' in her *Collected Poems* of 1925. In November she published the multi-section poem 'The Tribute' (pp. 165–7). ('Circe', which H.D. included in *Hymen*, followed in December, and with 'Tribute' was separately published at friend William Bubb's private Clerks Press of Cleveland, Ohio, in 1917.) Then the eponymous poem, 'The God' and 'Adonis', appeared in January 1917, followed by 'Pygmalion' in February, and 'Eurydice' in May.

From April 1916 until November 1917, Wyndham Lewis' *Tarr* ran serially in *The Egoist*, in abridged form, but these were arrangements made directly between Harriet Weaver and Ezra Pound, acting on behalf of Lewis.[17]

During this time, H.D.'s personal life was accumulating a level of stress that would eventually become intolerable. On 24 July 1916, she confided to Flint from Corfe Castle, 'I am desperate – but I say to myself "be strong for the sake of the others – for Richard's sake". I want to go on with my work, with Richard's work!' (Pondrom 1969, p. 576). Matters did not improve when Aldington was actually shipped overseas on 21 December 1916, for his letters were often despairing (Zilboorg, p. 28). Although she herself was already at work on her contribution, the *Ion* of Euripides,[18] it proved impossible to put together a second 'Poets' Translation Series' at this time. The January 1917 issue of *The Egoist* conceded that 'The Second Series [of the Poets' Translation project] is unavoidably postponed.' H.D. could not present the March 1917 issue of *The Egoist* because of the 'late arrival of part of the matter for our March number' (p. 37) and before the June issue, at the request of Harriet Weaver, H.D. and Richard had been replaced by the up-and-coming new poet, T.S. Eliot.[19]

Throughout these same years, H.D. played a major role in the editing of the three annual anthologies of *Some Imagist Poets, 1915, 1916* and *1917*.[20] In July 1914, after two successive dinners at the Dieudonné at which Amy Lowell felt the butt of the jokes, Lowell assembled John Gould

Fletcher (who had been left out of *Des Imagistes*), H.D., Aldington and D.H. Lawrence in her rooms at the Berkeley Hotel to propose establishing a new imagist anthology,[21] and on the next day she circulated their proposal to Flint, Ford Madox Hueffer [Ford] and Pound himself. The group proposed that there should be no editor – in a clear rebuff to Pound's autocracy – and that the poets should select their contributions themselves, in concert with the others, as a committee. In response, Pound retorted:

> You offer to find a publisher, that is a better publisher, if I abrogate my privileges, if I give way to, or saddle myself with, a dam'd contentious, probably incompetent committee. If I tacitly . . . accept a certain number of people as my critical and creative equals, and publish the acceptance.
>
> I don't see the use. Moreover, I should like the name 'Imagisme' to retain some sort of a meaning. It stands, or I should like it to stand for hard light, clear edges. I can not trust any democratized committee to maintain that standard.[22]

The committee principle was probably the thing the imagists most wanted to keep, for they all had been stung from time to time by Pound's high-handedness. Keep it they did, without Pound's participation. Lowell saw to arrangements for publication in Boston, and Aldington and H.D. sent her lengthy letters of suggestions – but most of the imagists were in London, and there was subtle consensus, sometimes explicit in reviews of imagist work and sometimes implicit, that H.D. was the 'purest' imagist, perhaps (though they bucked at such rankings), the 'best' imagist poet. Initially, both Aldington and H.D. sought to collect contributions, but as Aldington grew more and more distracted by the prospect of his imminent call-up to war, and then by his induction, H.D. willingly accepted what they chose to treat as his 'delegation' of chief responsibility. Thus, she was positioned to provide editing by a first among equals to the imagists who contributed to the three anthologies.

This position is exemplified as early as a letter of 9 December 1914, from H.D. to Flint, during the planning for *Some Imagist Poets 1915*. Beginning 'Dear Brother Bard', H.D. conveys Richard's invitation to Flint to join them the next evening and explains: 'We have a new plan for the anthology and want – need – to talk it over with you before writing Amy. This is important! – Our arrangements have been disturbed – can you guess by whom? But we will talk it over. – ' (Pondrom 1969, p. 562). The disruption was a consequence of Pound's assertion of control over the *imagiste* label, an obstacle made clear in H.D.'s letter to Amy Lowell of 17 December 1914:

> Things gets worser and worser! Our great & good friend is taking up 'Imagism' again – don't you think *we'd* better drop it? . . . E.P. is making it ridiculous – . . . Ford . . . says the only thing to do – is to drop the title

> 'Imagism!' – We have talked it over – all of us here – and we think a good title – 'the Six' – Then underneath if you want 'An Anthology' [*sic*].[23]

As the first anthology was already well along in its assembly, in the same letter H.D. proposed that the 'Preface' stay as it is except 'just cut out the bit about Ezra & insert . . . that these tenets have been proposed by some of us as imagism, but . . . we do not use it either as a title or a group denomination'. The matter was resolved by the selection of the title *Some Imagist Poets 1915* and the anthology was published by Houghton Mifflin in April 1915. Arranged alphabetically, it included seven poems each by Aldington, H.D., Flint, Lawrence and Lowell, and two multipart titles by Fletcher, and each was accorded roughly similar space, ranging from nine pages to sixteen. The preface stipulated that not all of the contributors were 'imagists', but all the poets collectively subscribed to six principles, including a commitment 'to produce poetry that is hard and clear' and concentrated, that 'use[s] the language of common speech . . . the *exact* word', and that 'present[s] an image', to convey any subject of the poet's choosing (whether typical or not), in 'new rhythms', although not necessarily in *vers libre*.[24]

H.D.'s challenge in managing intergroup relations of the imagists swiftly grew larger, when in a letter to Flint of 2 July 1915, Pound termed Flint's 'History of Imagism' in the May issue of *The Egoist* 'BULLSHIT'.[25] 'Don't – don't worry about that beastly letter from E.P.', H.D. wrote to Flint in early July 1915. 'Don't even answer it', she continued, as she arranged for Flint to visit and talk over the situation with both Richard and herself (Pondrom 1969, pp. 562–3). The flap over *The Egoist* Imagist Special Issue did not deter the group from producing another anthology in the following year, but the first anthology had occasioned its own hurt feelings. Harriet Monroe protested that *Poetry* magazine was insufficiently recognised in the first volume, so Amy Lowell promised her a special acknowledgement in the second volume – which appeared as follows:

> To *Poetry* belongs the credit of having introduced Imagism to the world: it seems fitting, therefore, that the authors should record their thanks in this place for the constant interest and encouragement shown them by its editor, Miss Harriet Monroe.[26]

The remaining group members were outraged, since most of the formation of imagism had been centred in London and Harriet Monroe had been *cajoled* by Pound into publishing the first poems, and H.D. had her hands full smoothing over the resentment. She explained to Flint in a letter of 22 March 1916:

> Fletcher wrote, A.[my] had promised Harriet to put into the new I. A. a special acknowledgment to Poetry. It seems very rotten – F.[letcher] did his best to

> get it out – but H. said Amy had promised it! – There is nothing to be done, but I thought you ought to know. Do not row Amy please as it is too late anyhow . . . A. wrote R.[ichard] a suitable apology & we'd best let sleeping dogs lie! – (Pondrom 1969, p. 566)

Some Imagist Poets 1916 was soon out, and on 25 May 1916, H.D. relayed to Flint a clipping of its appreciative review by William Stanley Braithwaite in the *Boston Evening Transcript* of 6 May 1916 (pp. 572–4). The volume was now subtitled 'An Annual Anthology'; it maintained the format of the preceding year: a substantial preface and an alphabetical listing of the six poets, each allocated thirteen–fourteen pages, save for Lawrence and Aldington who had seven and ten, respectively. The preface this time was a forthright effort to explain imagism to ordinary readers who did not understand what the movement was about, beginning: '. . . "Imagism" does not mean merely the presentation of pictures. "Imagism" refers to the manner of presentation, not to the subject.'[27]

The following April the imagists produced the third and last volume, *Some Imagist Poets 1917*. H.D.'s contributions were the four poems published January–May in *The Egoist* – 'The God', 'Adonis', 'Pygmalion' and 'Eurydice'. This volume had no preface, but was otherwise generally similar to the previous ones, offering the same six poets, alphabetically, with somewhat similar space accorded to each. It was to be the last of the imagist anthologies issued by the poets themselves.

As Richard Aldington anticipated the end of the war, he began to think of reviving the Poets' Translation Series as a way of securing some employment. He wrote to H.D. on 22 September 1918, that he had encouraged Bryher to consider translating Greek for the new series 'if we can get it going again' (Zilboorg 1992, p. 140) and, notwithstanding their marital problems (which, with H.D.'s pregnancy, were now excruciating), formally asked her to collaborate on 1 December (p. 160). His plans for the new series were elaborate, envisioning volumes in modern as well as classical languages, H.D. as 'Greek editor', and a major publisher. When Aldington had returned to England and managed to re-establish publishing opportunities, he abandoned the elaborate series (Zilboorg 1992, pp. 164–71, 195), and eventually the only outcome of the proposal was publication by The Egoist Press of a few volumes which chiefly reprinted earlier numbers of the first series in expanded form. To this, H.D. contributed, as number 3, translations of the choruses of Euripides' *Hippolytus*, which were included with the republication of her *Choruses from 'Iphigeneia in Aulis'* from the earlier series. Glenway Westcott in his review of both series for *Poetry* in August 1921, saw the work of other contributors as tending towards the 'sweet and discreetly sentimental' (p. 286), but found H.D. the 'solitary exception', a poet who 'writes English as hard as Anglo-Saxon' (p. 287).

Over the next several years H.D. devoted herself to poetry, which she submitted to magazines and published as small collections, and undertook new efforts at experimental prose. She returned to active involvement in the production of avant-garde magazines only when Bryher and second husband Kenneth MacPherson established *Close Up* in July 1927 in Switzerland as a vehicle for serious analysis of the new experimental medium of the cinema.[28] Although H.D. was not formally listed as an editor of the journal – MacPherson was editor and Bryher, who funded it, was the assistant editor – H.D. participated in soliciting contributions, and during the first two years made major contributions herself, in the form both of poetry and of acute reviews of contemporary films. On 6 June 1927, for example, she wrote to Viola Jordan about plans for the journal and her own great interest in cinematic art and suggested that Jordan write 'us an article for our movie paper'.[29] The first issue contains her important poem 'Projector' and the first instalment of her critical essay 'The Cinema and the Classics', as well as essays by Bryher, MacPherson and their good friend Dorothy Richardson. Soon, there were contributions by other friends, like Gertrude Stein, Osbert Sitwell, Havelock Ellis and Robert Herring, a British film critic who was to become a significant figure in the Bryher circle. H.D. herself provided essays and reviews for ten of the fifteen issues between the journal's founding in July 1927, and September 1928, including the poem 'Projector II (Chang)' and two additional instalments of 'The Cinema and the Classics' (August and November 1927), which contained important ideas linking modernism and the cinema.[30] After this, H.D. remained active with POOL Productions, Bryher and MacPherson's vehicle for publication and film, and was a principal actress in the film *Borderline* in 1930, but she contributed only two other pieces to *Close Up* before it ceased publication in December 1933.

In 1934, H.D. and Bryher took an apartment at 49 Lowndes Square in London (Guest 1984, p. 223), where H.D. would spend the majority of her time until 1946, and Bryher took over the staggering journal *Life and Letters Today*, where she installed Robert Herring and, for a time, Petrie Townshend as editors. They explained in September 1935 (13.1), 'In taking it over our first aim has been to preserve, both for readers and writers, one of the few literary papers remaining since the amalgamation and cessation of so many journals.' The first issues after their entrance looked somewhat like *Close Up*, and many of the same writers appeared – Gertrude Stein, Osbert Sitwell, Havelock Ellis, Kenneth MacPherson, Sergei Eisenstein and, very importantly, H.D. Her contribution to Herring's first issue was the long poem 'The Dancer', followed by 'The Poet' in December (13.2). Imaginary dialogues between a poet-speaker and another artist – a dancer modelled on Isadora Duncan and a poet reflective of D.H. Lawrence – these two poems anticipate the visionary range that H.D. was to manifest in *Trilogy.* Several of her prose contributions and reviews for the journal during these pre-war years were made under the pen names 'D.A. Hill', 'Sylvania Penn' or 'S. Penn'. *Life and Letters Today* was one of the few literary magazines that managed to survive the hard years at the beginning of the Second World War, moving its editorial headquarters to a location 'Somewhere in Sussex' that Herring did not disclose. It was the journal of choice for some of H.D.'s most important Second World War work. In April 1942, under the title 'Introduction to the Coming One', H.D. published the opening poem of *The Walls do Not Fall*, accompanied by two poems envisioning Amen-Ra, 'the sun-disk, / the re-born Sun', now numbered 21 and 22 in the *Walls* sequence. Two more poems from the sequence, 'Sea Shell' and 'Worm' (now numbers 4, 6) appeared in the issues for October and November 1942. The second elicited from Edith Sitwell, with whom H.D. and Bryher were in steady correspondence, the exclamation: 'The new poem in *Life and Letters* is lovely, as all your work is lovely, – oh the end! It is *wonderful* – and "I profit / By every calamity" – is so great . . . Yes, that short poem has the whole of time in it.'[31]

The next efflorescence of H.D.'s work in *Life and Letters Today* came in 1944–5, when in July 1944, she published 'Seven Poems' from the first half of *Tribute to the Angels* (pp. 1, 4–5, 15, 18–20) and May–September 1945, four of five instalments of 'Writing on the Wall (To Sigmund Freud)', which became *Tribute to Freud.* She completed 'Writing on the Wall' in the issue for January 1946, shortly before Bryher took her to Klinic Bruner in Küsnacht to recuperate from the emotional breakdown that was the culmination of vision and war stress of the last six years.

Edith Sitwell's reaction to the crucial visionary poems of *Tribute to the Angels* which appeared in July 1944, suggests both the importance of H.D.'s contributions to avant-garde magazines like *Life and Letters Today* and the significance of the support she received from the friends and associates who surrounded them. Congratulating H.D. upon the book publication of *Tribute to the Angels* on 11 April 1945, Sitwell recalled her first exposure to two of the key poems in *Life and Letters Today* in the issue for July 1944:

> I can only say, you yourself can't have been more excited than I was this morning when the book arrived . . . I know this book so well, *and yet* print has

given it even a finer body . . . Yours is the supreme apple tree, the flowering apple. I shall never forget the day when I saw these poems first – but the feeling remains exactly the same. I shall never see any flowering tree again without thinking of that revelation.[32]

NOTES

1 For a comprehensive view of all H.D.'s periodical contributions, see M. Boughn, *H.D.: A Bibliography, 1905–1990* (Charlottesville: University Press of Virginia, 1993).
2 Ezra Pound, 'To Harriet Monroe', 13 August [1913]. In D.D. Paige (ed.), *The Letters of Ezra Pound 1907–1941* (London: Faber, 1951), p. 58.
3 Pound, 'To William Carlos Williams', 19 December [1913], *The Letters of Ezra Pound*, p. 65.
4 L.H. Silverstein, 'Herself Delineated: Chronological Highlights of H.D.', in S.S. Friedman and R.B. DuPlessis (eds.), *Signets: Reading H.D.* (Madison: University of Wisconsin Press, 1990), p. 35.
5 Quoted in C.N. Pondrom, 'Marianne Moore and H.D.: Female Community and Poetic Achievement', in P.C. Willis (ed.), *Marianne Moore: Woman and Poet* (National Poetry Foundation: Orono, 1990), p. 373.
6 'H.D. to Norman Holmes Pearson, 29 January [1949]' in D. Krolik Hollenberg (ed.), *Between History and Poetry: The Letters of H.D. and Norman Holmes Pearson* (Iowa City: University of Iowa Press, 1997), p. 86.
7 Signed, holograph, undated letter, Rosenbach Library, postmarked '21 Aug 1915 Hampshire'.
8 C. Zilboorg (ed.), *Richard Aldington & H.D.: The Early Years in Letters* (Bloomington: Indiana University Press, 1992), p. 226.
9 *Times Literary Supplement*, 4 May 1916, p. 210. Quoted in 'Selected Letters from H.D. to F.S. Flint: A Commentary on the Imagist Period', in C.N. Pondrom (ed.), *Contemporary Literature*, 10.4 (Autumn, 1969), 570.
10 'H.D. to Frankie', [17/5/16] in Pondrom, *Contemporary Literature*, p. 572.
11 H.D. to Moore, 15 April 1916, holograph signed ms., Rosenbach Library.
12 Moore to H.D., 9 August 1916, typed unsigned carbon, Rosenbach Library.
13 H.D. to Moore, 3 September [1916], holograph, signed ms., Rosenbach Library.
14 H.D. to Amy Lowell, 27 April 1915, Houghton Library. Quoted in G. Hanscombe and V.L. Smyers, *Writing for Their Lives: The Modernist Women 1910–1940* (Boston: Northeastern University Press, 1987), p. 175.
15 Quoted by William Carlos Williams, 'Prologue' to *Kora in Hell*, in W. Schott (ed.), *Imaginations* (New York: New Directions, 1970), pp. 12–13.
16 *The Collected Poems of William Carlos Williams, Volume I, 1909–1939*, W. Litz and C. MacGowan (eds.) (New York: New Directions, 1986), pp. 493–5.
17 T. Materer (ed.), *Pound/Lewis: The Letters of Ezra Pound and Wyndham Lewis*, (New York: New Directions, 1985), pp. 17–21.
18 B. Guest, *Herself Defined: The Poet H.D. and Her World* (New York: Doubleday, 1984), p. 82.
19 'Notice', 4.5 (June 1917), 69; and Zilboorg, *Early Years*, p. 28.
20 *Some Imagist Poets 1915* (Boston: Houghton Mifflin, 1915).

21 H. Carpenter, *A Serious Character: The Life of Ezra Pound* [1988] (New York: Doubleday/Delta, 1990), pp. 252–4.
22 Pound to Amy Lowell, 1 August [1914], in Paige (ed.), *Letters*, p. 78.
23 Hilda to Amy, 17 December 1914 in 'H.D. (1886–1961)', in S.S. Friedman (ed.), *The Gender of Modernism: A Critical Anthology*, B. Kime Scott (ed.) (Bloomington: Indiana University Press, 1990), p. 134.
24 'Preface' in *Some Imagist Poets 1915*, pp. vi–vii.
25 Quoted by C. Middleton, 'Documents on Imagism from the Papers of F.S. Flint', *The Review*, 15 (April 1965), 41.
26 *Some Imagist Poets 1916*, p. 1.
27 'Preface' in *Some Imagist Poets 1916: An Anthology* (Boston: Houghton Mifflin, 1916), p. v.
28 Bryher, *The Heart to Artemis* (Ashfield, MA: Paris Press, 2006), p. 289.
29 Viola Jordan Papers, Beinecke Library, quoted in J.E. Marek, *Women Editing Modernism* (Lexington, KY: University Press of Kentucky, 1995), p. 129, n. 62, p. 219.
30 For substantial discussion of H.D.'s contributions to understanding the relationship of the cinema and literature, see 'H.D.'s Borderline Bodies' in S. McCabe, *Cinematic Modernism* (Cambridge University Press, 2005), pp. 133–83.
31 Autograph ms. n.d., Beinecke Library.
32 Autograph ms., Beinecke Library. The reference is to poems 19 and 20 of *Tribute to the Angels*.

4

POLINA MACKAY

H.D.'s modernism

It is very hard to detach H.D.'s name from literary modernism. Indeed, her oeuvre demonstrates the fundamental themes, poetics and ideological standpoints of that movement: the change from Victorian norms to a modern world primarily concerned with science, technology and the nature of modernity itself; the coinage of innovative poetics; and the challenging of existing stereotypes through new discourses, in H.D.'s case through the ideology of early to mid twentieth-century feminism.

Indeed, H.D.'s relationship with modernism has been explored at great length. Among the most sophisticated analyses is Cassandra Laity's reading of H.D. in light of Romantic and Victorian literary values. Laity argues that the poet embraces the sexuality-driven poetic masks of hermaphrodism, androgeneity and homoeroticism previously propagated by decadent Romantics such as A.C. Swinburne and Walter Pater, and suggests that H.D. appropriates these personae to 'fashion a modernist poetic of female desire'.[1] Georgina Taylor's subsequent study, *H.D. and the Public Sphere of Modernist Women Writers* (2001), demonstrates the author's centrality in the modernist public sphere of literary women.[2] With other female authors – among them, Amy Lowell, Edith Wyatt and Marianne Moore – H.D. had a hand in promoting modernist work primarily through the editorship of self-published magazines such as *The Egoist*, *Little Review* and *Poetry*. Both Laity and Taylor see H.D.'s work through the lens of identity politics, whereby aesthetics and poetic masks speak for communities of women. More recently, Adalaide Kirby Morris attempts to explore H.D. outside the field of gender studies. In *How to Live/What to Do: H.D.'s Cultural Poetics* (2003), Morris talks of H.D.'s 'radical modernisms': a retrospective reading of the author through the work of some of those she influenced, including contemporary poets Nathaniel Mackey, Jack Spicer and Leslie Scalapino. This approach, Morris suggests, 'opens a new angle into [H.D.'s] creativity, one that yields fresh access to the strengths and limitations of the work, puts into question conventional divisions between modernism and postmodernism, and reaches across the boundaries built up by the identity politics within which H.D. has been most recently read'.[3] Morris' thesis illuminates the potency of H.D.'s work and its relevance to new generations of writers and readers.

The studies I summarised above commonly treat H.D. as a central figure of modernism. Reading H.D. in this context illuminates her thinking and aesthetic. As I show below, her work engages with the major theories or knowledges, such as psychoanalysis and sexology, that influenced modernist writers. Her early poetry, in particular, exemplifies the principles of the modernist practice of imagism, while her use of gendered perspectives and her sustained focus on the modern woman contributes towards the crafting of a female version of modernism.

H.D. as modern thinker

In what ways is H.D. a modernist writer? First and foremost, H.D. is a modern thinker, evident primarily in her adoption of the language of psychoanalysis, her connection between the artist's vision and spirituality and her elaborate interest in sexuality and sexual expression.

H.D. was greatly influenced by new narratives and theories of the modern psyche. The impact of psychoanalytic theory and practice on the author is primarily manifested in her connection with Freud. She had several sessions with Freud in the 1930s, during which he tried to help her work through some unresolved issues with her past. She wrote reports of some of these meetings in her journal, published as part of her prose memoir, *Tribute to Freud* (1956). The book, which in Susan Stanford Friedman's words is 'a modernist reflection on psyche and society',[4] reveals that the poet saw less in Freud's ability to 'cure' her and more in the potential of psychoanalysis to inspire a new language. H.D. writes in her journal in 1933: 'I must find new words as the Professor found or coined new words to explain certain as yet unrecorded states of mind or being.'[5] H.D. saw great potential in this new visionary language; as Tony Trigilio has noted, she perceived it as a tool powerful enough to eventually give the poet prophetic authority.[6] The author is not able to clearly label this vision prophecy before *Tribute to Freud* (p. 51), but she first begins to conceptualise writing as a kind of visionary process in *Notes on Thoughts and Vision* (1919). Here, long before her sessions with Freud, H.D. uses the language of psychoanalysis to determine the role of the modern aesthete; she argues, for instance, that 'The realization of [the] over-conscious world is the concern of the artist.'[7]

The poems in *Sea Garden* (1916), written around the same time as *Notes*, are haunted by the need to discover the psyche. 'Sheltered Garden', for example, begins with a quest to pause for thought ('I have had enough. / I gasp for breath') and continues with the realisation that 'Every way ends, every road, / every foot-path leads at last / to the hill-crest- / then you retrace your steps, / or find the same slope on the other side, / precipitate.'[8] Here, the poet's hiatus enables her to retrace her steps, to read the self's place in time. These lines display what Claire Buck has observed of H.D.'s connection with Freud: 'the central insight which H.D. takes from psychoanalysis is that the self is a text to be read'.[9] These instances of psychoanalytic discourse in H.D. – from *Notes* to the poems in *Sea Garden* – which are not merely created by the poet's partial assessment of her own analysis by Freud but also enhanced by her use of terminology associated with the discipline to explicate her literary practice, show that the author was, if not directly influenced by narratives of modern psychology, actively engaging with this context.[10]

Besides an urgent sense of self-discovery, for H.D. another concern of the artist is (or should be) to possess and express a spirituality that is based on modern ideals. Like many of her contemporaries, H.D. was influenced by J.G. Frazer's seminal text, *The Golden Bough: A Study in Magic and Religion* (1890; 1906–1915), which saw religion as a cultural phenomenon as opposed to a subject of theology. T.S. Eliot, for instance, called *The Golden Bough* in *Vanity Fair* in 1924 'a work of no less importance for our own time than the complementary work of Freud – throwing its light on the obscurities of the soul from a different angle'.[11] H.D. elaborates on the nature of the modern soul in *Notes on Thoughts and Vision* where she reaches a similar conclusion to *The Golden Bough*: spirituality has not to do with religion but rather, with culture and myth. Towards the end of *Notes*, H.D. realises that the spirit 'is a seed'; man 'can retard its growth by neglect of his body because the body of man as the body of nature is the ground into which the seed or spirit is cast' (*Notes*, p. 52). She expands on this point by referring to myth in the next sentence: 'This is the mystery of Demeter, the Earth Mother. The body of the Eleusinian initiate had become one with the earth, as his soul had become one with the seeds enclosed in the earth' (H.D., *Notes*, p. 52). In the following paragraph – the one that ends *Notes* – H.D. recounts the story of Christ as myth: 'Christ and his father, or as the Eleusinian mystic would have said, his mother, were one. Christ was the grapes that hung against the sun-lit walls of that mountain garden, Nazareth . . . He was the body of nature, the vine, the Dionysus, as he was the soul of nature' (H.D., *Notes*, pp. 52–3). In H.D.'s discourse the earth and myth (storytelling) nurture the spirit; when this process is crystallised in the mind (as in her example of the story of Christ), the writer becomes aware of the spirit's overall function for humanity ('the spirit, we realize, is a seed') and achieves the desired spirituality (H.D., *Notes*, p. 52). As evident in H.D.'s critical prose, this state of heightened spirituality has less to do with religion and more with good knowledge and appreciation of cultural history and mythology.[12]

We should not mistake, however, H.D.'s high regard for spiritual awareness as a call to disregard the body. In fact, the poet acknowledges the body's centrality throughout her work, particularly in her writings on spirituality. She writes in *Notes on Thought and Vision*: 'Perhaps so we cannot have spirit without body, the body of nature, or the body of individual men and women' (H.D., *Notes*, p. 48). For H.D. the body is not just a physical entity (the body of an individual); it is also a natural phenomenon, which stores and mediates energy, and an artefact (e.g. the Greek sculptures) the lines of which 'may be used as an approach to the over-mind or universal mind' (H.D., *Notes*, p. 47). Even more important is the body's role in the process of achieving spiritual fulfilment: 'Once we become aware of this pearl, this seed [the spirit – that is], our centre of consciousness shifts. Our concern is with the body' (H.D., *Notes*, p. 50).

H.D.'s focus on the body in her writings on spirituality is indicative of her wider connection between the spirit and sexual expression. She links the notions of body and spirit to the practice of sex in the modern age. In the opening page of *Notes*, she announces that 'All reasoning, normal, sane and balanced men and women need and seek at certain times of their lives, certain definite physical relationships' (H.D., *Notes*, p. 17). But this fact, H.D. suggests later on, should not hinder humanity's striving towards the realisation of a state of consciousness which encompasses the kind of spirituality that she seeks and seems to have found in the final pages of *Notes*. Not only do sexual instincts not become an obstacle to the achievement of this new state of being, they initiate it. H.D. explains in *Notes* that 'The brain and the womb are both centres of consciousness, equally important', having just labelled the womb as 'the love-region of the body' in the paragraphs preceding this statement (H.D., *Notes*, pp. 21, 20). In other words, sexual expression and a consciousness aware of the centrality of both body and spirit are indivisible.

H.D.'s argument that a mature consciousness and sexuality are inseparable is built on the work of another modern thinker who also influenced modernism to a large extent, the British sexologist Havelock Ellis. H.D. first met Ellis in 1919 around the time she was writing *Notes*.[13] She and Bryher became interested in his theories, and corresponded with him for a number of years.[14] Ellis, a pioneer in the study of human sexuality, argues in 1890 that 'The chief and central function of life – the omnipresent process of sex, ever wonderful, ever lovely, as it is woven into the whole texture of our man's or woman's body – is the pattern of all the process of our life.'[15] Like H.D., Ellis links sexual impulses with spiritual fulfilment, and both of these thinkers are examples of their era's fusion of science, sexology and spirituality.[16]

H.D.'s interaction with Freud and Ellis shows that early twentieth-century modernity was as much of a product of ideas as of a circle of friends. This dialogue, evident in letters, memoirs and journals, makes up a modern discourse – a language, a way of thinking, a cue for further debate – which H.D. also appropriates in her literature.

H.D.'s modernist aesthetic

H.D.'s modernism is primarily manifested in her literary practice. The best place to start looking into the poet's modernist aesthetic is in her early poetry, heavily influenced as it was by Ezra Pound. Her onetime fiancé became interested in H.D.'s poetic ability, and had her skills in mind in envisioning imagism. Legend has it that Pound and H.D. met in the tea room of the British museum in 1912 when, upon seeing her work, he came up with the infamous signature 'H.D. Imagiste'.[17] Pound then sent three poems, 'Hermes of the Ways', 'Orchard' and 'Epigram', to Harriet Monroe, editor of *Poetry*, with this note: 'This is the sort of American stuff that I can show here and in Paris without its being ridiculed. Objective – no slither; direct – no excessive use of adjectives, no metaphors that won't permit examination. It's straight talk, straight as the Greek!'[18] The poems were published in 1913 in the January issue of *Poetry*, while the March volume of the same year contained F.S. Flint's and Pound's summary of imagism. This expanded on Pound's sense of directness and lack of excess in writing, adding a few principles for those starting to write poetry:

1. Direct treatment of the 'thing', whether subjective or objective.
2. To use absolutely no word that did not contribute to the presentation.
3. As regarding rhythm: to compose in sequence of the musical phrase, not in sequence of a metronome.[19]

At the centre of imagist practice is the poet's treatment of the image. Pound argues in the same piece:

> An 'Image' is that which presents an intellectual and emotional complex in an instant of time . . . It is the presentation of such a 'complex' instantaneously which gives that sense of sudden liberation; that sense of freedom from time limits and space limits; that sense of sudden growth, which we experience in the presence of the greatest works of art. (Rainey 2005, p. 95)

The three poems H.D. published in *Poetry* demonstrate the methods Pound outlined. 'Orchard', in particular, never strays from its subject matter – an orchard – presenting the reader with a series of images created by the poet's gaze upon the thicket as it zooms in to a pear ('I saw the first pear / as it fell'), as it tunes in to the sound of 'the honey-seeking' and as it illuminates a scenery of ripe fruit (H.D., *CP*, pp. 28–9). It is the first poem in *Sea Garden*, 'Sea Rose', however, which displays best the imagist complexity Pound seeks in poetry. The sea rose, a 'thing' directly crafted as the centre of the poem's image, is presented from multiple angles as it makes its impression on the poet:

> Rose, harsh rose,
> marred and with stint of petals,
> meagre flower, thin,
> sparse of leaf,
> . . .
>
> Stunted, with small leaf,
> you are flung on the sand,
> you are lifted
> in the crisp sand
> that drives in the wind. (p. 5)

The poet both translates for the reader the significance of this natural image, where a sea rose is transformed from a stunted flower lying on the sand into the focus of the scenery, and goes through intellectual and emotional searching evident in the question that closes the poem: 'Can the spice-rose / drip such acrid fragrance / hardened in a leaf?' (p. 5). Posed like a philosophical puzzle, it is the contemplation of such a query that matters, not the actual answer.

'Hermes of the Ways' and 'Epigram', two poems that Pound included in the anthology *Des Imagistes* in 1914,[20] show early signs of where H.D. was to take her imagism. The two exemplify H.D.'s combination of imagist principles with Greek myths and themes. 'Hermes of the Ways' elaborates on the central image of a Greek mythical figure, Hermes, waiting by the shore. 'Epigram', a free adaptation of Epigram XLVI from J.W. Mackail's *Select Epigrams from the Greek Anthology* (1907),[21] exemplifies Pound's 'straight as the Greek' in its careful and measured free translation of the Greek original. David Ayers perceptively notes that H.D. produces in her own poem a 'loose version in which aesthetic goals related to the ideals of the Greek epigram are reconfigured as a modern poetics which specifically seeks to substitute a laconic detachment for what was perceived as the emotional effusiveness of the late Victorian poets' (Ayers 2004, p. 4).

'Epigram' was not included in *Sea Garden* when it was first published. However, many other poems (besides 'Hermes of the Ways') in *Sea Garden* utilise the three imagist principles to reflect on Greek themes. 'The Helmsman' and 'The Shrine' develop sea imagery, while 'Pursuit', 'The Wind Sleepers', 'Huntress' and 'Sea Gods' are centrally concerned with the figure of the Nymph. These not only invoke recognisable Greek motifs, such as Gods, seafarers and rites of passage, but also display a deeper understanding of the ancient Greek discourse evident in the poems' Sapphic layers. Eileen Gregory rightly points out that Sappho herself 'is a latent mythic presence' in these poems.[22] *Sea Garden* shares with Sappho a definite sense of the 'Poetess' and a focus on landscape. Even in the flower poems, where the Greek discourse is somewhat suppressed, H.D. builds in a Sapphic presence. 'Sea Rose', 'Sea Lily' or 'Sea Violet', Gregory suggests,

> reveal the spiritual potency residing in a surrender to the process of 'sea-change'. The flowers represent, like those of Sappho, a pure openness to life; however, rather than the fresh, natural virgin threshold of the young girls in Lesbos, these show a virginity, an integrity, *achieved* within desire. (Gregory 1986, pp. 539–40)

Diana Collecott's later meticulous study of Sapphic elements in H.D. builds on these early manifestations to read the author as an exemplary of Sapphic modernism who negotiates gender, sexuality, lesbian poetics as well as literary tradition.[23] This appropriation is, as Gregory would later observe, part of H.D.'s wider engagement with Hellenism. Her analysis in *H.D. and Hellenism* takes in the author's most recognisable Hellenic narratives, *Hippolytus Temporizes* (1927), *Ion* (1937) and *Helen in Egypt*, as well as her other work to show how H.D. increasingly became self-conscious about her Hellenism with an akin sense of the classic, Romantic and modern.

H.D.'s acute sense of the modern comes through in the aesthetics of *Sea Garden*, where she replaces the elaborate imagery of natural beauty, so admired by late Romantics such as Swinburne (e.g. in his poem 'A Forsaken Garden'), with the sharpness of a rose 'cut in rock' in the landscape of 'rocks fitted to dark, to silver granite, . . . clean cut, white against white' (H.D., *CP*, pp. 24, 26).[24] She gestures towards a wider modern world which assumes the characteristics of granite: this is a world which is both hard and craftable, both durable and transitory. *Sea Garden* uses language which illuminates modernity's dualities. The poems use adjectives such as 'slashed' and 'torn' (p. 14); nouns such as 'ridge' and 'rock-edge'; and verbs such as 'split' and 'crack' (pp. 18, 26, 21, 36). Despite the inherent ambiguity in things that are slashed and torn and in places that are on the rock-edge, H.D. manages to build in the poems clarity and sharpness. Objects in *Sea*

Garden are 'crisp', 'cropped' and 'curved' (pp. 5, 13, 14), framed by the recurring and dominating image of cutting (pp. 9, 11, 13, 14, 19, 22, 24, 25, 26, 33, 34). H.D.'s aesthetic reflects a world where objects – and by association entire landscapes – are artefacts made with extreme effort and skill. The poet's task in *Sea Garden* is to emphasise the long-standing beauty of nature by illuminating the craftsmanship of the natural landscape.

Sea Garden can be read as a celebration of the power of observation. This hermeneutic possibility is immediately visible in the collection's first poem, 'Sea Rose'. Here, the speaker closely examines the sea rose ('Rose, harsh rose, / marred and with stint of petals, / meagre flower, thin / sparse of leaf'), which counteracts the fact that the flower is meant to be 'flung on the sand', easily missed by passers-by (H.D., *CP*, p. 5). H.D. repeats this method in 'Sea Lily', where the reed's merciless crushing against the wind is transformed into the sea lily's act of defiance: 'Yet though the whole wind / slash at your bark, you are lifted up' (p. 14). The implication in the poem, as in 'Sea Rose', is that the flower's situation is reconceptualised because it is being witnessed.

H.D. perhaps inherited these techniques from nineteenth-century Realism, and, in particular, from Gustave Flaubert's observant narrator in *Madame Bovary* (1857) or the relentless search for order by observation and deduction in the Sherlock Holmes stories. What makes H.D.'s aesthetic recognisably modernist in *Sea Garden*, however, is her ability to turn a seemingly objective camera eye into the most significant agent in the poetic process. It is the poet and his/her particularised perspective that create the beautifully crafted landscape. The sea rose becomes 'precious' through one eye at one moment in time in 'Sea Rose'; the same happens in 'Sea Lily', in 'Sea Poppies', in 'Sea Violet' and in 'Sea Iris' (H.D., *CP*, pp. 5, 14, 21, 25, 36). In using the sea as the key background, H.D. suggests that the poetic gaze, despite its ability to focus on one small flower, is as passing as water, for H.D. inverts the scientific method of observation into the kind of impressionistic writing that not only illuminates the subjective nature of seeing but also extends this subjectivity to the entire shot. In 'Evening' (pp. 18–19), for instance, the poet offers a developing picture of light and shadow on flowers witnessed by a speaker whose sense of gain and loss increases as the kinetic image develops.

H.D.'s modernist aesthetic, as it is shaped in *Sea Garden* in particular, expands the imagist principles of directness and lack of excess into wide-ranging engagement with literary traditions – from Greek mythology to Sappho's poems and beyond – without ever losing sight of its own modernity, of its own place in time. As Hermes is waiting by the sea in 'Hermes of the Ways' surrounded by the vast uncertainty of water, the poet, in the sharp language of 'The hard sand [that] breaks, and the grains of it / are clear as wine', can appreciate the specificity of this subject in time:

But more than the many-foamed ways
of the sea,
I know him
Of the triple path-ways
Hermes,
who awaits. (H.D., *CP*, p. 37)

Even the vast sea itself knows Hermes' name: 'Hermes, Hermes, / the great sea foamed' (p. 39).

H.D.'s gendered modernism

I believe in the modern woman.
(Mrs Carter in *Bid Me to Live*)[25]

Many male writers contributed to the formation and expansion of modernism; among them, Ezra Pound, T.S. Eliot, D.H. Lawrence and William Carlos Williams. Nowadays, it is recognised that literary women also helped to augment and disseminate modernist discourses. This list includes Virginia Woolf, whose writings wrestle with the notion of woman in early twentieth-century modernity, and poets like Harriet Monroe and Marianne Moore whose poetry and editing illuminate the role of the female poet in literary production. H.D.'s input to women's modernism matches the achievement of the aforementioned female authors: like Woolf, she concentrates on women's perspectives while at the same time interrogating the idea of gender essentialism (see Woolf's *Orlando* (1928) and H.D.'s *Hippolytus Temporizes* (1927)); and like Monroe and Moore, she understands that literary production is as significant as the propagation of that material and becomes involved in the creation and distribution of literary journals. H.D.'s entwining of 'woman and poet' (as Michael King puts it in the title of one of the first collections of essays on the author)[26] is indicative of her aesthetic, which strives to craft a female version of modernism. This aspect of H.D.'s modernism goes beyond the turn from male to female points of view, offering, to echo Cassandra Laity's argument in *H.D. and the Victorian Fin de Siècle*, complex discourses of femininity and masculinity such as androgyny and abjection.

H.D.'s literature, especially after *Sea Garden*, uses gendered perspectives to comment on modernity. This artistic concern is particularly evident in her prose; as Friedman has noted:

[G]ender in her early poetic discourse was suppressed – still there, but buried, screened. Her prose discourse, in contrast, as the language of history, unveiled

> the woman and directly narrated the story of her social relations in the world. Precisely because H.D.'s prose was relational, set in the narrative of history, it was more directly gendered than her poetic discourse.[27]

The story of woman that H.D. wishes to tell in her prose focuses on the woman as storyteller in the modern world. In *Palimpsest*, for instance, the three protagonists of the three novellas that comprise the novel are all women who write: Hipparchia is a translator of Greek texts; Raymonde is a poet influenced by the Greek; Helen is a scholar of Greaco-Roman archives. Echoing H.D.'s own biography, they all struggle to come to terms with life in an era of immense destruction around the time of the Great War. H.D. conflates these Greaco-Roman layers of her narrative with what is presented as harsh modern times, and in doing so she draws attention both to the role of female authorship in the discovery and sustainment of literary tradition as well as to her new responsibilities as she writes her way through modernity.

H.D.'s *Madrigal* novels – *HERmione*, *Bid Me to Live*, *Paint It Today* and *Asphodel* – also explore gender to varying degrees. These texts draw more clearly and definitively on H.D.'s biography, addressing the growth and maturing of the woman artist in the modern world. Thus, in *HERmione*, for instance, the female protagonist, who is an author, moves from reading about the woman as object in male-centred narratives to writing her as subject who not only speaks for herself but also reflects on and revises the myths of patriarchy.

H.D.'s gendered writing, however, would mature in her later work. In *Helen in Egypt* (written between 1952 and 1954 and first published in 1961),[28] H.D. reshapes Euripides' *Helen* partly from Helen of Troy's perspective and thus illuminates the role of woman in the epic story of male heroes and legends. H.D. writes directly against Homer by placing Helen not in Troy but in Egypt. This is the first indication of H.D.'s intention to challenge epic tradition. Since this genre is that which is mostly associated with male writing, *Helen in Egypt* counteracts classic male-authored literature and its tendency to either ignore or deliberately silence women. In her own modern epic, H.D.'s objective is to revise Helen's story by filling in gaps left wide open by male epicists who came before her. Coinciding with similar work in women's literature near the same time (Sylvia Plath's challenge of misogynist attitudes in *Ariel* (1965), Joanne Kyger's focus on the waiting Penelope in *Tapestry and the Web* (1965) or Anne Sexton's deconstruction and eventual rejection of the Cinderella story in 'Cinderella' [1971]), *Helen in Egypt* contributes to a recovery of women and female voices in literary tradition.

Helen in Egypt is a recreation of the Greek myth of soul-searching in light of war and destruction in modern terms. In the prefatory note to the third poem in the book, where H.D. directly challenges Homeric 'truth' by writing Helen's presence in Troy as a mere 'reflection' (for as the poet takes it she was never there), she describes the Trojan War as the 'holocaust of the Greeks' (H.D., *Helen in Egypt*, p. 5). The poet's labelling of the Trojan War in terms of the most traumatic instance of mass killing in modern history reveals *Helen in Egypt*'s grounding in modernity, a discourse which H.D. sees as both sharing universal concerns of humanity, such as the physical and mental disintegration of societies brought about by war, and with a language of its own. H.D.'s project of engendering her modernist literary practices is centred around her sense of this modernity, a fascination with which she never lost from her first imagist pieces to her later prose and poetry.

NOTES

1 C. Laity, *H.D. and the Victorian Fin de Siècle: Gender, Modernism, Decadence* (Cambridge and New York: Cambridge University Press, 1996), p. xi.
2 G. Taylor, *H.D. and the Public Sphere of Modernist Women Writers 1913–1946. Talking Women* (Oxford: University Press, 2001).
3 A. Morris, *How to Live/What to Do: H.D.'s Cultural Poetics* (Urbana: Illinois University Press, 2003), p. 185.
4 S.S. Friedman, *Penelope's Web: Gender, Modernity, H.D.'s Fiction* (Cambridge and New York: Cambridge University Press, 1990), p. 298.
5 H.D., *Tribute to Freud* (New York: New Directions, 1972), p. 145.
6 T. Trigilio, *'Strange Prophecies Anew': Rereading Apocalypse in Blake, H.D., and Ginsberg* (Cranbury, London and Ontario: Associated University Presses, 2000), p. 86.
7 H.D., *Notes on Thought and Vision & The Wise Sappho* (San Francisco: City Lights Books, 1982), p. 40.
8 H.D., in L.L. Martz (ed.), *Collected Poems 1912–1944* (New York: New Directions, 1983), p. 19. Henceforth abbreviated as *CP* in the main text.
9 C. Buck, *H.D. and Freud: Bisexuality and a Feminine Discourse* (Hemel Hempstead: Harvester Wheatsheaf, 1991), p. 99.
10 For an analysis of H.D.'s post-imagist poems and autobiographical prose writings in light of Freudian concepts such as transference and narcissism, see D. Chisholm, *H.D.'s Freudian Poetics: Psychoanalysis in Translation* (Ithaca: Cornell University Press, 1992).
11 Cited in D. Perkins, *A History of Modern Poetry: From the 1890s to the High Modernist Mode* (Cambridge, MA, and London: The Belknap Press of Harvard, 1976), p. 509. The influence of *The Golden Bough* on modernist writers, particularly on Eliot, Yeats, Joyce and Lawrence, has been established by J.B. Vickery in his classic work of literary criticism, *The Literary Impact of 'The Golden Bough'* (Princeton University Press, 1973).

12 For H.D.'s Hellenic spirituality, see E. Gregory, *H.D. and Hellenism: Classic Lines* (Cambridge and New York: Cambridge University Press, 1997), especially pp. 75–128. Other studies have highlighted H.D.'s interest in the occult: for seminal work; see S.S. Friedman, *Psyche Reborn: The Emergence of H.D.* (Bloomington: Indiana University Press, 1981), pp. 157–206.
13 A. Gelpi, 'Introduction: The Thistle and the Serpent' in H.D., *Notes*, p. 13.
14 See S.S. Friedman (ed.), *Analyzing Freud: The Letters of H.D., Bryher, and Their Circle* (New York: New Directions, 2002), pp. 10–11, 14–16, 17–18, 86–8, 245–6, 361–2, 376–7, 403–4, 423, 500–4, 523–4.
15 H. Ellis, *The New Spirit* (Boston, MA: Elibron Classics, 2004), p. 129.
16 On this, see R. Pappas, 'H.D. and Havelock Ellis: Popular Science and the Gendering of *Thought and Vision*', *Women's Studies*, 38.2 (March 2009), 151–82.
17 H.D., in N. Holmes Pearson and M. King (eds.), *End to Torment: A Memoir of Ezra Pound* (New York: New Directions, 1979), p. 40.
18 H. Monroe, *A Poet's Life: Seventy Years in a Changing World* (New York: Macmillan, 1938), p. 264.
19 L.S. Rainey (ed.) *Modernism: An Anthology* (Oxford: Blackwell Publishing, 2005), p. 94.
20 The other H.D. poems in *Des Imagistes* of 1914 are: 'Sitalkas', 'Priapus', 'Acon' and 'Hermonax'. See *Des Imagistes: An Anthology* (New York: Albert and Charles Boni, 1914). Available at: www.archive.org/details/desimagistesananooalberich. Accessed 15 May 2010.
21 D. Ayers, *Modernism: A Short Introduction* (Oxford: Blackwell Publishing, 2004), p. 3.
22 E. Gregory, 'Rose Cut in Rock: Sappho and H.D.'s "Sea Garden"', *Contemporary Literature*, 27.4, H.D. Centennial Issue (Winter 1986), 525–52 (529).
23 D. Collecott, *H.D. and Sapphic Modernism 1910–1950* (Cambridge University Press, 1999).
24 I owe this insight to Diana Collecott. See essay in this Companion.
25 H.D., *Bid Me to Live (A Madrigal)* (New York: Grove Press, 1960), p. 97.
26 M. King (ed.) *H.D.: Woman and Poet* (Orono: The National Poetry Foundation, 1986).
27 S.S. Friedman, *Penelope's Web: Gender, Modernity, H.D.'s Fiction* (Cambridge and New York: Cambridge University Press, 1990), p. 6.
28 H.D., *Helen in Egypt* (New York: New Directions, 1974).

5

GEORGIA JOHNSTON

H.D. and gender: queering the reading

HERmione, H.D.'s early autobiographical novel, provides an excellent case study through which to explore the author's connections between gender, text and reader. In *HER*, H.D. exposes patriarchal textual gendering and, then, inserts texts alternative to the patriarchal ones. Mirrors, both literal and metaphorical, allow her women characters to read themselves and each other in spaces that produce lesbian eroticism, female subjectivity and a woman's writing. By framing through reflection, H.D. questions a patriarchal 'normal' subjectivity, subjectivity defined in terms of a unitary individualised self. Her reflecting, textualised women protagonists, paramount in her writing, illuminate, through the texts they create, a stirring gendered link between female subjectivity and creativity. For H.D., gender is a text to be read.

Patriarchal foundations

H.D.'s early fictional autobiographies – *HERmione* (1927), *Paint it Today* (1921) and *Asphodel* (1922) – portray (in that order, in sequential chronology) H.D.'s early years as a writer – when she first writes poetry, when Ezra Pound became her fiancé and mentor, when she meets her lovers Frances Gregg, Richard Aldington (her husband), Cecil Gray, then Winifred Ellerman (Bryher). Susan Stanford Friedman's and Rachel Blau DuPlessis' plot synopsis of these interlocking novels emphasises the gendered complications of their scripts: 'This story moves from intense love of both man and woman, centers in the experiences of loss and betrayal engendered by heterosexual relationships in a patriarchal context, and ends in the celebration of a *love for a woman* and the birth of a girl child.'[1] The heterosexual

I thank Polina Mackay and Nephie Christodoulides for their invitation to write the essay for this volume and for their insightful comments upon an early draft. I thank Saint Louis University, which provided a Summer Research Award, funding this essay's final research and writing.

losses and betrayals emphasise a woman's failure within patriarchy, while lesbian betrayals and 'celebration[s]', both, meaningfully expand the female protagonists' understandings of themselves. The female protagonist in each text fails in patriarchy, but fails for the woman only if read in terms of patriarchy. That repetition of failed scripting[2] evokes a gendering, which enacts itself within the referent of patriarchy. In contrast to the patriarchy as referent, the '*love for a woman*' in these early novels, whether circumscribed by patriarchal claims and disapproval or freed from them, steadies and maintains subjectivities for women that sustain their writing.

In *HERmione* the protagonist 'Her' fails in every available patriarchal script, and each failure takes away more of her scripted subjectivity. She fails to succeed as a student at Bryn Mawr, paralleling her inabilities to understand her father's and brother's equations. She fails to fit as daughter and sister in her family, discovering that she 'can not stay' in the family home;[3] 'if she stayed, she would be suffocated' (H.D., *HER*, p. 9). She tries to 'escape' by becoming engaged to George, who will take her away to Europe, not at first realising that she would exchange one patriarchal text for another. Even though 'Hermione realized George [her fiancé] wanted now to help Her' and, so, she tries 'to reach forward to some stabilized world they might create between them' (p. 68), George's sexuality imposes his own reality on hers, obliterating her: '[k]isses forced her into soft moss'. Her becomes 'smudged out'. 'I am smudged out' she repeats (p. 73). Because he cannot understand her, Her ends their engagement.[4]

From the beginning, Her fails 'to conform to expectation'. The authorial narrator, compassionately reevaluating Her's failures from a future point of view, explains that 'Hermione Gart could not then know' that her 'failure to conform to expectations was perhaps some subtle form of courage' (*HER*, p. 4). Her cannot realise this, because the failures do not seem like 'courage'; they seem self-annihilating. The novel begins with a 'stuttering' repetition of the name 'Her', a 'stuttering' that, for Diana Collecott, 'represents the heroine's ruptured speech and ruptured subjectivity'.[5] 'Her Gart went round in circles. "I am Her", she said to herself; she repeated, "Her, Her, Her".' The phrase 'went round in circles' suggests a miring in self-reflection, seemingly without exit.

The repetition, however, also suggests that Her repeats her name as if a talisman to keep herself clear, with the repetition maintaining Her despite all odds. By repeating her name, Her textualises herself, powerfully connecting self to writing. Her's act of textualisation becomes clearer when Her forcefully repeats the complete phrases at the beginning of a new section: 'I am Her Gart. I am Hermione Gart. I am going round and round in circles.' She has been 'forced along slippery lines of exact definition', but she's aware of the 'dementia'. Her can begin to escape that 'definition' when she names herself and repeats her name, mapping the patriarchal subjectivity. By marking the name as text intrinsically connected with herself, Her stays alive within the patriarchal equation that woman is object (H.D., *HER*, pp. 4, 3).[6] Her begins to give herself other identities, presenting other possibilities. For example, living in the state of Pennsylvania, she recognises the etymology of 'Sylvania. Trees. Trees. Trees . . . Trees are in people. People are in trees' (p. 5). Naming herself, then, 'Tree', she alters her objectification within the patriarchy (Her) with a new subject, 'tree': 'I am a tree planted by rivers of water. I am . . . I am . . . HER' (p. 70, original ellipses). Her never objectifies herself into a name, as the patriarchy does. Instead, the text itself has a subjectivity for her that leads her to identify herself with the text, with the word: 'She said, "HER, HER, HER. I am Her, I am Hermione . . . I am the word AUM"' (p. 32, original ellipsis). By presenting her name as text within the context of subjectivity, she begins to give herself alternate possible subjectivities, to identify with her name while altering her role in relation to it.

Her's emphasis on her own naming suggests that patriarchy and her failures within it have exposed the imposed relationship between name and named. Her extends her awareness to patriarchy's general practice of using names to maintain a woman's gendered role. When Her announces to her father that she will marry George Lowndes, her father addresses her by her family role: '"I mean – what are you saying, daughter?" He called her daughter . . . like God saying *daughter I say unto you arise*' (H.D., *HER*, p. 100). 'Daughter' places her in the patriarchal category, immediately gendered. By naming Her 'daughter', Her's father defines her in the patriarchal system by role. With that name, patriarchy can exchange her. Already this family has taken in 'Minnie Hurloe' (p. 19), who has become 'Minnie Gart' by marrying Her's brother, Bertrand. Minnie has become a sister to Her, a relationship Her cannot accept; Minnie 'isn't and never could be my sister' (p. 122).

Family relationships (such as Minnie as Her's sister) are defined for women whether or not they have biological referents, and patriarchy extends these referents to textual ones. Her is not only her father's specific daughter, but also an extended textual daughter, through the Biblical referents ('God saying *daughter I say unto you arise*'). Her, through her own recognition of patriarchy's earlier texts, is the daughter of Jairus, whom Jesus takes by the hand after she has died, commanding her 'Damsel I say unto thee arise',[7] as well as God's daughter as Nation from the Old Testament – 'Arise . . . O daughter of Zion . . . and thou shalt beat in pieces many people.'[8] Her, as daughter, arises out of a nascent insular subjectivity, one recognised by the patriarchy only as death. The daughter rises out of death (as does Jairus' daughter) back into life, and, as Nation, 'Arise[s]' in order to give death. The patriarch (the Father, Jesus, God) decides life and death, not the woman. The patriarchal role of daughter establishes woman's subjectivity as an extension out of and towards death. Both in Her's own body and through established biblical texts, the patriarchy creates and extends the daughter. In a patriarchal script, so goes the underlying message, the woman will be dead to 'I' even while called back into putative life. Her would need to change the previous patriarchal texts or their signification of 'daughter' in order to step outside the assigned meaning.

By exposing connections in patriarchy of name to gender, simultaneously Her begins to question those texts. Considering her name changing from Gart to Lowndes when she will marry George Lowndes, Hermione thinks, 'it wasn't right. People are in things, things are in people. I can't be called Lowndes' (H.D., *HER*, p. 112). Patriarchal gendering emerges from patriarchy's naming women, thereby creating assigned subjectivity, not subjectivity intrinsic to the individual woman. Her's realisation that she cannot change her name from Gart to Lowndes comments directly upon the exchange of women in a gender system that establishes patriarchy.[9] The system has created an untenable situation, because patriarchy has institutionalised the name, as mutable text, not as the thing itself. Her would disappear with the new name. In contrast, Her points out that a name is a material 'thing' as much as a 'tree'. She varies this phrase (as when she thinks 'People were in things, things were in people. Names were in things, things were in names') throughout the novel, paralleling 'things' with 'trees' and 'names' in their relation to people. Her learns to use her name rather than let others use it to define her, begins to alter her relationship to her name, and thereby creates a differently gendered subjectivity, since 'people are in things, things are in people' – Her's name is one of those 'things'.[10] When Her reads her own name, she, not the patriarchy, controls it. But to read herself, she must reject the patriarchal naming, which relies upon dense textual traditions. She must change her relationship to text, making text as much subject as object in relation to herself.

Entering new texts

These readings show the vigour with which H.D. contested patriarchy's gendered scripts, through Her's failure to conform to them. Instead of capitulating to 'romantic thralldom' to men, a pattern that H.D. reveals within patriarchal structures,[11] Her resists the gendering ascribed to her through patriarchal institutionalised plots. H.D. shows how two different systems situate economies of desire. In patriarchy, men's desire positions the women as objects. Her, for example, is a 'decorative' object for George (H.D., *HER*, pp. 167, 172). In contrast, H.D. uses Her to create an alternative system of textualising and gendering, an alternative text producing concomitant subject/object, so that Her is neither and both. H.D. writes this alternative text in three dimensions, one spatially (with Fayne Raab), one temporally (with a future 'I') and one across writings (with Sappho).

Fayne/Her and the mirror

Only after Her leaves patriarchal expectations does text seem capable of producing alternative gender roles. Through an erotic friendship with Fayne Raab, Her learns to 'see' – to read gender differently from patriarchy. She can then defy patriarchal gendering. Her first sees Fayne through a 'convex Victorian mirror' (H.D., *HER*, p. 51). Fayne sits opposite Her, so Her sees Fayne with her 'back to the little slightly convex mirror, facing Her'. Through the mirror, Her witnesses her own act of seeing, and she experiences beyond a physical reality into that textual one. That new text *genders* a new reality for Her, through spatial reorganising. The new reality appears in the literal mirror, and extends to her mind: 'her head – the bit here, the bit there, the way it fitted bit to bit – was two convex mirrors placed back to back. The two convex mirrors placed back to back became one mirror . . . as Fayne Rabb entered' (p. 138, original ellipsis).

Fayne Raab sees Her also: 'The girl *was* seeing Her' (H.D., *HER*, pp. 71, 52, original emphasis). Literal *seeing* creates both subjectivity and eroticism for the women, where Fayne is 'this thing that made the floor sink beneath her feet and the wall rise to infinity above her head'. Her will not look into Fayne's eyes at first, admonishing herself, 'Don't look', but then 'forced eyes back till they met eyes' (pp. 52, 56, repeated p. 74). In contrast to Her's inabilities to maintain a subjectivity in patriarchy, Her creates a mutual subjectivity with Fayne, wherein 'she is HER and I am HER' (p. 131). Her does not take on a new name; the two women have the same positioning in patriarchy as object. Their parallel alignment highlights an extreme awareness of self-identity through Her's identification with Fayne. Her's self-identity depends upon that connection, for 'I am in Her' (p. 173). Her new subjectivity, then, aligns with the self-created and multiply identified text, which queers the institution of patriarchy. Her and Fayne 'see' each other, their own desire queering patriarchal objectification by positing simultaneous subject and object, textualising themselves while reading themselves, both reader and read.

When characters like Her step aside from the scripts given them by the patriarchy, they voice what 'does not yet exist' or has been silenced, 'unspeakable differences'.[12] Desires outside patriarchy create alternative identity, with desire and identity intersecting through textual creation. Elisabeth Meese notes that, 'Writing the lesbian means writing someone who does not yet exist',[13] which suggestively describes Her's situation. Despite the patriarchal narratives in Her's family life, Her and Fayne, 'see[ing]', are able to read themselves as concurrent subjects. Reading the self and the other woman extends the subjectivity of the female self into heretofore non-existent texts; but alternative female texts are not self-evident. Her must read Fayne and vice versa. Fayne corroborates their recognition of each other, saying to Her, '"You make me see things"' (H.D., *HER*, p. 158). Her moves from the third person to the first: 'Fayne being me, I was her' (p. 210). The patriarchy will no longer be able to exchange these women, with daughters moving from one family to another, taking the old roles with their new families, as Minnie has done in changing from Hurloe to Gart. Instead, the women in terms of one another sustain a text that the patriarchy cannot read. George, for instance, reacts to the women by saying that they should be 'burnt for witchcraft' (pp. 165, 168), representing the patriarchal assertion that women should be killed if they do not gender themselves according to the patriarchal roles.

In contrast to patriarchal objectification, the woman's self doubles, and then a split self joins as does an 'amoeba' (H.D., *HER*, p. 120). The processes of splitting, doubling and reflecting take place both outside and inside the self. Using the 'convex mirror' does not collapse subject into object. The word 'Her' inscribes a seeming collapse, since 'her' is the objective form grammatically, even while the word names the subject 'Her', as Rachel Blau DuPlessis has explained.[14] Instead of collapse, the mirror creates a second intermediary text. That new dichotomy creates a self as both creator and text. No longer avoiding Fayne Raab's eyes, Her turns to her, and Fayne's 'wild eyes' were the 'only sane eyes' that 'Hermione had yet seen' (pp. 57–8). They begin to speak together, and Her's 'words now were a gambler's heritage, heady things, they would win for her, they would lose for her'. These words with Fayne, 'the very speaking of the words, conjured up proper answering sigil [a magical sign]. A whole world was open' (pp. 61–2, 62). The relational female text (established first through mirror, then through eyes, then through words) negotiates the division between subject and object, identifying this queer subjectivity with a woman's creativity, with her words as 'heady things'.

Helen McNeil writes that 'In *HER* both narrative and metaphor argue that the self's need for a mirror, for "image", is fulfilled by communion with another woman.'[15] That 'need . . . for image' extends to the need of a new reality, for without Fayne, Her, 'avid and eager' could only try to communicate 'into an empty area' (H.D., *HER*, p. 214). Without the 'dream' that is Her and Fayne, Her will give up her new self; she will 'keep Her under'. She 'will incarcerate Her. Her won't anymore be'; no subjectivity exists (p. 216). With Fayne, in contrast, by framing her self and Fayne together within the mirror, Her creates a new gender based on subjectivity that combines subject and object, through new self-textualisation, outside patriarchy: 'She is Her. I am Her. Her is Fayne. Fayne is Her. I will not let them hurt HER' (p. 181). While, in patriarchy, woman is positioned as object and the woman's subjectivity can be 'hurt', Her can protect both herself and Fayne when together they produce subjects.

This new relationship to name produces new texts. Hermione does not at first recognise her own potential power to create, not only through name but through her writing, an alternate text from patriarchy's. Instead, '[w]riting had somehow got connected up with George Lowndes' (H.D., *HER*, p. 71). She waits for George 'to acclaim her, to say, bravissimo'. She accepts his recognition of her writing ('"*this is writing*"', he says of her poetry). She accepts his evaluation when he says her poetry is '"like the choriambics of a forgotten Melic"' (p. 136, original spacing, p. 149). Patriarchy filters through textuality with George as its spokesman. Then, through Her's new textualisation with Fayne, 'writing' will move from the associations with George to Fayne, when Her will eventually 'try and put the thing [with Fayne] in writing' (p. 71).

Her realises, thinking of the 'dream' of Fayne Raab, that 'Solid and visible form was what she had been seeking. I will put this into visible language' (H.D., *HER*, p. 213). Through the subjectivity formed with Fayne Raab, Her emerges as a writer. Her new text with another woman genders a new subjectivity, which leads her to create art, to 'put into stark language' (p. 213). She needs the other woman for this subjectivity. When she loses Fayne – when Her and Fayne have been separated by Fayne's mother, by George's and Fayne's betrayal of Her, and by Her's three-month emotional breakdown – then she momentarily puts aside the writing self, even though she knows she 'could have really written'. When she loses Fayne, she would re-enter the roles of patriarchy, and thus she would lose herself.

Juxtaposing the split between 'I' and Her

Losing Fayne does not terminate Her's ability to elude patriarchy, however, because another woman (herself) enters the text. Her retains an alternate subjectivity after the loss of Fayne. By inserting an 'I', H.D. replaces Her's and Fayne's spatial multiple identity with a temporal multiple identity.

'I' and Her recreate the multiple but split identities that are able to sustain each other. To extend the 'I' temporally, H.D. inserts 'I', who enters alongside Her, and who takes a position similar to Fayne's. Her precedes this future 'I' but also assimilates 'I', as revealed in this section of the text, with its movements between 'I', 'She', 'her' and 'Her': 'Every year all my life, I have discovered something really in the winter . . . The stars are shining all of them, but I can't see any. She felt like a star invisible in daylight. Then her thought widened . . . Her saw Her as a star shining' (H.D., *HER*, p. 225). In 'I''s 'discover[y]', 'I' actively genders a new female text against patriarchal gendering of unitary 'I'. While 'I can't see any' of the 'stars', the past version of 'I' (Her) is able to see herself 'as a star shining', even while 'invisible in daylight', a 'discovery' that occurs because 'her thought widened'. Her expansion of 'thought' allows her to 'see' despite the 'daylight' that makes 'star[s] invisible'. 'I' both observes and experiences Her's 'discover[y]', one of the discover[ies] 'I' has made 'every year'.

Repeatedly, 'I' enters to observe and read Her while simultaneously experiencing Her's situation, supportively standing beside her. Her seems unsure at these points in the text, as in the case when Her steps outside patriarchy with Fayne. As if 'I' guards past selves, H.D. inserts 'me' and 'we': 'It frightens me to hear Fayne. It happens just as we are near coming together in some realm of appreciation' (H.D., *HER*, p. 146). 'I' moves from commenting on Her's position to taking her place when Her is threatened physically, when Her resists George's violent attempt at seduction, as if a future self needs to insist, 'I am stronger. I turn and twist out of those iron arms because if he had held me, I would have been crushed' (p. 173). After the danger is over, Her re-enters the text as 'she': 'She said "Please put the light on".' 'I' figures woman as text who can both protect and be protected, read and be read, facilitating flexible positions for gender to emerge outside patriarchal control. As did Her of Fayne, the 'I' acts as if to say, 'I will not let them hurt HER' (p. 181). As Her did with Fayne, 'I' parallels Her, but never collapses into Her, even when she momentarily takes Her's place. Similar to the mirror formation of Her with Fayne, the new textual formation changes the positioning of space to time. Gender functions through juxtaposed experience, rather than expected object roles. The 'I' reads and helps Her from *within* the novel's frame, from *future* experiential knowledge, outside Her.[16] The older self (one who can comment on 'every year all my life', who can state 'Things can't happen that aren't meant to happen' (p. 174)) comes in to observe and validate the earlier self.

'I' allows Her to exist in multiply gendered roles. When Her is standing at her and George's engagement party, guests come up to Her and say things like '"Yes, I knew George" giggling "when he wore lace collars" and "Yes, you are the sort of person George *would* like."' These inanities make reality freeze for Her. Her 'saw it now . . . Something that had been going . . . became . . . static'. At this juncture, when 'static' overwhelms Her, the 'I' appears: 'I am standing here for someone has come in, more people have come in.' The 'I' is in the same place at the party, yet this transient, momentary appearance of 'I' allows Her relief, while still (barely) existing at the party as George's fiancée (H.D., *HER*, pp. 105–6). The relief allows Her to perceive her role as fiancée as 'static'.

As Her and Fayne have in the mirror, 'I' and Her extend a woman's subjectivity. Yet, even when 'I' is a future 'I', the relationship is not a retrospective one. When 'I' enters, both character and 'I' exist at that novelistic moment, while, because 'I' *is* separate from the story, 'I' has the capacity to read this other (chronologically earlier but textually simultaneous) self.[17] At the party, 'Hermione couldn't follow' and Hermione did not 'trouble to answer'. But 'I' acts as ghost-like female text, establishing a presence that allows Her to exist both inside and outside patriarchy. The guests cannot see Her as she is; she is 'the sort of person George *would* like' to them, a Her defined in terms of George. Inability to read outside the patriarchy recalls Terry Castle's proposition that, in twentieth-century fictions, the 'lesbian has been "ghosted" – or made to seem invisible – by culture itself',[18] and 'I' seems to work in those terms. Countering cultural excision of Her as an individual subject, the 'I' intensely recognises her previous incarnation, validating in the earlier self that which is outside patriarchy.

'I' validates a textual future beyond Her's dilemmas, even while Her experiences her present, and 'I' represents Her's deliverance. 'I' and Her together reflect larger-than-one-life subjects, traversing time, through reflection. Rather than displacing Her, 'I' needs the earlier self as part of the epistemologies of reading. The combination of 'I' and character Her allows a subjectivity that depends upon the other. For instance, 'I' is 'free for . . . memories' because of Her, for Her appears to 'I' as 'an image standing by a crossroad'. 'I' states she 'never knew her', but Her's experiences, which George's 'Hibiscus kisses smudged out', alter, not just Her, but 'I' – both 'smudg[ing memory] out' and leaving 'me free for... memories' (H.D., *HER*, p. 121, original ellipses). Patriarchy (represented by George's 'kisses') entraps neither Her nor 'I', because through reflection Her and 'I' create alternate female text and alternate gender.

Sappho's desired text

By becoming a text alongside and with Fayne, alongside and with 'I', Her develops erotic lesbian space. Teresa de Lauretis' work on erotic lesbian space helps to conceptualise this space as space of *address*, a space in which women can communicate with other women, since, 'in the very act of assuming and speaking from the position of subject, a woman could concurrently recognize women as subjects *and* as objects of female desire'.[19] Marilyn Frye's point that, 'If the lesbian sees the woman, the woman may see the lesbian seeing her . . . may learn that she *can be* seen',[20] is exactly Her's act when the mirror combines Her and Fayne and when 'I' returns to observe, replace and protect Her. 'Seeing' and 'learn[ing] that she *can* be seen' is exactly what Her accomplishes when Her and 'I' read the text of themselves, observing and validating each other, positioning desire outside patriarchal terms.

This queer aesthetic validates Diana Collecott's argument that H.D.'s 'entire oeuvre can be read as a creative dialogue with Sappho' (*Sapphic*, p. 3).[21] Collecott reads H.D.'s use of Sappho as 'commemoration' of the earlier poet and as 'reincorporation' of 'a lesbian poetics' (p. 10). In her 1924 volume of poems, *Heliodora*, for example, H.D. includes variations on four of Sappho's fragments. She reworks the fragments freely, as if she is the medium through which the lost poem returns. When reclaiming Sappho's texts, H.D. revitalises the fragments left from the virulent destruction of Sappho's works. Her poem based on Sappho's 'Fragment thirty-six', 'I know not what to do: / my mind is divided',[22] is one of erotic upheaval, measuring 'the rage that burns' against girl's 'song's gift'. The girl inspires the speaker's 'wild longing', which produces multiple 'minds' in the speaker: 'My mind is quite divided, / my minds hesitate.'

Images of division and reflection in patriarchy invoke death and loss, but division and reflection become, through H.D.'s extensions through Sappho, images of immense plenitude. This split reproduces in one body the doubled subjectivity of Her/Fayne and I/Her, a Sapphic generative subjectivity of division and communion. These 'minds' 'strive' with each other, 'so my mind waits / to grapple with my mind'. The split in desire parallels the moment when Her becomes aware of her own divided mind, split and joined like the convex mirror. As in the poem, two subjective positions, within the same body, 'grapple' with each other in passionate desire, so that Her's mind, 'separated' in itself, was 'astonished to perceive how she could turn, perceive as a mirror the whole of the fantasy of the world reversed and in that mirror a wide room opening' (H.D., *HER*, pp. 120, 118, 76). The dilemma as H.D. characterises it across her writing, while external at the beginning, becomes internalised, creating the song inside the self, as the 'mind hesitates / above my mind, / listening to song's delight'. This new subjectivity, eroticised, has become, to draw on de Lauretis' thinking once again, lesbian 'erotic space' – 'a space of contradiction requiring constant reaffirmation and painful renegotiation' (Abelove *et al.* 1993, p. 142).

Through these writings that 'reaffirm' and 'renegotiat[e]' Sappho, H.D. marks lesbian 'erotic space' and time. She emphatically connects female subjectivity and creativity across generations, embracing Sappho's texts *as* gendered texts, alternative to patriarchy's insistence on unified subjectivity, alternative to an 'I' who cannot embrace a relinquishing of that subjectivity into object formation. As in her use of the mirror to frame Her and Fayne and of 'I' to stand beside and observe the earlier selves within the novelistic frame, Sappho's words stand beside H.D.'s as titles to her poems and, then, through extended images, in the novels. The texts juxtapose the two writers, in an 'intertextuality' that, Collecott observes, 'reinforces a female – and even matrisexual – bond' (Collecott 2008, p. 33). H.D. textually embraces Sappho to reposition her own self, to embody Sappho. Helen McNeil points out that in the 'male romantic tradition, the muse or epipsychicion was female' (McNeil 1983, p. x). In contrast to that tradition, H.D. neither enters the male position to use a female as muse, nor does she herself act as one. Sappho is not H.D.'s muse or inspiration. Instead, H.D. radically 'reaffirm[s]' Sappho's voice across space and time, crossing vast expanses.[23] By creating a symmetry of textuality with the earlier poet, H.D. embodies an alternate subjectivity through an alternate female text, the lesbian 'erotic space' of the woman writer. Sappho herself becomes a female text that provides this woman modernist with a model, a gendered figuring of herself, which the modernist men around her (Pound and Lawrence especially) denied her. Eluding the roles they would have her play, she claims the queer writer (Sappho – and by extension herself – H.D.) for modernism.

H.D.'s sophisticated understandings of herself in literary cultural terms are stunning in their complexity. Her's subject position with Fayne, her regeneration through 'I', as well as her embodiment of Sappho's split desires occupy space and place in the text *as* a text, a material position which patriarchy would deny. H.D., thus, develops an erotic space that defies patriarchal gendering. She deliberately reconfigures gender through reconsidering of name, identity and textuality, by realigning Her with Fayne and Her with 'I', and by taking on the Sapphic position. H.D. writes from and extends self-identity, redefining fragment and whole, so that she genders women beyond patriarchy, 'see'ing, reading, and writing anew. By contesting patriarchy's identifications and definitions, she adds multiple locations of woman's subjectivity and objectivity within the text, thereby creating alternate female subjectivity through spatial and temporal refiguring.

NOTES

1 S.S. Friedman and R.B. DuPlessis (eds.), '"I Had Two Loves Separate": The Sexualities of H.D.'s *HER*', in *Signets: Reading H.D.* (Madison: University of Wisconsin Press, 1990), p. 207, my emphasis.
2 I use the term 'script' deliberately to recall Carolyn Heilbrun's work on autobiography: *Writing a Woman's Life* (New York: Norton, 1988). The cultural requirements of gender, she reveals, compel particular life scripts.
3 H.D., *HERmione* (New York: New Directions, 1981), p. 94. Hereafter abbreviated to *HER* and referred to in the main text.
4 Susan Stanford Friedman rightly associates rising family 'social approbation' of the marriage and Her's discomfort with that proposed marriage. *Psyche Reborn: The Emergence of H.D.* (Bloomington: Indiana University Press, 1981), p. 40. Friedman, however, suggests that the 'approbation' *causes* Her's wish to end the engagement. Her's reaction, however, is not due to the family's acceptance, but to her own recognition of her obliteration. In contrast to Her's repudiation of conformity, the family begins to accept the marriage when they realise that the marriage will require Hermione to conform.
5 D. Collecott, *H.D. and Sapphic Modernism: 1910–1950* (Cambridge University Press, 1999), p. 61.
6 Her continues to repeat her name throughout the text when she is bolstering her sense of self against patriarchal attempts to circumscribe her and later when she begins the relationship with Fayne. See *HER*, pp. 29, 32, 33, 158, 177, 181.
7 Mark 5:41: 'And he took the damsel by the hand, and said unto her, Talithacumi; which is, being interpreted, Damsel, I say unto thee arise.'
8 *Micah* 4:13.
9 For Gayle Rubin, the 'exchange' enforces women's subjection to patriarchy. 'The Traffic in Women: Notes on the "Political Economy" of Sex', in R.R. Reiter (ed.), *Towards an Anthropology of Women* (New York: Monthly Review Press, 1975), pp. 157–210.
10 This phrase and its variations repeat throughout *HERmione*, pp. 5, 74, 131, 134.
11 See DuPlessis' work on 'thralldom', 'Romantic Thralldom in H.D.', *Contemporary Literature*, 20.2 (Summer 1979), 178–203.
12 I deliberately use Julia Watson's terms for what cannot be said in lesbian autobiography. 'Unspeakable Differences: The Politics of Gender in Lesbian and Heterosexual Women's Autobiographies', in S. Smith and J. Watson (eds.), *De/Colonizing the Subject: The Politics of Gender in Women's Autobiography* (Minneapolis: University of Minnesota Press, 1992), pp. 139–68.
13 E.A. Meese, *(sem)erotics: theorizing lesbian writing* (New York University Press, 1992), p. 3.
14 The name marks her as both female subject and object, since grammatically it is the possessive form, 'in which', according to S. Travis, 'subject and object refuse to split'. 'A Crack in the Ice: Subjectivity and the Mirror in H.D.'s *HER*', *Sagetrieb*, 6.2 (1987), 126. DuPlessis discusses the object/subject dichotomy of the word 'Her' at length in 'Romantic Thralldom in H.D.'
15 H. McNeil, 'Introduction' in *HERmione* (London: Virago, 1983), p. x.

16 The same process occurs in C. Laity (ed.), *Paint It Today* (New York University Press, 1992).

17 H.D. queers time through 'I', as Judith Halberstam defines 'queer temporality', which, according to Halberstam, 'disrupts the normative narratives of time that form the base of nearly every definition of the human', *In a Queer Time & Place* (New York University Press, 2005), p. 152.

18 T. Castle, *The Apparitional Lesbian: Female Homosexuality and Modern Culture* (New York: Columbia University Press, 1993), p. 4.

19 'Sexual Indifference and Lesbian Representation' in H. Abelove, M. Aina Barale and D.M. Halperin (eds.), *The Lesbian and Gay Studies Reader* (New York: Routledge, 1993), pp. 141–2. See Georgina Taylor for accounts of H.D.'s historical audiences that diverge from patriarchal ones, *H.D. and the Public Sphere of Modernist Women Writers, 1913–1946: Talking Women* (Oxford University Press, 2001).

20 M. Frye, 'To Be and Be Seen: The Politics of Reality', in *The Politics of Reality: Essays in Feminist Theory* (Freedom, CA: The Crossing Press, 1983), p. 172.

21 DuPlessis' and Friedman's point that *HER*'s 'exploration of . . . the lesbian . . . served as a center of identity' also corroborates reading queerly ('Two Loves', p. 227). McCabe cites H.D.'s work from 1914 to reconceptualise modernism as a 'lesbian period' ['"A Queer Lot" and the Lesbians of 1914: Amy Lowell, H.D., and Gertrude Stein', in J.W. Warren and M. Dickie (eds.), *Challenging Boundaries: Gender and Periodization* (Athens: University of Georgia Press, 2000), p. 64], and that reconceptualisation also highlights a reading of queer in *HER*.

22 H.D., 'Fragment Thirty-six', in *Heliodora and Other Poems* (London: Jonathan Cape, 1924), pp. 44–7.

23 H.D. does not limit her representation of extensions of self across space and time to that with Sappho. In *The Gift*, H.D. steps aside from boundaries of individual memory, history and bodies. See G. Johnston, *The Formation of 20th-Century Queer Autobiography* (New York: Palgrave, 2007), pp. 113–22. Anna Banti has also used this technique, of one woman embodying another across space and time, in her 'biography' of Artemisia Gentileschi. See M. Fuch, *The Text Is Myself: Women's Life Writing and Catastrophe* (Madison: University of Wisconsin Press, 2004), pp. 109–38.

6

JO GILL

Reading H.D.: influence and legacy

'Hermione lived her life and lives in history.' So murmurs the speaker of H.D.'s long, reflective sequence 'Winter Love'.[1] This melancholy note provides an apt starting point for a study of H.D.'s legacy for a number of related reasons.

First, the publication history of this particular poem evidences one of the obstacles to establishing definitive lines of influence in H.D.'s case. Written in 1959 and conceived, as Norman Pearsall reports, as the 'coda' to 1961's *Helen in Egypt*, 'Winter Love' was not finally published until 1972 (H.D., *Hermetic*, p. viii).[2] This sizeable – although not in H.D.'s oeuvre unusual – delay means that what may appear at first to be striking similarities (for instance, between the structure, voice and imagery of this poem and examples from Sylvia Plath's work) should be dismissed on the grounds that Plath predeceased the publication of 'Winter Love', or argued on rather different premises. In like manner, H.D.'s *Asphodel*, written in the early 1920s, remained unpublished until 1992. Although editor Robert Spoo identifies in it a 'high modernis[t]' tendency 'toward strong formal control and experimental abandon', its attenuated publication history makes it problematic to argue for its explicit influence on the wider development of a modernist aesthetic.[3]

The second reason for taking 'Winter Love' as a point of departure lies in the speaker's recognition that one might live two different lives simultaneously or palimpsestically, to use one of H.D.'s favoured figures. Hermione, in the line quoted above, has a life in the present and a legacy (a life in history) that succeeds her, spreading outwards and beyond like ripples in a pool. Interestingly, T.S. Eliot uses a similar image in his description of imagism, the aim of which was 'to induce a peculiar concentration upon something visual, and to set in motion an expanding succession of concentric feelings'.[4] The line from 'Winter Love' thus provides a striking metaphor for H.D.'s own reception and legacy.

This chapter will argue for H.D.'s sustained influence in a number of different fields. It will begin by briefly establishing the importance of H.D.'s work to the development of the modernist movement, the founding of imagism, and the subsequent establishment of an avant-garde poetics. Thereafter, the chapter will turn to address the influence of H.D.'s work on the emergence and refinement of feminist and lesbian critical practice. In this respect her poetry, more perhaps than that of any other single writer, has provided a stimulus and a test case for the range of theoretical positions that came to prominence in the closing decades of the twentieth century. It has demanded new ways of reading, and these new perspectives have, in turn, caused readers to look afresh at once-familiar H.D. texts, to bring hitherto overlooked texts to light and, with H.D.'s example in mind, to apply these insights and reading practices to a range of other poets. In the case of her influence on lesbian and queer poetics in particular, as we will see later with reference to Robert Duncan's work, H.D.'s example pushes us to ask new questions and to think in unfamiliar ways. Some of this new critical work may, of course, have emerged without H.D.'s specific example. Nevertheless, in H.D. we find a touchstone and a point of departure. In her own words: 'My sign posts are not yours, but if I blaze my own trail, it may help to give you confidence and urge you to get out of the murky, dead, old, thousand-times explored old world, the dead world of overworked emotions and thoughts.'[5] The allusion to Duncan above takes us to the final and most substantial section of the chapter – a discussion of H.D.'s influence on a range of individual poets. This touches on her relationship with well-known and long-established contemporaries such as Marianne Moore, but primarily focuses on her legacy to later poets such as Adrienne Rich, Diane di Prima, Denise Levertov, Margaret Atwood and, more unexpectedly perhaps, Lorine Niedecker, Anne Sexton and Carol Anne Duffy.

Imagism/modernism

The dedication that opens Bonnie Kime-Scott's 1990 anthology, *The Gender of Modernism*, is to 'the forgotten and silenced makers of modernism'. The epitaph crystallises the various processes by which what we define as 'modernism' has been constructed, disseminated and latterly challenged. The present essay is not the place to revisit this history, or to reopen related debates about periodisation, aesthetics and ethics; these issues are addressed elsewhere in this volume. For now, and in brief, our interest is in noting H.D.'s specific contribution to the emergence and character of modernism, howsoever we might choose to define the term. As Georgina Taylor notes, H.D.'s centrality to modernist thought and practice is beyond question:

> H.D. can be located at the heart of a network of women writers spanning the Anglo-American divide; through discussion, and often through disagreement, these writers came to challenge expectations of women's writing and collectively to work on new ways of expressing and exploring subjectivity, of engaging with socio-political reality and of stretching the possibilities of the literary form in new directions.[6]

The same case might be made for H.D.'s involvement in the emergence of 'imagism'. The history of this particular movement is as contested as that of the larger umbrella of modernism (and is similarly considered in other essays in this collection).[7] Regardless of the detail of its origins, three things bear stating. The first is that H.D. rapidly acquired a seemingly unassailable position as, in Peter Brooker and Simon Perril's terms, the 'premier imagist' who 'belongs at the centre of modernist poetry'.[8] The second is that imagism itself was fundamental to the direction that the larger modernist movement was to take. In Jacob Korg's words: 'Imagism's technical innovations may be said to have played a significant part in authorizing what was meant by "modernism" in twentieth-century poetry, and they were not without effect in the novel as well.'[9] The third is that, as Korg's point suggests, imagism has had an influence beyond its own cultural moment. As we will see shortly, poets such as Plath and Sexton have – perhaps unexpectedly, given their embracing of the personal voice eschewed by H.D. – learnt much from her taut, spare lines. They appropriate many of her images (of ice, heat, crystal, mirrors and so on) and adopt similar personae (the figure of Daphne, to name just one). Subsequent movements such as objectivism can trace a debt to imagism's, and thereby H.D.'s, radical rethinking of the limits of language. Such linguistic self-consciousness foreshadows the work of poets such as Susan Howe or Lyn Hejinian. This self-consciousness about language – seen, for example, in *Hermetic Definition*'s 'my verse / I can't get away from it, I've tried to; . . . why must I write?' (p. 7) – although shared by other modernist poets (notably T.S. Eliot whose 'East Coker' laments the poet's 'intolerable wrestle / With words and meanings'), truly flourishes in the writing of avant-garde successors.[10]

The lyric voice

One of H.D.'s lasting legacies to modernist and subsequent poetic movements lies in her radical rethinking of the role of the subjective lyric voice. In her early imagist writing, the eschewal of a conventional lyric speaking position is evidenced by the paring away of voice and identity such that only spare, elemental images remain. H.D.'s poetry emerged into a post-Victorian, neo-Georgian world which still associated female and lyric poetry with a sentimental voice. According to Taylor, one of the first texts to challenge this convention was H.D.'s 'Hermes of the Ways', a move which, as Taylor proceeds to argue, paved the way for 'the significant developments in women's writing that were to follow' ('Public Sphere', pp. 47, 68). In later work, a distinctive and distinctively female speaking position re-emerges, but is dramatically rethought. It is presented by multiple personae or masks, by fragmented and dispersed subjectivities, by the bold embracing of hitherto marginalised or objectivised perspectives and, in many cases, by an unusual willingness to speak about female desire. Poets from Niedecker through di Prima and Atwood to Hejinian evidence the influence of H.D.'s work in this respect.

As Rachel Blau DuPlessis argues, 'H.D. reworked the beginning of the Western lyric in the Greek Anthology.'[11] By turning to the ancient Greek poet Sappho and 'reanimat[ing]' (DuPlessis 1986, p. 23) her shattered and thereby distorted fragments, H.D. re-energises and hones the lyric line which had, over time, lost its power. In DuPlessis' words: 'The reinterpretation of female hero/ines is a culturally empowering action for a woman writer who moves this hero/ine into subject place, foregrounding her voice, justifying her choices, making her story emotionally and politically plausible' (DuPlessis 1986, pp. 27–8). This understanding that the aesthetic is also the personal and the political is, in many ways, one of H.D.'s most important and lasting legacies – informing, as we will see, the emergence of feminist and queer critical practice and the work of individual poets including Rich, Judy Grahn and Duncan.

Beyond imagism

For Friedman and DuPlessis, H.D.'s influence on the poetry that followed derives not from her markedly imagist poetry alone but from the whole of her 'rich and varied oeuvre'.[12] Prose texts such as the 1919 essay 'Notes on Thoughts and Vision' (published in 1982), proffer a startling manifesto for her own poetic process, one which yokes the intellectual and the physical and roots creativity in the female body. It thereby anticipates in important ways the work of later thinkers including, most significantly, feminist theorists such as Hélène Cixous and Luce Irigaray. H.D.'s willingness to traverse boundaries of genre is itself an important point of influence. As Helen Sword proposes, her effacement of conventional thresholds marks one of H.D.'s contributions to modernism and to the emergence of contemporary feminist poetics.[13]

For Susan Gubar, it is H.D.'s epic writing that most deserves acclaim: 'These female epics', she argues, 'have been almost completely ignored by a critical establishment that reads her verse couplets only one way, from the monolithic perspective of the twentieth-century trinity of imagism, psychoanalysis, and modernism.'[14] So, too, her sustained use of mythology and appropriation of mythic masks merits attention because of its prefiguring of the work of generations of later poets including Atwood (to whose *Circe/Mud Poems* we will return) and Carol Anne Duffy. The latter's *The World's Wife*, although often tongue-in-cheek, nevertheless retains the radical political edge and the same sure sense of its own daring as H.D.'s mythic writing.[15] Anne Sexton's *Transformations* – her knowing revision of Grimm's fairytales for the postmodern age – inherits from H.D. a willingness, in Dickie's description of the latter's work, to move 'outside the process of male myth-making to comment on its silencing of women'.[16] In *Transformations*, myths of femininity, domesticity, romance and consumerism are undermined by a succession of rebellious or dysfunctional heroines, all of whose voices are controlled by the narrative voice of the 'middle-aged witch, me'.[17]

Gender

One of H.D.'s key contributions to modern culture has been her evocation, or perhaps invocation, of a complex female subjectivity and thereby her countering of that culture's deep-rooted idealisation of a passive femininity. For Rich, Grahn and others, H.D. is the foremother who has given them figurative permission to explore their own genders and sexualities as, for example, in Rich's *Dreams of a Common Language*. DuPlessis suggests that H.D.'s writing 'effects a major cultural displacement by insistently making the matriarchal female power of the mother-goddess dominant'. There is arguably a risk of essentialism here. Nevertheless, as DuPlessis shows, H.D.'s use of such symbols is not unqualified: 'H.D., quite able to negotiate in classical Greek, assumed its cultural authority in a critical way' (DuPlessis 1986, pp. 16, 17).

In debating H.D.'s influence in this context, it is vital to consider her own inheritance from Sappho. H.D.'s use of Sappho is important for a number of reasons. She restores to view a range of Sapphic fragments, embedding them in her own writing and thereby revitalising them.[18] In so doing, she influences a number of later poets including Judy Grahn and Nicole Brossard who, as Collecott shows, also uses such fragments as a way of assembling the lesbian body. Moreover, H.D.'s turn to Sappho demands of the reader a new approach to the literary text. Much of her 'Sapphic' work resists being understood from a conventional (for which read heteronormative) position and must be approached differently. Collecott suggests comparing H.D.'s poem 'I Said' with Audre Lorde's 'Love Poem' as a way of illustrating this reorientation. Here, interestingly, questions about chronology and publication history noted earlier illuminate a pleasing reciprocity of influence. Lorde and H.D.'s poems, although written several decades apart, appeared in print at the same time in the early 1980s. From this, Collecott deduces that 'the "coming out" of North American writers such as Rich and Lorde created a climate for the publication of [H.D.'s] previously suppressed work' (*Sapphic*, p. 201). In other words, Lorde's writing paved the way for H.D.'s, just as H.D.'s larger project may have inspired Lorde. Other poets, including Rich (discussed in more detail below) have continued this work. Grahn is perhaps the best-known of H.D.'s successors to pursue explicitly the queer line. Her 1987 verse play *The Queen of Swords* (subtitled: 'A Play with Poetic Myth') references *Helen in Egypt* through its reworking of Helen's story as a new myth of desire and power set in an 'underground lesbian bar'.[19]

Inheritance

The ambition and complexity of H.D.'s work (evidenced in its occasional austerity of tone and willingness to risk hermeticism, its daring appropriation of multiple masks, its bold traversing of genres and its self-conscious attentiveness to language) challenges expectations of what poetry is, and might be – to the advantage of writers and readers alike. In addition to the influence on the development of imagism and modernism, and the emergence of successive waves of feminist and lesbian-identified criticism, outlined thus far, H.D.'s work has proved important to a number of individual poets from contemporaries Lowell and Moore to present-day writers such as Atwood and Amy Clampitt.

The relationship between H.D., Lowell and Moore has been well-documented elsewhere in this book and in the wider critical field (for example, in Jane Dowson's book *Women, Modernism, and British Poetry 1910–1939: Resisting Femininity* and Taylor's *H.D. and the Public Sphere of Modernist Women Writers 1913–1946: Talking Women*). The main focus of the rest of this chapter is on H.D.'s bequest to the poets who followed this group of peers – some well-known, others less so.

Adrienne Rich

Adrienne Rich's debt to H.D., expressed in critical essays such as 'When We Dead Awaken', has already been acknowledged. According to Susan Stanford Friedman, 'H.D.'s rich presence nourished the evolution of the younger woman's poetic vision toward the woman-identified, gynocentric feminism of *The Dream of a Common Language*.'[20] This collection takes lines from H.D.'s *The Flowering of the Rod* as its epigraph:

> I go where I love and where I am loved,
> into the snow;
>
> I go to the things I Love
> with no thought of duty or pity.[21]

A number of poems in Rich's book look back to H.D.'s example. 'Cartographies of Silence', for instance, develops H.D.'s characteristic use of motifs of ice, snow and frozen stasis (the 'ice-floe split' of section 1) which it contrasts with images of life and energy: 'blood' in the penultimate stanza of this section; 'raw sounds' in section 3; a 'lifted head / alight with dew' in section 7, and the 'newborn infant's mouth / violent with hunger' in the final section. Diane di Prima's poem 'For H.D.' uses similar images – of water ('tears' and 'still water') which is transmuted from 'ice' which is, in turn, connected with 'crystal', 'quartz' and 'diamonds' and contrasted with 'heat', 'the burning cauldron' and the 'burning bushes' – in a homage to H.D. which is also an evocation of the visceral price of creativity.[22] To return to Rich's 'Cartographies of Silence', though, the struggle throughout, as also in some of H.D.'s poems, is to break the silence or, more properly, perhaps, to hear the silence speak; the plangency of silence is an important element of H.D.'s bequest to later poets. To quote Marianne Moore from her 1961 obituary of the poet, 'H.D. contrived in the short line to magnetize the reader by what was not said – .'[23] The profound self-reflexivity of moments such as these, evidenced too in texts such as H.D.'s 'H.D. by Delia Alton', is rendered explicit in Rich's poem where 'Language Cannot Do Everything' (section 7). Images of fragmentation throughout the poem (from the 'ice-floe split' onwards) further parallel H.D.'s interest in the dispersal of the speaking, experiencing subject. A similar movement is apparent in Rich's 'Splittings' where H.D.'s woman-identified poetics is implicitly referenced:

> My body opens over San Francisco like the day –
> light raining down   each pore crying the change of light
> I am not with her   I have been waking off and on
> all night to that pain[.]   (Rich 1978, p. 10)

This poem also establishes the centrality of the mother–daughter bond ('Does the infant memorize the body of the mother / and create her in absence?') in a manner disturbingly relevant to H.D.'s own biographical experience with her daughter, and commensurate with some of her explorations of this area – and picked up in the present day in the work of poets such as Sexton and Sharon Olds.

The penultimate poem in Rich's collection, 'Toward the Solstice', bears comparison with the final poem of H.D.'s 'Winter Love'. The same contemplative tone is common to both and both use a moment of quiet, cold stillness as the occasion to recollect, in the words cited at the beginning of this chapter, a life lived in history. Both make repeated use of the conditional 'if': 'If I could make sense' and 'if I could know' in Rich's poem and 'If I thought of you' in H.D.'s. Both speakers concede the limits of their own memory and understanding; H.D.'s 'I did not remember, I did not remember' (section 4) is echoed in Rich's speaker's search for an 'unremembered clearing / I am meant to have found'. Jan Montefiore identifies a stylistic debt to H.D. both in *Dream of A Common Language* and in the sequence 'From an Old House in America':

> Rich's genius for vivid fragments has, I surmise, been assisted by her reading in the poetry of H.D., especially *Trilogy*: the free verse couplets and the mode of presenting junkshop rubbish recall the meditative opening of 'The Walls Do Not Fall' where bombed houses are seen as Egyptian tombs opened up by investigators.[24]

Trilogy offered Rich and other post-Second World War women poets a model of how to realise a public and political voice. In a period dominated first by the quiet academic voice of, say, Richard Wilbur and then by the intimate, taboo-breaking impetus of confessionalism, *Trilogy* stands as an example of how to speak politically while also retaining a sense of personal (and gendered) experience. As I have argued elsewhere:

> The catastrophe of the Second World War is explored in the context of individual, localised, immediate experience which is also so much more than that – which has long historical and cultural roots. Birth and death, beginnings and endings, the material and the spiritual, the immediate and the historical, the experiential and the abstract – all are encompassed and explored in this poem which stands alongside, say, T.S. Eliot's *The Waste Land* as an account of modern despair and potential salvation.[25]

Rich's achievement in late twentieth-century poetry has been to extend this legacy. By her own admission, her early work was cautious, conventional and quiet, but she was able to imbibe enough from the 'peculiar keenness and ambivalence' of H.D. and her predecessors (including Sappho) to dare to nurture a new voice – one which tackles issues of violence and oppression from a markedly female, and historicised, position (H.D., 'When', p. 39). Nick Halpern makes a similar point, arguing for H.D.'s influence on Rich's

'Orion' (with its echoes of 'The Walls Do Not Fall') and suggesting that: 'H.D. writes about living through the London blitz. Rich wants to remind the reader of the reality of invisible domestic explosions while at the same time evoking the courage of the people of that time.'[26]

Denise Levertov

Denise Levertov has similarly credited H.D. with directing her to a new way of writing at a crucial moment in her career: 'She showed a way to penetrate mystery; which means, not to flood darkness with light so that darkness is destroyed, but to *enter into* darkness, mystery, so that it is experienced.'[27] As Levertov herself recounts, she was born in England in 1923 and thus shared H.D.'s experience of London life during the Blitz; but it was a later encounter with the latter's poetry of this time that newly opened up the initial experience to Levertov's own consciousness (Levertov 1973, pp. 244–8). For Levertov, as for a number of other poets associated with the LANGUAGE and Black Mountain schools and other avant-garde movements, it is H.D.'s deconstruction of language which resonates. Of H.D,'s 'Sagesse', Levertov writes:

> In 'Sagesse', the photograph of an owl [. . .] starts a train of thought and feeling which leads poet and reader far back into childhood, by way of word origins and word-sound associations, and back again to a present more resonant, more full of possibilities and subtle awareness, because of that journey. The interpenetration of past and present, of mundane reality and intangible reality, is typical of H.D. (Levertov 1973, p. 244).

In Lorine Niedecker's poetry, too, we see an attempt to distil language and thereby to examine its meaning (see 'Mourning Dove', 'Poet's Work' and *Subliminal*, for instance). Niedecker's *If I Were A Bird* is explicit about its debt to H.D.: its opening stanza continues the proposition of the title:

> I'd be a dainty contained cool
> Greek figurette
> On a morning shore –
> H.D.[28]

In a later essay, Levertov again cites H.D. as an influence, describing her 'great importance to me as a *writer*, not only as a reader' [Levertov's emphasis].[29] We can detect this writerly influence in poems such as Levertov's 'The Wound', whose spare economy of language and invocation of a figure from nature in a moment of intense crisis or change is wholly reminiscent of H.D.'s 'Sea Violet' or 'Storm' (H.D., *Selected*, pp. 8, 12).

Levertov's taut three-line poem 'Bruckner' similarly invokes 'Oread' and 'The Garden'. All three texts are charged with a latent energy which threatens at any moment to exceed their own tight parameters. Levertov's 'Agon' and 'The Lyre-Tree' more explicitly echo some of the themes and voices of H.D.'s work, for example, of 'Cassandra' and 'Towards the Piraeus'. According to Susan Gubar, H.D.'s example permitted Levertov to explore a female vision: 'The "other side, the Hiddenness" that H.D. and Levertov seek to penetrate consists precisely of those experiences unique to women that have been denied a place in our publicly acknowledged culture, specifically the experiences of female sexuality and motherhood' (H.D., 'Echoing', p. 206).

Anne Sexton and Sylvia Plath

Gubar argues for H.D.'s extensive influence on a range of modern poets, noting that she:

> serves as a paradigm for contemporary women writers like Marge Piercy, whose sequence of poems 'The Spring Offensive of the Snail' celebrates encircling, blossoming lovers, and Monique Wittig, who makes the circle an emblem of her Amazon utopia, and Margaret Atwood, who focuses on circularity in her revision of the myth of Circe's island, and Adrienne Rich, who circles around the wreck with a book of outworn myths. (Gubar 1979, p. 217)

To this list we might add Anne Sexton, whose 'The Fierceness of Female' and 'The Consecrating Mother' speak from a place of female desire, and embrace the power of circling and recirculating pulses self-reflexively to explore the sources of women's creativity (Sexton 1981, p. 546). However, it is also possible to argue that H.D.'s refusal to be defined by or restricted to her own subjective experience has offered an important alternative model to the poets who succeeded her. The cool, clipped lines of her early poems, the construction of multiple personae which, like the voices of John Berryman's *The Dream Songs*, are 'essentially about an imaginary character (not the poet, not me)', and the later use of epic or – in Nick Halpern's terms, 'prophetic' – modes (*Everyday*) indicate that H.D.'s significance has been more complex than simply offering women poets a way of talking about female experience.[30]

The first-person speaker of H.D.'s 1957 sequence *Sagesse* arguably establishes an important precedent for the work of later 'confessional' poets, Sexton and Plath. The laconic, dead-pan opening line ('You look at me, a hut or cage contains / your fantasy, your frantic stare;') followed by the careful, detailed and precisely dated evaluation of a set of circumstances, and the admission of confusion or uncertainty or guilt (sections 3 and 5, for example), bring to mind Sexton's poems including 'Little Girl, My String Bean, My Lovely Woman', 'A Little Uncomplicated Hymn', 'Christmas Eve' and 'Eighteen Days Without You'. So, too, the invocation of angels in *Sagesse* (section 6) anticipates Sexton's use of the same figures in poems such as 'Consorting with Angels' and the sequence *Angels of the Love Affair.*[31] May Swenson also reclaims the potential of the angel in her poem 'Angels at "Unsubdued"', although here they are addressed with more familiarity than in either H.D.'s or Sexton's work.

Another unexpected line of influence runs from *Sagesse* to Elizabeth Bishop's 'In the Waiting Room', which also takes a chance sighting of a magazine article as a catalyst for an exploration of trauma and change. In his Foreword to *Hermetic Definition*, editor Norman Pearsall recollects that H.D. told him that the source of *Sagesse* was seeing 'a picture of an owl in the London zoo, published in *The Listener* for May 9, 1957' (H.D., *Hermetic*, p. vii). Similarly, the use of an image of an animal as the starting point for a meditation on time, change and human existence is to be found in poems ranging from Bishop's 'The Fish' to Plath's 'Black Rook in Rainy Weather'. The 'rainbow, rainbow, rainbow' and 'coarse white flesh / packed in like feathers' of the former, incidentally, resemble the 'rainbow feathers' of the final section of *Tribute to the Angels*.

Sagesse offers a model to Plath in a number of other ways. The use of catoptric (reflective) surfaces in Section 10 of the sequence alongside that in earlier poems such as 'Priest' (to which H.D. refers as 'a mirror-poem, a moon poem' ('Delia Alton', p. 216)) and the prismatic closing section of *Tribute*, cited above, anticipate Plath's 'Crossing the Water', 'Mirror' and 'Mussel Hunter at Rock Harbor'. Similarly, H.D.'s use of images of glass and crystal is echoed in Anne Sexton's deployment of similar metaphors, for example, of the simultaneously reflective and refractive glass bowl in 'For John, Who Begs Me Not to Enquire Further'. As Gubar proposes:

> In the final book of *The Trilogy*, the escaping fragrance of such flowering within the pristine glass of a jar represents the poet's success in finding a form that can contain without confining. No longer surrounded by splintered shards, H.D. makes of her jars a symbol of aesthetic shape not unlike those of Wallace Stevens or Hart Crane, beautiful and complete objects but also transparencies through which a healing content is made manifest. (H.D., 'Echoing', p. 211).

Margaret Atwood's *Circe/Mud Poems* further develop these metaphors, adding chilling images of cold whiteness as though further to distil the meaning. In her 'Head Against White':

> In the mirror, face to glass face,
> neon, the winter light strikes

through the window, your eyes flare, the city
burns whitely behind us. Blood flows
under the molten skin.

And in 'Book of Ancestors':

Midwinter, the window
Is luminous with blown snow, the fire
Burns inside its bars.[32]

Stylistically, 'Winter Love', like other poems such as *Helen in Egypt*, provides a valuable example to Plath of the use of three-line verse stanzas. In both poets, the employment of the tercet encourages an economy and precision of expression and a fluency of narrative as the poem develops (see, for example, Plath's 'Lorelei'). In thematic terms, 'Winter Love's' use of the bee motif (seen also in *The Flowering of the Rod*) provides an important precedent for Plath's refinement of similar images in such poems as 'The Bee Meeting', 'Stings', 'The Arrival of the Bee Box' and 'Wintering'. Also present in both H.D.'s and Plath's work are unsettling images of crows, rooks and similar corvine creatures (see, for example, the latter's early poem 'The Shrike', where the speaker attempts to mythologise her fears). H.D. has also bequeathed to Plath an important colour palette. The reds, blacks and whites of the former's 'Eurydice' and the 'spectrum blue' of *The Walls Do Not Fall* (section 13) are echoed in the latter's 'Edge', 'Daddy', 'Ariel' and 'Whiteness, I Remember', among others. So, too, the translucent, pearl-like tones of H.D.'s *Trilogy* (see, for example, section 4 of *The Walls Do Not Fall*) are reflected in Plath's poems 'Contusion' and 'Lady Lazarus'.[33] The metaphor of the shell or pearl, incidentally, appears in some of Moore and Bishop's work, often signifying a tantalising troubling of vision or palimpsestic layering of meanings.

Plath continues the work that H.D. started in reimagining the identities and experiences of figures from ancient mythology in suggestive new ways. The former's 'On the Decline of Oracles' invokes, among others, the story of Leda and the swan and the sacking of Troy – both, of course, features of H.D.'s poetry. Plath's near-contemporary Mona Van Duyn also has poems entitled 'Leda' and 'Leda Reconsidered'.[34] The figure of Daphne evoked in H.D.'s 'If You Will Let me Sing' is echoed in Plath's rather troubling 'Virgin in a Tree'. Sexton appropriates Daphne's circumscribed voice in 'Where I Live in This Honorable House of the Laurel Tree', while May Swenson takes the myth as the starting point for a wistful fantasy of creative freedom in 'A Dream'.[35]

Successive women poets have followed H.D.'s example (see, among others, *The Flowering of the Rod*) in using the figure of the echo – or the character of 'Echo' from Ovid's *Metamorphoses* – as a way of exploring ideas about voice and silence, agency and passivity. For Sexton, the echo provides the structure of a number of poems which – like some of H.D.'s – puzzle over the mother–daughter bond (see, for example, Sexton's 'The Double Image' or 'Little Girl, My String Bean, My Lovely Woman'). She uses it, too, in her poem-cum-manifesto 'For John, Who Begs Me Not to Enquire Further', where the figure of the echo provides a way of exploring the borderland between language and silence, self and other, I and you (Sexton 1981, pp. 546, 35, 145, 34).

And beyond . . .

In the generation after Plath and Sexton, American poet Amy Clampitt shares H.D.'s starting point – a sure knowledge of ancient Greek sources – but brings these forward into the present day. The title poem of her 1987 collection, *Archaic Figure*, situates the discovery of an ancient statue ('no goddess / but a named mere girl') in post-Second World War East Berlin. The collection thereby signals, in a way which H.D. would surely have recognised, the contiguity of past and present, and the persistence of powerful oppressive forces. Poems such as 'Medusa', 'The Olive Grove of Thasos' and 'Perseus Airborn' share common roots with H.D.'s work. Clampitt's 'Athena' uses the *terza rima* form which, as we have already seen, is present in both Plath's and H.D.'s poetry.[36]

As indicated earlier, one of the most significant of H.D.'s bequests has been to the avant-garde writing which succeeded the imagist and modernist movements. Korg and Jones both identify specific lines of influence from H.D. through William Carlos Williams to Olson *et al.* (Jones 1972, p. 38; Korg, in Roberts 2001, p. 135).[37] Similarly, Friedman notes that in the middle decades of the twentieth century, 'while the academic community moved H.D. to the periphery of modernism, some of the innovative poets of the 1950s and 1960s, such as Robert Duncan, Denise Levertov, and Allen Ginsberg, continued to read and deeply admire H.D.'s work' (Friedman and DuPlessis 1990, p. xiii).

Chief among H.D.'s inheritors – and interpreters – has been poet Robert Duncan. In a series of essays latterly collected as *The H.D. Book*, Duncan traces the profound and persistent influence exerted by H.D. on his own creative practice.[38] Part 1 of *The H.D. Book* ('Beginnings') recalls the poet's first encounter with H.D.'s poetry in a sleepy high-school classroom. Duncan's teacher was reading from 'Heat'. The poem, Duncan reveals, 'came as an offering' (p. 5); it 'seemed to contain a personal revelation' (p. 6) and for the nascent poet, unlocked some vital dimension of his own subjectivity. In structural terms, the loosely connected paragraphs and utterances of the later sections of *The H.D. Book* closely resemble some of the statements and contemplations of H.D.'s later prose. Thematically, H.D.'s use of mythology and her queer sensibility have proved equally influential while *The War Trilogy*, which Duncan first encountered in the years immediately after the cessation of the Second World War, provided him with 'an anatomy of what Poetry must be' (p. 138). By this point in his career, H.D. had become for Duncan 'my master here in the art of writing; and . . . my master here in spirit' (p. 130). His subsequent work – both his own poetry, and his critical work on H.D. (the two being barely divisible) – represents a meeting of minds, a reciprocity across the decades which has simultaneously engendered his own creativity and brought H.D.'s writing to new audiences at the end of the twentieth century.

In this way, to return to the quotation with which this chapter opened, H.D.'s work 'lives in history'. Her poetry has influenced movements (imagism and modernism) and ways of reading (feminist and queer criticism) and has brought the themes and voices of the ancient past to new generations of readers and writers. Poets from Amy Lowell and Marianne Moore through Lorine Niedecker and Sylvia Plath to Adrienne Rich and Robert Duncan are clear beneficiaries of her gift. The ripples continue to spread as new generations of poets, informed by H.D.'s own writing, and by the interpretations of her successors, come into their inheritance.

NOTES

1 H.D., *Hermetic Definition* (South Hinksey, Oxford: Carcanet, 1972), pp. 85–117 (112).
2 For a chronology of H.D.'s writing and publication, see S.S. Friedman, *Penelope's Web: Gender, Modernity, H.D.'s Fiction* (Cambridge and New York: Cambridge University Press, 1990), pp. 360–6.
3 H.D., in R. Spoo (ed.), *Asphodel* (Durham and London: Duke University Press, 1992), p. xiii.
4 T.S. Eliot, 'Introduction to Marianne Moore's *Selected Poems*', in B. Kime-Scott (ed.), *The Gender of Modernism: A Critical Anthology* (Bloomington and Indianapolis: Indiana University Press, 1990), pp. 149–54 (152).
5 H.D., 'Notes on Thoughts and Vision', in Kime-Scott, *Gender*, p. 96.
6 G. Taylor, *H.D. and the Public Sphere of Modernist Women Writers 1913–1946: Talking Women* (Oxford University Press, 2001), pp. 1–2.
7 Helen Carr's recent study, *The Verse Revolutionaries: Ezra Pound, H.D. and the Imagists* (London: Jonathan Cape, 2009) offers perhaps the closest to a definitive view of imagism's genesis.
8 P. Brooker and S. Perill, 'Modernist Poetry and its Precursors', in N. Roberts (ed.), *A Companion to Twentieth-century Poetry* (Oxford: Blackwell, 2001), p. 33.

9 J. Korg, 'Imagism', in Roberts, *Companion*, p. 135.
10 T.S. Eliot, *Collected Poems 1909–1962* (London: Faber & Faber, 1974), p. 198.
11 R.B. DuPlessis, *H.D.: The Career of That Struggle* (Brighton: Harvester Press, 1986), p. 18.
12 S.S. Friedman and R.B. DuPlessis, *Signets: Reading H.D.* (Madison: University of Wisconsin Press, 1990), p. xi.
13 H. Sword, *Ghostwriting Modernism* (Ithaca, NY, and London: Cornell University Press, 2002), p. 131.
14 S. Gubar, 'The Echoing Spell of H.D.'s *Trilogy*', in S.M. Gilbert and S. Gubar (eds.), *Shakespeare's Sisters: Feminist Essays on Women Poets* (Bloomington: Indiana University Press, 1979), p. 201.
15 C.A. Duffy, *The World's Wife* (London: Picador, 1999).
16 M. Dickie, 'Women Poets and the Emergence of Modernism', in J. Parini and B.C. Millier (eds.), *The Columbia History of American Poetry: From the Puritans to Our Time* (New York: MJF Books, 1993), pp. 233–59 (246).
17 A. Sexton, *The Complete Poems* (Boston: Houghton Mifflin, 1981), p. 223.
18 Diana Collecott's book, *H.D. and Sapphic Modernism 1910–1950* (Cambridge University Press, 1999) provides a useful account of this process while Ellen Greene's edited collection, *Reading Sappho: Contemporary Approaches* (Berkeley: University of California Press, 1996) offers evidence of Sappho's wider importance in modern culture.
19 J. Grahn, *The Queen of Swords* (Boston: Beacon Press, 1987), p. 3.
20 S.S. Friedman, '"I Go Where I Love": An Intertextual Study of H.D. and Adrienne Rich', *Signs: Journal of Women in Culture and Society*, 9.2 (1983), 228–45 (p. 228).
21 A. Rich, *The Dream of a Common Language: Poems 1974–1977* (New York: W.W. Norton, 1978).
22 D. di Prima, *Pieces of a Song: Selected Poems* (San Francisco: City Lights, 1990), pp. 120–2.
23 M. Moore, in Patricia C. Willis (ed.), *The Complete Prose of Marianne Moore* (London: Faber & Faber, 1987), p. 558.
24 J. Montefiore, *Feminism and Poetry: Language, Experience, Identity in Women's Writing*, revd edn (London: Pandora, 2004), p. 86.
25 J. Gill, *Women's Poetry* (Edinburgh Critical Guides Series) (Edinburgh University Press, 2007), pp. 156–7.
26 N. Halpern, *Everyday and Prophetic: The Poetry of Lowell, Ammons, Merrill, and Rich* (Madison: University of Wisconsin Press, 2003), pp. 209–10.
27 D. Levertov, 'H.D.: An Appreciation', in *The Poet in the World* (New York: New Directions, 1973), p. 246.
28 L. Niedecker, in Jenny Penberthy (ed.), *Collected Works* (Berkeley: University of California Press, 2002), pp. 23, 194, 287, 130.
29 D. Levertov, 'The Untaught Teacher', *Poet in the World*, p. 178.
30 J. Berryman, *The Dream Songs* (London: Faber & Faber, 1990), p. vi.
31 For more on Sexton's use of the angel, see D. Rees-Jones, *Consorting with Angels: Essays on Modern Women Poets* (Tarset, Northumberland: Bloodaxe, 2005), pp. 128–44.
32 M. Atwood, *Selected Poems* (Toronto: Oxford University Press, 1976).

33 Reñee Curry's *White Women Writing White: H.D., Elizabeth Bishop, Sylvia Plath and Whiteness* (Westport, CT: Greenwood Press, 2000) draws attention to the problems associated with reading H.D.'s use of images of whiteness from a twenty-first century perspective. See pp. 21ff.
34 M. Van Duyn, *Selected Poems* (New York: Knopf, 2003), pp. 57, 89.
35 M. Swenson, *Nature: Poems Old and New* (Boston: Houghton Mifflin, 1994), p. 21.
36 A. Clampitt, *Archaic Figure* (London: Faber & Faber, 1988).
37 P. Jones (ed.), *Imagist Poetry* (London: Penguin, 1972).
38 R. Duncan, *The H.D. Book* (np: Frontier Press, 1984). Available at: www.ccca.ca/history/ozz/english/books/hd_book/HD_Book_by_Robert_Duncan.pdf. Accessed 9 October 2009.

PART II

Works

7

DIANA COLLECOTT

H.D.'s transformative poetics

I

At the heart of *Sea Garden*, H.D.'s first published book, is the desire:

> . . . to find a new beauty
> in some terrible
> wind-tortured place.[1]

Published in 1916, in the midst of war, *Sea Garden* is a site of conflict and of transformation. Its very title is contradictory, like Sappho's celebrated oxymoron *bittersweet*, which resonates through this and subsequent volumes in expressions like 'scented and stinging / . . . sweet and salt' (H.D., *CP*, p. 36).[2] In an inspired essay, Eileen Gregory has asserted that the poet Sappho is a 'latent mythic presence' in *Sea Garden*, while I have suggested elsewhere that a Sapphic aesthetic of variegation patterns this poetry and is carried into H.D.'s later work.[3] Both insights identify her poetics with an ancient tradition, reaching back to the pre-classical era in Greece, but also active in renaissance England.

H.D.'s way of writing *is* very old, but it is also very new, with the shocking, iconoclastic newness that prefers rupture to perfection, kinesis to stasis. Ezra Pound immediately recognised this and, as he turned his attention from imagism to Vorticism, used H.D.'s 'Oread' to illustrate its aesthetic of moving energies.[4] That much-anthologised poem is not in *Sea Garden*, but contemporary with it, like the rest of those gathered in *The God*.[5] The poetry of this early period, which is the foundation of all H.D.'s later work, is modern in its abruptness and brevity, its unpredictable open form, its natural language, its inherent riskiness. Such poems demonstrate the imagist principles summarised in 1913 by F.S. Flint:

1. Direct treatment of the 'thing' whether objective or subjective.
2. To use absolutely no word that does not contribute to the presentation.
3. As regarding rhythm: to compose to the sequence of the musical phrase not in sequence of a metronome.[6]

'Direct treatment of the thing' describes a practice capable of dismantling the entire structure of symbolic resemblance that dominated English poetry from the sixteenth to the nineteenth centuries. The keystone of that structure was metaphor. According to Aristotle, the making of metaphors requires 'an eye for resemblances'; Sidney, following Aristotle, called it 'figuring forth' or speaking metaphorically, that is, transferring meaning from the literal to the figurative plane.[7]

In the first half of the twentieth century, critics informed by linguistics acknowledged the frequent difficulty (in normal usage and in literature) of distinguishing between the literal and the figurative. Introducing the terms 'tenor' and 'vehicle' into Practical Criticism, I.A. Richards nevertheless recognised the significance of context in determining the meaning of words; he described metaphor as 'a transaction between contexts', in which (we might argue) the energies of resemblance interact with those of literalness, as they do in everyday speech (Richards 1965, p. 94). By contrast, Ramon Jakobson insisted on a radical opposition between metaphor and metonymy (which had previously been seen as a form of metaphor). In his account, both are based on the substitution of one meaning for another, but metaphor involves the substitution of figurative for literal meaning, while metonymy may involve the substitution of one non-figurative meaning for another, often referential or contiguous.[8] This follows Boris Eichenbaum's distinction between the way metaphor functions at a 'supra-linguistic' level, that of ideas, while metonymy functions by means of 'a displacement, or lateral semantic shift, that lends words new meanings without leaving the literal plane'.[9] It led Jakobson to distinguish also between literary movements, identifying metaphor as the master-trope of romanticism, with its emphasis on allegory and symbolism, and metonymy as the master-trope of realism, with its emphasis on the literal and material. Paul De Man went even further, stressing the contingent or accidental aspect of metonymy, as opposed to the transcendent and unifying pressure of metaphor.[10]

In English-speaking modernism, both of these tendencies are present. A case can be made for placing T.S. Eliot and W.C. Williams, two American-born poets of the same generation as H.D., at almost opposite ends of Jakobson's metaphoric and metonymic poles. Williams' well-known 'By the road to the contagious hospital' from *Spring and All* (1923), with its focus on the accidence of 'twiggy / stuff' and 'outline of leaf', hazards a personification of 'dazed spring', but does not press the metaphor of rebirth, let alone the symbolic implications (especially in an American context) of 'They enter a new world naked'. Instead, he keeps the car on the road, and the poem on the plane of contiguity.[11] By contrast, Eliot, in the opening of *The Waste Land*

(1922), uses a range of tactics to propel the reader onto the plane of resemblance, and to set up strong resonances with earlier literary works.

The published version of Eliot's poem, stripped of much allusion and parody by Pound's editing, is supported by authorial notes; these refer the poem's title and 'incidental symbolism' to *From Ritual to Romance*, the initial subtitle ('The Burial of the Dead') to the Anglican liturgy, and identify the quotations from Petronius and Dante in the epigraphs.[12] Therefore, so the notes offer us a series of metaphorical fences to shy at, as does the deliberate symbolism of: 'April is the cruellest month, breeding / Lilacs out of the dead land, mixing / Memory and desire, stirring / Dull roots with spring rain' (Eliot 1963, p. 63). Revising the vigorous opening of Chaucer's Prologue to the *Canterbury Tales*, these lines get their full significance from a recognition of that historic source, setting the hopeless tone of the whole poem, and also establishing its relentless strategy of contrast between an idealised past and a dystopian present. In Roland Barthes' terms, *The Waste Land* is a 'readerly' text, its ideal reader having access to all the codes that make it intelligible; by comparison, Williams' poem from *Spring and All* is a 'writerly' text: in Barthes' words, such texts are 'read with difficulty, unless I completely transform my reading regime'.[13] While Barthes refutes the notion of a naive or 'innocent' reader who is unaware of other texts, his theory acknowledges writing that articulates the possibilities of a culture, and in doing so creates a new discursive space not bounded by past 'monuments'.[14] H.D.'s lines in my opening quotation occupy just such a space.

2

The 'wind-tortured place' in which the speaker of 'Sheltered Garden' seeks 'a new beauty' is both inside and out: within the mind and exposed to the elements.[15] Critics agree that H.D. sited her earliest writings on the borderline between human consciousness and natural objects, divine beings and elemental forces. It is the relationship between these binaries that is contested. N.H. Pearson's remark that H.D. 'writes the most intensely personal poems using Greek myth as metaphor', though perceptive, may be taken as an instance of an unreformed 'reading regime', in its assured pre-Richards distinction between the literal and the figurative.[16] In her ground-breaking study *Psyche Reborn*, Susan Friedman asserts that most of H.D.'s imagist poems are 'about consciousness, not the world of objects external to consciousness' (Friedman 1981, p. 56), but she does so as a reader informed by Freud's understanding of the operations of *condensation* and *displacement*: the first enables a single dream-image, like an oxymoron, to express 'contraries' and even 'contradictions'; the second enables the analysand or writer to displace emotions onto objects, the self onto others (pp. 57–8). In both cases, there is an equivalence between the object and the emotion; this is recognised in the term 'image' and distinguishes it from the comparison or resemblance represented by the terms 'metaphor' and 'simile' in classical rhetoric. Patrick McGuinness notes that one of imagism's 'primary methods . . . is to abolish the division (one might say the hierarchy) between tenor and vehicle'.[17] This is obvious in the first poem of *Sea Garden*, 'Sea Rose', in which emotion is embedded in the sensory image of a 'harsh rose, / . . . / sparse of leaf' and cannot be separated from it. As May Sinclair acutely remarked, defending imagism in general and H.D.'s practice in particular: 'The Image is not a substitute; it does not stand for anything but itself. Presentation, not representation, is the watchword of the school.'[18]

A novelist with a transatlantic reputation when she championed the imagists, Sinclair was also a proponent of psychoanalysis and helped to establish the London centre for psychotherapy that later became the Tavistock Clinic.[19] Eichenbaum himself was informed by psychoanalysis when writing his 1923 study of Anna Akhmatova; by adopting Freud's term *displacement* in his definition of metonymy, as a 'lateral' shift on the literal level of meaning, rather than a (so to say) 'vertical' shift on the metaphorical level, he too, prepared the way for new readings of modern poetry. According to Jakobson, moreover, poets who tend to metonymy rather than metaphor typically project their sense of self onto an outer reality that is displaced from the normal by heightened emotion and perception.[20] Such criteria place H.D.'s poetics in a disturbing discursive space where intensely felt inner and outer worlds meet and transform one another, and where (despite her passion for myth and mystery) the mode of writing is more often metonymic than metaphorical.

This can be seen in 'Hermes of the Ways', which does not begin with an invocation of the god, but with a sharply focused close-up on grains of sand. The rhetorical equivalent of a cinematic close-up is the synecdoche, in which the part is substituted for the whole. For Jakobson, synecdoche was a kind of metonymy, because there is a material or contingent connection between the part and the whole it designates. In Freudian terms, this image of the sand presents itself as a displacement of attention from a larger complex of ideas and feelings to a physical detail. At the same time, the words H.D. has placed on the page remind the reader that a poem itself is a physical construct. The first line of 'Hermes of the Ways' consists of four monosyllables: 'The hard sand breaks' (H.D., *CP*, p. 37). These words are as discrete as the image that follows, and as hard-edged as consonants can make them; their syntax is precisely that of normal speech, yet the almost equal stress on all but the definite article, and the way the line breaks on 'breaks' alerts us to formal artifice.

The Hermes of this poem is neither the messenger of the Greek gods, in rapid transit between heaven, earth and the underworld; nor the alchemists' Hermes Trismegistus, who will make an appearance in the *Trilogy*; nor is he the statue of a voluptuous young hermaphrodite (named for its parents, Hermes and Aphrodite) that H.D. and Frances Gregg had seen in Paris and Rome.[21] Rather, we are presented with a truncated *herm*: a standing stone, sometimes bearing the vestiges of both sexes, used as a way-mark: 'Dubious, facing three ways, / welcoming wayfarers' (H.D., *CP*, p. 38). The stone is less an image of the god, than a sign of his absence; to adapt Gregory's insight, Hermes (like Sappho) is a 'latent' presence in *Sea Garden*, hinted at in the poem's title and the expression 'him / of the triple pathways'.[22] Set up where 'Wind rushes / over the dunes', the herm marks the doubtful boundary between earth and sea: that transitional space in which, by turns, one becomes the other. This space is at the edge of meaning. Hermeneutics, the science of interpretation, concerns itself with borderlines such as this, where Hermes might well be invoked.

H.L. Gates introduces us to a comparable figure from African myth, the trickster known as Exu, Esu or Echu, whom he identifies with the oxymoronic Signifying Monkey of African-American folklore: 'he who dwells at the margins of discourse, ever punning, ever troping, ever embodying the ambiguities of language'.[23] Hermes, like Exu, embodies these linguistic ambiguities, while his offspring, Hermaphroditus, embodies those of gender. At the close of H.D.'s poem, he is directly addressed: 'Hermes, Hermes, / . . . / . . . you have waited, / where sea-grass tangles with / shore-grass' (H.D., *CP*, p. 39). The transformation of 'sea-grass' into 'shore-grass', by substituting one word of similar sound but different meaning for another, precisely places this figure 'at the margins of discourse', while the repetition of 'grass' in two contexts insists that this marginal place is (if a pun be permitted) both *littoral* and *literal*. In these ways, 'Hermes of the Ways' serves as a synecdoche for *Sea Garden* as a whole, with its persistent displacement, its generative wordplay and dynamic soundscapes. Remarking that poems like these are 'liminal state[s], without ordinary determinations of gender, person or tense', Gregory adds that the voice of these poems is 'hermaphroditic' (Gregory in Friedman and DuPlessis 1990, p. 139), which could imply that H.D. was aware, at the very start of her career, that all utterance is 'dubious' in its need for, and resistance to, interpretation.

3

Psychologists derive the word 'liminal' from Latin *limen*, 'threshold'. It was the early twentieth-century anthropologist Arnold van Gennep who used the same term to describe that middle stage in rites of passage (such as coming-of-age or marriage), which he identified as a place of transition, transgression and transformation.[24] Later in the same century, Victor Turner developed this concept in further studies of the ritual process, where he described liminal individuals as 'neither here nor there', but 'betwixt and between the positions assigned and arrayed by law, custom, convention and ceremonial'.[25] Whereas other anthropologists identified individuals in this transitional phase as dangerous and polluting, hence risky for society as a whole, Turner saw their potentiality in a positive light, defining liminality as 'a realm of pure possibility'.[26] With reference to this definition, we might see the accounts of narrative structure offered by literary theorists such as Tzvetan Todorov as having a stage, between beginning and ending, which depicts transgressive events or entertains new possibilities, such that the transition from start to finish of a text may involve a radical shift in perceptions of normality and a willingness to abandon old ideas and identities in order to take on new ones. Such transformations occur in the trajectories of poems like 'Mid-Day' and, more extremely, in 'Sheltered Garden'. In the essay already cited, Eileen Gregory has argued that they also occur in the affective structure of *Sea Garden* as a whole; and we shall see that they are the very purpose of the *Trilogy*.

Van Gennep discusses religious rites of passage in the context of territorial frontiers, noting the way that 'the boundary is marked by an object – a stake, portal or upright rock', or, indeed, a statue, and that these consecrated signs are 'set only at points of passage, on paths and at crossroads' (Van Gennep 1960, pp. 15–17). He also notes the significance of doors and thresholds as markers of the boundary between public and domestic spaces or, 'in the case of a temple', the sacred and the profane (p. 20). Transitional places have physical markers in literary texts also: for western culture, the key *topos* is the threshold. In the marriage songs of ancient Greece and Rome and hence, in the poems of Sappho and Catullus, the bride is carried by the groom across the 'polished threshold' of the marital home, signifying not only the ritual passage from one stage of life to another, but also sexual initiation. The same motif occurs, with a difference, in ancient Chinese poetry: if Ezra Pound's 'Liu Ch'e' is to be believed, the sixth Han emperor 'presented the "Image"' of his lost lover as 'A wet leaf that clings to the threshold'.[27] The way this last lingering line is separated from the rest of the poem, marking the transition between life and death – but delaying closure – gives it a liminal quality: in an early Canto, Pound called it 'My lintel, and Liu Ch'e's lintel'.[28] He achieved a similarly uncanny effect by the use of space in the original 1913 format of 'In a Station of the Metro', where the first line appears as: 'The apparition of these faces in the crowd'. Pound commented: 'In a poem of this sort one is trying to record the precise moment when a thing outward and subjective transforms itself, or darts into a thing inward and subjective.'[29] Commenting on 'In a Station of the Metro' and on 'Oread', McGuinness remarks: 'At its best . . . Imagist poetry is about . . . the porous threshold between inner and outer, abstract and concrete, the intimate and the glitteringly impersonal' (McGuinness in Bradshaw and Dettmar 2006, p. 187).

Our readings of H.D. bear this out, registering both that outer 'sense of a finite place' we find in *Sea Garden* (Gregory in Friedman and DuPlessis 1990, p. 139), and that sense of infinite space, of timeless time, that is the inward experience of certain rites of passage. In her persuasive analysis of the 'ritual intent of the whole volume', Gregory identifies the beaches and rocks of the shoreline and the inland gardens and orchards, as well as the series of sacred spaces invoked in poems such as 'The Shrine' and 'The Cliff-Temple' (Gregory in Friedman and DuPlessis 1990, p. 139). The shrine is on a headland ('that edge, / that front of rock') while its goddess is addressed as 'spirit between the headlands / and the further rocks' (H.D., *CP*, p. 9), recalling Turner's designation 'betwixt and between'. Central to the volume is the temple, that 'Great white portal' on its 'shelf of rock'; it is a 'pillar for the sky-arch', marking not just the 'rock-edge' but the 'world-edge' (p. 26). In 'Sea Gods', the rock shelf becomes a 'sand-shelf', and the *portal* a 'lintel of wet sand' (p. 31).

Like Pound's *lintel*, H.D.'s *portal*, together with her repeated use of *pillar*, *porch*, *arch*, *gate*, *edge* and *ledge*, underline not only the marginality of these imaginary spaces, but their transitional quality. Two poems that, in their subject matter, stand apart from *Sea Garden*, nevertheless share this quality. One is 'Cities', which is at the very end of the volume, beyond 'Hermes of the Ways' and the 'Pear Tree' that marks a further boundary.[30] Sited in the poet's urban present, 'Cities' is H.D.'s own, not wholly successful, piece of 'waste land'; its collective *cri-de-cœur* is for the sacred architecture of ancient Greece: '. . . the beauty of temple / and space before temple, / arch upon perfect arch, / of pillars and corridors that led out / to strange court-yards and porches' (H.D., *CP*, p. 40). Similar terms occur in 'Prisoners', whose speaker recalls his lover in Sapphic terms ('your hyacinth-circlet', etc.) as he urges this lover, now a fellow prisoner, to: 'stand near to the gate, / . . . Press close to the portal, / . . . As I pass down the corridor' (pp. 33–4); these physical structures mark the momentary passage from life to death for the speaker on his way to execution.

Sea Garden itself is a *gate* or *portal*: our place of entry into 'a realm . . . of possibility'. This first volume was positioned by H.D. at the start of her *Collected Poems* of 1925, as it is in the *Collected Poems* of 1983.[31] It does not merely initiate her poetry for new readers; it transforms sympathetic readers into initiates. *The God* has a similar position in both of the *Collected Poems*, as a second gate or inner courtyard after that of *Sea Garden*. As initiates, we are transported to a familiar/unfamiliar place ('neither here nor there' in Turner's phrase) and stripped of our preconceptions. With heightened senses, we experience its intense particularity (the 'split leaf' of 'Mid-Day', the 'broken shells' of 'The Wind Sleepers') but, like the speakers of 'The Helmsman', are without bearings: 'We wandered . . . / We forgot . . .' (H.D., *CP*, p. 6). We are beset by wrecks, caught up in battles, confronted by natural barriers, unable to find shelter. The voice that leads us on is itself confused, distressed, exhausted: 'I am startled – / I am scattered . . .' (p. 10); 'I perish on the path . . .' (p. 10); 'I am almost lost . . .' (p. 12); 'I have had enough. / I gasp for breath' (p. 19).

This speaker abandons the pursuit and feels defeated by the ordeal: 'I said: / for ever and for ever, must I follow you / through the stones? . . . I was splintered and torn: / the hill-path mounted / swifter than my feet' (H.D., *CP*, p. 27). Yet the poet is always sure-footed, placing the words with precision, forcing us to follow the path 'patterned in . . . letters' (p. 34), however disorientating its movement.[32] For example, the speaker scrambling up to 'The Cliff-Temple' is dizzy at the sight of it, and despairs of reaching it. By contrast, the reader of this poem must descend deftly like a climber, from rock to rock:

> shelf of rock,
> rocks fitted in long ledges,
> rocks fitted to dark, to silver granite,
> to lighter rock –
> clean cut . . .   (H.D., *CP*, p. 26)

The irregular lines jut out into space, as the 'jagged cliff' juts into the air, but we leave histrionics to the poem's speaker: 'Shall I hurl myself from here, / shall I leap and be nearer you?' (p. 27).[33] Our task as readers is to keep our heads as we move over the surface of the verse, following like footholds the subtle shifts of sound and meaning: from *shelf* to *ledges*; from *rock* to *rocks fitted in* . . . to *rocks fitted to* . . . and back to *rock*; from the two syllables of *granite*, exposed at its line end, to those of *clean cut*.

4

There is certainly a mimetic aspect to H.D.'s writing, which makes it surprising that so few phenomenological readings have been attempted. With Turner in mind, we could cite repeated instances of betweenness, such as the nouns *crevices* (H.D., *CP*, p. 10), *clefts* (pp. 6, 24), *fissures* (p. 26), as well as many verbs: *split* (p. 21), *rend* (p. 25), *cut* (pp. 24, 30, 33), *break* (pp. 20, 29, 57), *crack* (p. 36), and so on. Expressions like these form a continuum that includes *Sea Garden* and *The God* and reflects an aesthetic that recognises the specificity of objects, as well as the transitional nature of their existence. Despite the Sapphic register, we are not in the blurred, late romantic world of Swinburne's 'foam-flowers' and 'rose-blossoms',[34] but the brittle modern world of 'grass-tip' (p. 18) and 'straight tool-edge' (p. 12). The poetic focus is consistently sharp, not soft; its cinematic equivalent is not the dissolve, but the jump-cut. H.D.'s speakers reject the scented abundance of the 'Sheltered Garden' and seek instead the 'astringent', the 'scent of resin' that sets their senses on edge (p. 19). Similarly, the speech of her poetry retains (at best) a 'cutting edge' like Sappho's, described by Anne Carson: 'As eros insists upon the edges of human beings and of the spaces between them,' she writes, 'the written consonant imposes edge on the sounds of human speech and insists on the reality of that edge, although it has its origins in the reading and writing imagination.'[35]

Repetition reinforces this phenomenon, generating a progressive range of sonic variations; at the same time it sustains a coherence of thought and intent. Reviewing the *Collected Poems* of 1925, Marianne Moore praised 'a secure, advancing exactness of thought and speech'.[36] At this early stage of her poetic development, H.D. has discovered a way of writing that presents brokenness, without participating in it; this enables her to incorporate Sapphic fragments in the body of her own work, instead of quoting them or alluding to them.[37] Reiteration is vital, at every level, to this lyric process, reinforcing sensation and multiplying meaning as the lexis links one 'clean cut' line to the next, or ties a series of poems into a larger architectonic structure. Thus, in two consecutive poems from *Sea Garden*, 'Loss' and 'Huntress', we read: 'feet cut steel on the paths' (H.D., *CP*, p. 22) and 'feet cut into the crust' (p. 24). A third poem, 'Garden' transposes the same verb to a different context, moving swiftly from 'Rose, cut in rock' to a reiterated injunction: '. . . rend open the heat / cut apart the heat / . . . cut the heat' (p. 25). The simple repetition of 'the heat', at the end of each of these three lines, becomes more complex when they are read aloud. We then notice how, from line to line, the second stress buckles under the speaker's urgency – '**rend op**en the **heat** / **cut** a**part** the **heat**' – then is lost as the line abruptly reduces from three stresses to two: '**cut** the **heat**'. This is terser because the previous commands have used compound expressions involving more vowels, and because 'cut the heat' compresses the five syllables of 'cut apart the heat' into three. A reprise of the same motif initiates a sea change in 'Sea Gods': 'you are **cut** a**part** / by **wave-break** upon **wave-break** / . . . you are mis**shap**en by the **sharp rocks**, / **brok**en by the **rasp** and **after rasp**' (p. 29). While the simple repetitions are evident, shifting stresses create a texture which weaves together a double pattern of assonance: 'wave-break . . . rocks, broken', and 'apart . . . misshapen . . . sharp . . . rasp after rasp'.

Remarking on phonic overlap in the *Trilogy*, and noting how often in that work repetition is an agent of transformation, Alicia Ostriker adds: 'To "echo" is to repeat while changing, or to change while repeating, so as to be understood.'[38] She also points out that H.D. uses echo 'to suggest a reality that emanates from a mysterious source, endures through transformations, and may ultimately communicate to the receptive ear a sacred truth' (Ostriker in Friedman and DuPlessis 1990 p. 349). *Echo*, then, has a capacity for resonance beyond mere *repetition*, as a technique that unites the deep structure of H.D.'s poetry with its surface structure. Adalaide Morris has amply demonstrated this in her 'phonemic reading' of 'Storm', finding that its 'patterned energy' sets up 'a seemingly interminable . . . proliferation of meanings' and concluding: 'its soundscape enacts a philosophy, an epistemology, even an ethics of generativity to which H.D.'s work returns again and again'.[39]

5

'The Imagist poem . . . expands from compression' says McGuinness (p. 185), and the compressed power of short poems such as 'Storm' was not lost when H.D. made the transition from imagism to the more expansive mode of *The God*, *Hymen* (1921) and *Heliodora* (1924). Pound railed against H.D. for having, after 1916, 'let loose dilutations and repetitions'.[40] By contrast, May Sinclair, reviewing the *Collected Poems* of 1925, understood that the 'lucid, sharp simplicity' of 'pure imagism' was already giving way – in poems such as 'The Cliff-Temple', 'Loss' and 'The Shrine' – to a transitional phase of 'greater intricacy', in preparation for the 'profounder vision' of her later work ('H.D.', pp. 462–3). Gathering together poems published between 1913 and 1917, *The God* embraces the brief fusion of 'Oread' and the extended fission of 'Eurydice'. Rejected by Pound in his objection to H.D.'s having 'gone on' from imagism, this long dramatic monologue in a mythic female voice belongs with the translations and revisionary narratives of the period 1915 to 1925. H.D.'s decision to juxtapose it with 'Oread' in the text of her first *Collected Poems* implies a challenge to Pound, her former fiancé and mentor, just as the speech of Eurydice challenges Orpheus, her partner and the god of poetry:

So you have swept me back,
I who could have walked with the live souls
above the earth,
I who could have slept among the live flowers
at last;
. . .
At least I have the flowers of myself
and my thoughts, no god
can take that;
I have the fervour of myself for a presence
and my own spirit for a light;

and my spirit with its loss
know this;
. . .
hell must break before I am lost;
before I am lost,
hell must open like a red rose
for the dead to pass. (H.D., *CP*, p. 55)

Ideas such as 'presence' and 'loss' echo throughout this text. Repetition with variation spits out the speaker's outrage: 'myself . . . my thoughts . . . myself for a presence / . . . my own spirit for a light; // . . . my spirit with its loss'; chiasmus announces her defiance: 'hell must break before I am lost; // before I am lost, / hell must open . . .' By means of reiteration, alliteration, parallelism and reversal, the text mirrors that catastrophic moment when Orpheus looked back at Eurydice, as he was leading her out of hell:

What was it that crossed my face
with the light from yours
and your glance?
what was it you saw in my face?
the light of your own face,
the fire of your own presence? (H.D., *CP*, p. 52)

There is, of course, a larger reversal at work here: the revisionary movement that, as Rachel DuPlessis has shown, reconstructs the Orpheus myth and 'puts the woman as hero at the centre of the story'.[41] In this way, H.D. challenges one of the foundational narratives of western culture and anticipates the major projects of her maturity: the synergistic rereading of the

New Testament in *Trilogy*, and 'the re-writing of the Trojan War and epic in *Helen in Egypt*'.[42] Texts like these are 'palimpsests', to use the poet's own term, referring to parchments 'from which one writing has been erased to make room for another'.[43] Morris has described the actual process of textual transformation that we have witnessed from word to word, as well as from one narrative to another, as palimpsestic, and argued that 'palimpsestic overwritings undo existing cultural agreements' by rewriting concepts fundamental to received culture (Morris 2004, p. 210).

6

'Eurydice' enacts a rite of passage in two senses: by dramatically crossing from death to life and back again, and as a transitional poem between H.D.'s earlier and later work. The *Trilogy*, composed under aerial bombardment during the Second World War, emerges from the ordeal of the London Blitz, as Eurydice herself emerged from the underworld. Its three parts – *The Walls Do Not Fall* (1944), *Tribute to the Angels* (1945) and *The Flowering of the Rod* (1946) – are linked by textual echoes. The second part begins by citing the final lines of the first: '*possibly we will reach haven, / heaven*' (H.D., *CP*, p. 547). The third part repeats those of the second: '. . . *we pause to give / thanks that we rise again from death and live*' (p. 577). The entire work has the aspect of a perilous journey, a physical and spiritual ordeal. Appropriately, in each of the three parts, writer shares with reader an awareness of liminal places, among them the 'shrine . . . open to the sky' of *The Walls Do Not Fall* (p. 509), the 'charred portico' of *Tribute to the Angels* (p. 559) and the 'half-open door' of *The Flowering of the Rod* (p. 589).[44]

Though pivotal in all three poems, this awareness of liminality is most impressive and most sustained at the start of *The Walls Do Not Fall*. That is because it is presented as a shared experience, and also because it has a known historic context. Referring, in passing, to ancient Egypt and the destruction of Pompei, the poet's attention is nevertheless on 'London 1942':

> An incident here and there,
> and rails gone (for guns)
> from your (and my) old town square: (H.D., *CP*, p. 509)

With this opening triplet, we are in the midst of modern war, with its indiscriminateness and its capacity for traumatic change. The insidious slant rhyme in 'gone (for guns)' enacts a local transformation from peace-time to wartime. Moreover, the now unfenced square gardens represent both the destruction of 'old habit' (p. 521), and the opening up of new possibilities (political and ontological). This double movement is soon reinforced:

there, as here, ruin opens
the tomb, the temple; enter,
there as here, there are no doors: (H.D., *CP*, p. 509)

Alicia Ostriker has identified 'the *here-there* off-rhyme' as one of the many 'threads of sound' that set up varied echoes throughout this lyric passage, citing '*square, colour . . . enter, doors, endure, everywhere*'; at first, she says, these expressions feel 'casual and spatial', but gradually they reinforce the motif of 'struggle, fear and disorientation': '*fire, floor, terror, ember, dismembered*' (Ostriker in Friedman and DuPlessis 1990, p. 342). In ways such as these, what Ostriker calls 'the poet's insistence on a poetics, and a politics, of openness' becomes a shared project with her readers.

In *The Gift*, her profound meditation on origins that was contemporary with the *Trilogy*, H.D. wrote: 'Shut the door and you have a neat flat picture. Leave all the doors open and you are almost out-of-doors, almost within the un-walled province of the fourth-dimensional.'[45] When this metaphorical passage is set beside her long poem's doors and walls, we are struck by their metonymic accidence, their literal contiguity. Among the many more far-fetched images of enclosure and exposure in *The Walls Do Not Fall*, the 'sliced wall' of a bombed house has the immediacy of lived experience.[46] This is achieved, in part, by word-placement; in the triplet just quoted, 'opens', 'enter' and 'no doors' all gain significance from their position at line-ends. The same is true of these lines: 'yet the frame held: / we passed the flame: we wonder / what saved us? what for?' (H.D., *CP*, p. 511). The colons are markers of liminality, pauses to catch one's breath on the edge of terror; the whole triplet is like a stepping-stone, or stopping-stone, on the brink of possible extinction; the near-repeats 'frame' and 'flame' draw attention to themselves, suggesting symbolism, yet clearly refer to the body under threat and the threat of fire.

H.D.'s handling of accidence, learned in the crafting of *Sea Garden*, is also evident when the 'old town square' of *The Walls Do Not Fall* is recapitulated as 'an old garden-square' of *Tribute to the Angels*:

we entered a house through a wall;

then still not knowing
whether (like the wall)

we were there or not-there,
we saw the tree flowering; (H.D., *CP*, p. 559)

The process by which this 'half-burnt-out apple-tree, / blossoming' (p. 561) is recognised as a sign, even a 'vision', of renewal is quite open. It allows us to acknowledge, as we read, the numinous simplicity of these quoted lines.

Between the opening statement ('we entered') and the closing statement ('we saw') is a little narrative, with a middle stage much like that in Turner's account of the ritual process; its condition is uncertainty, disorientation, loss of self (Turner's 'neither here nor there' is uncannily rendered between the two negatives: 'not knowing . . . not-there'); but this is not a dream-image, or an imagined place; it is an accessible state of mind rendered by what Eliot would have called an 'objective correlative'.[47] H.D.'s preferred term was 'spiritual realism' (H.D., *CP*, p. 537). As a threshold between the ordinary and the visionary, the unwalled garden-square of *Tribute to the Angels* takes the place of the once-sacred spaces that precede it in the poem: 'the lane is empty but the levelled wall / is purple as with purple spread / upon an altar' (p. 551). While H.D. was writing this poem in Knightsbridge, Bryher was exploring the ruins of bombed-out city churches, transformed by weeds into gardens and playgrounds.[48] This process has its linguistic parallels in what Eileen Gregory calls the 'transforming artifice' of H.D.'s poetry (Gregory in Friedman and DuPlessis 1990, p. 150); hence, a 'tree flowering' becomes the 'flowering of the wood', then the 'flowering of the rood' and thence *The Flowering of the Rod*.

Denise Levertov praised H.D. for providing 'doors, ways in, tunnels through', adding: 'She showed a way . . . to enter into darkness, mystery, so that it is experienced.'[49] In English, 'mystery' has two meanings: (a) knowledge that is imparted only to the initiated and otherwise unknown; (b), in archaic usage, the discipline of a particular craft or occupation. Both were significant to H.D.: her novel *The Mystery* concerns the secrets of Moravianism, and her interest in the Eleusinian mysteries (among other ancient rites) is well documented.[50] As for the other meaning of 'mystery', H.D. stated, in an oblique rejoinder to Pound: 'Imagism was something that was important for poets learning their craft early in this century. But after learning his [*sic*] craft, the poet will find his true direction.'[51] This knowledge of the craft is the way in to the deepest levels of her poetry, and forms the interface between those levels and its intricate surface. It is also the common ground between writer and reader: 'my mind (yours), / your way of thought (mine), / each has its peculiar intricate map', she writes in the *Trilogy* (H.D., *CP*, p. 539), even while as 'discoverers / of the not known, / . . . / we have no map' (p. 543).

NOTES

1 'Sheltered Garden', H.D., in L.L. Martz (ed.), *Collected Poems 1912–1944* (New York: New Directions, 1983), p. 21. Abbreviated henceforth as *CP* and cited in the main text.

2 See my *H.D. and Sapphic Modernism, 1910–1950* (Cambridge University Press, 1999), pp. 193–4, on the inscription of Sappho's Eros in other poems by H.D.

3 E. Gregory, 'Rose Cut in Rock: Sappho and H.D.'s *Sea Garden*', in S. Friedman and R.B. DuPlessis (eds.), *Signets: Reading H.D.* (Madison: University of Wisconsin Press, 1990), pp. 129–54 (132).

4 See E. Pound, *Gaudier-Brzeska* [1916] (New York: New Directions, 1970).

5 *The God* was never published as a separate volume, but H.D. presented it as a distinct section in her *Collected Poems* of 1925; Louis Martz preserved this structure in his posthumous edition of her *Collected Poems* in 1983. Italics are used here to distinguish the section from the title poem 'The God' (H.D., *CP*, pp. 45–7).

6 F.S. Flint's 'Imagisme' appeared in *Poetry* I (March 1913); H.D.'s earliest published poems, including 'Hermes of the Ways' and 'Orchard' and signed 'H.D. Imagiste', had appeared in the same magazine in January 1913.

7 Aristotle, *Poetics*, cited by I.A. Richards, *The Philosophy of Rhetoric* [1936] (New York: Oxford University Press, 1965), p. 89. P. Sidney, *An Apology for Poetry* [1595] (Manchester University Press, 1973), p. 101.

8 See R. Jakobson and M. Halle, 'The Metaphoric and Metonymic Poles', in *Fundamentals of Language* [1956] (The Hague: Mouton, 1971), pp. 90–6.

9 B. Eichenbaum, *Anna Akhmatova* (1923), cited in A. Preminger and T.V.F. Brogan (eds.), *The New Princeton Encyclopaedia of Poetry and Poetics* (Princeton University Press, 1993), p. 784.

10 See P. De Man, *Allegories of Reading* (New Haven and London: Yale University Press, 1979).

11 W.C. Williams, in A. Walton Litz and C. MacGowan (eds.), *Collected Poems I, 1909–1939* (Manchester: Carcanet Press, 1987), p. 183. In some anthologies, this first untitled poem from *Spring and All* (1923) is given the title of the whole volume.

12 T.S. Eliot, *Collected Poems, 1909–1962* (London: Faber & Faber, 1963), pp. 61, 80.

13 R. Barthes, *S/Z* (1970), cited by A. Morris, *How to Live/What to Do: H.D.'s Cultural Poetics* (Urbana and Chicago: Illinois University Press, 2003), p. 35.

14 T.S. Eliot: 'The existing monuments form an ideal order among themselves . . .' etc. 'Tradition and the Individual Talent' (1919) in F. Kermode (ed.), *Selected Prose* (London: Faber & Faber, 1975), p. 37.

15 For example, Louis Martz: 'Her poetry and her prose, like her own psyche, live at the seething junction of opposing forces' (H.D., *CP*, p. xi). Compare Susan Friedman's in-depth discussion of H.D.'s borderlines in *Penelope's Web: Gender, Modernity, H.D.'s Fiction* (Cambridge and New York: Cambridge University Press, 1990), pp. 81–2 *et passim*.

16 Interview with L.S. Dembo, cited by S.S. Friedman in *Psyche Reborn: The Emergence of H.D.* (Bloomington: Indiana University Press, 1981), p. 59.

17 P. McGuinness, 'Imagism' in D. Bradshaw and K. Dettmar (eds.), *A Companion to Modernist Literature and Culture* (Oxford: Blackwell, 2006), pp. 183–8 (187).

18 M. Sinclair, review of H.D.'s *Collected Poems* of 1925 for the *Fortnightly Review* (1927), repr. in B. Kime Scott (ed.), *The Gender of Modernism* (Indiana University Press, 1990), pp. 453–67 (454). Cited henceforth as 'H.D.'

19 1913, the Medico-Psychological Clinic; see E. Showalter, *The Female Malady: Women, Madness and English Culture, 1830–1980* (London: Virago, 1987), ch. 8.

20 R. Jakobson, cited above, and D. Lodge, *The Modes of Modern Writing: Metaphor, Metonymy, and the Typology of Modern Literature* (London: Edward Arnold, 1977), pt. 2.

21 H.D., in C. Laity (ed.), *Paint it Today* (New York and London: New York University Press, 1992), pp. 64–5.

22 Among the gods of the ancient world, Hermes and Priapus marked boundaries; H.D. invokes both divinities in *Sea Garden*. 'Orchard' (*CP*, p. 28) was entitled, on first publication in 1913, 'Priapus / Keeper-of-Orchards'; in this poem, the 'rough-hewn / god of the orchard' is evidently a simple statue, as (I suggest) is Hermes in 'Hermes of the Ways'.

23 In H.L. Gates (ed.), *Black Literature and Literary Theory* (London: Methuen, 1984), p. 286; see also his *The Signifying Monkey: A Theory of African-American Literary Criticism* (Oxford University Press, 1988).

24 A. van Gennep, *The Rites of Passage*, trans. M. Vizedom and G. Caffee (London: Routledge & Kegan Paul, 1960), p. 21. *Les Rites de Passage* was first published in French in 1909; within a few years, 'liminality' had been included in the 1913 revised edition of *Webster's Unabridged Dictionary* of American English.

25 V. Turner, 'Liminality and Communitas', in *The Ritual Process: Structure and Anti-structure* (London: Routledge & Kegan Paul, 1969), p. 95.

26 Turner, 'Betwixt and Between: The Liminal Period in *Rites de Passage*', in *The Forest of Symbols* (Ithaca: Cornell University Press, 1967), p. 97.

27 *c.* 1914; E. Pound, *Selected Poems, 1908–1959* (London: Faber & Faber, 1975), p. 49.

28 Canto VII: Ezra Pound, *The Cantos* (London: Faber & Faber, 1975), p. 25.

29 *Gaudier-Brzeska*, p. 89; for the original format, as published in *Poetry* and the *New Freewoman*, see P. Brooker, *A Student's Guide to the Personae of Ezra Pound* (London: Faber & Faber, 1979), p. 103.

30 As Gregory puts it, the ecstatic image of 'Pear Tree' is 'outside the ordeal of the sea garden . . . past the boundaries marked by the god of thresholds' ('Rose Cut in Rock', in Friedman and DuPlessis 1990, p. 150).

31 See M. Boughn, *H.D.: A Bibliography, 1905–1990* (Charlottesville: University Press of Virginia, 1993) A6, A 38.

32 This basic distinction, between the poet and the speaker of the poem, must be insisted upon. Readers of Eliot and Pound do not confuse these poets with their 'personae', but readers of H.D. frequently do; for example, by equating the 'authorial self' of *Sea Garden* with the poems' scenarios of alienation and unfulfilled desire: C. Buck, *H.D. and Freud* (New York: St Martin's Press, 1991), p. 33.

33 Here, I differ from Eileen Gregory, who, eliding this speaker with Aphrodite and Sappho, also identifies him or her as the 'seer' (Gregory in Friedman and DuPlessis 1990, p. 149); my suggestion that H.D.'s readers are also initiates requires this separation.

34 A.C. Swinburne, 'A Forsaken Garden', in E. Gosse and T.J. Wise (eds.), *The Complete Works: Poetical Works* (London: Heinemann, 1925) III, p. 18. See my *H.D. and Sapphic Modernism*, p. 32.

35 A. Carson, *Eros the Bittersweet* (Princeton University Press, 1986), pp. 30, 50. For further samples of H.D.'s 'sonic cutting edge', see my *H.D. and Sapphic Modernism*, p. 259.

36 Moore, in P.M. Willis (ed.), *Complete Prose* (New York: Viking Penguin Books, 1986), p. 112.

37 See my 'Appendix: Fragments of Sappho in H.D.'s Poetry and Prose' (*H.D. and Sapphic Modernism*, n.p.), and compare Eliot's explicit use of allusion in *The Waste Land* with the despairing voice towards the end of his poem: 'these fragments I have shored against my ruins' (Eliot 1963, p. 79).

38 A. Ostriker, 'No Rule of Procedure: The Open Poetics of H.D.', in Friedman and DuPlessis 1990, pp. 336–51 (350).

39 A. Morris, *How to Live/What to Do*, pp. 34: see pp. 31–4 for her analysis of this short poem from *Sea Garden*, and also her far-reaching final chapter 'Transformations', pp. 204–27.

40 Writing to Margaret Anderson in July 1917, Pound instances 'some of the long things in the *Egoist*' (which could include 'Eurydice', published there in May 1917). *Pound/The Little Review: The Letters of Ezra Pound to Margaret Anderson* (New York: New Directions, 1988), p. 114.

41 DuPlessis, *Writing Beyond the Ending: Narrative Strategies of Twentieth-century Women Writers* (Bloomington: Indiana University Press, 1985), p. 70.

42 DuPlessis, *H.D.: The Career of That Struggle* (Brighton: Harvester Press, 1986), p. 84.

43 H.D., epigraph to *Palimpsest* (Carbondale: Southern Illinois University Press, 1968), n.p.

44 Other such markers are *doors*, *lintels*, the *meeting-house*, *cross-roads*, *path*, *gate*, *turning of the stair*, *open window*, and so on.

45 H.D., in J. Augustine (ed.), *The Gift: The Complete Text* (Gainesville: University Press of Florida, 1998), p. 84.

46 In the final chapter of *The Gift*, H.D. recounts her experience of surviving (with Bryher) an air raid on her London flat and asks: 'How could I see and be and live and endure these passionate and terrible hours of hovering between life and death, and at the same time, write about them?' (p. 213) We find in this prose 'sound threads' (*endure . . . terrible hours . . . hovering*') similar to those noticed by Ostriker in the poetry, as well as a powerful sense of ritual transition ('*between life and death*').

47 T.S. Eliot, 'Hamlet' (1919), *Selected Prose* in Kermode 1975, p. 48.

48 Compare Bryher, *The Days of Mars: A Memoir, 1940–46* (London: Marion Boyars, 1972), pp. 97–106: 'huge masses of the purple willow herb . . . made gardens of a still standing wall'. In my post-war childhood, rose-bay willow herb still grew profusely in the ruins of Wren churches.

49 'H.D.: An Appreciation', in D. Levertov, *The Poet in the World* (New York: New Directions, 1973), p. 246.

50 H.D.'s *The Mystery* has been edited and annotated by Jane Augustine (Gainesville: University Press of Florida, 2009). H.D. owned Lewis Farnell's five-volume *The Cults of the Greek States* (Oxford: Oxford University Press, 1907) and may well have read Jane Harrison's *Prolegomena to the Study of Greek Religion* (Cambridge University Press, 1903).

51 Letter to Norman Holmes Pearson, quoted in publisher's blurb, *Selected Poems of H.D.* (New York: New Directions, 1957), n.p.

8

SARAH GRAHAM

Hymen and *Trilogy*

In her essay 'Notes on Thought and Vision' (1919), H.D. asserts her belief that a small community of individuals, 'gathered together in the name of truth [and] beauty', could change the world: 'Two or three people, with healthy bodies and the right sort of receiving brains, could turn the whole tide of human thought.'[1] H.D.'s work suggests that she saw herself as a member of this group and believed in the revolutionary potential of poetry. In two of her major poetic works, *Hymen* and *Trilogy*, this belief is reflected in her revisionary portraits of women that challenge heteropatriarchy. While *Trilogy* (1944–6) is H.D.'s most discussed and highly regarded poem, *Hymen* (1921), her first substantial collection after the First World War, has received relatively little critical attention. Although *Hymen* shares with H.D.'s first collection, *Sea Garden* (1916), an interest in Greek Classicism, it signifies a distinct shift from the early work that established her as a poet and cemented her reputation as 'H.D. Imagiste'.[2] Most importantly, *Hymen* moves away from a focus on flowers and landscape to offer the first fully realised example of the emphatically woman-centred poetry for which H.D. has become known: its free-verse lyric poems are preoccupied with revising patriarchal images of women. Thus, in terms of both content and technique, *Hymen* is an important precursor to *Trilogy*, an epic poem that offers a spiritual response to war principally through the recuperation of biblical women, particularly Mary Magdalene. Together, these two texts exemplify H.D.'s poetic strategies and explore her main concerns: female identity and the impact of war on the modern world.

Composed between 1916 and 1921, *Hymen* reflects H.D.'s detailed knowledge of Greek myths, which she claimed were her 'foundation'.[3] While her poetry typifies the modernist preoccupation with the Classics illustrated by T.S. Eliot, Ezra Pound and, most famously, James Joyce's

I would like to express my gratitude to Emma Parker for her careful reading of this essay and invaluable suggestions for its revision.

Ulysses (1922), it is the reconsideration of female figures that distinguishes *Hymen* from the work of her male peers. This new use of Greek myth is anticipated by H.D.'s unconventional war-time translations of Euripides' *Iphigeneia in Aulis* and *Hippolytus*, which diverge from standard versions of the texts in their sympathetic representation of women such as Iphigeneia and Helen of Troy, who are sacrificed in war or blamed for its occurrence. *Hymen* also differs from *Sea Garden*, especially in its mood. As Eileen Gregory confirms, where the earlier work has a 'difficult and broken sense of beauty [and] sharp edge[s]', *Hymen* revels in sensuality and 'explicit eroticism' evoked by images of heat and the use of rich colour.[4] While Susan Stanford Friedman rightly insists that 'the poems can and should . . . be read without references to their analogues', it is worth noting that this new sensuousness parallels the end of H.D.'s marriage to Richard Aldington and the beginning of her passionate and lifelong intimacy with Winifred Ellerman, known as 'Bryher'.[5]

The woman-centredness of *Hymen* is underlined by the title of the collection (the term for the membrane across the vagina) and by its joint dedication to Bryher and to H.D.'s daughter Perdita. Nephie J. Christodoulides suggests that, since Hymen is the name of the Greek god of marriage, the dedication also 'celebrates [H.D.'s] marriage with them'.[6] The opening poem, which contests male views of an unidentified female figure, flows directly from the dedication, establishing the tenor of the collection. While the pronouns are not all explicitly gendered, 'she' and 'I' are set against a hostile other, 'they', and the allusion to war suggests that 'they' are men, since they 'have taken life . . . / blithely'.[7] The pain and destruction associated with 'they' through the rhyme of 'they said' with 'dead' and 'bled' is contrasted with the sensuality of the last stanza, indicated by its glowing flowers and colours, which suggests a cherished kinship between women capable of a special depth of feeling which 'they' cannot 'know' (H.D., *CP*, p. 101).

The dedication also reflects the woman-centredness of *Hymen* by highlighting the absence of men. Male voices are rarely heard in the collection, with the exception of Hippolytus (son of an Amazon and a devotee of the virgin goddess Artemis, who praises female beauty) and the boys who sing of the bride in 'Hymen'. One poem, 'Sea Heroes', is focused on male figures, but they are killed in battle, thus associating men with violence and loss. By contrast, an eroticised and celebrated community of women shape the collection. Indeed, Renée Curry proposes that connection is a central theme in *Hymen*, which venerates bonds – familial, spiritual and sexual – between women.[8]

'Hymen', the title poem, is an *epithalamion* (a song for a bride on her wedding-night) that focuses on the rituals leading up to the union between 'Love' and the bride. Rachel Blau DuPlessis sees the poem as 'a carefully mapped ritual of passage, for and by a community of women'.[9] However, Alicia Ostriker describes it as a 'somber meditation on the predatory pattern of heterosexuality', and Georgina Taylor contends that it 'equates an assimilation into the role of wife with a violent sexual initiation that has nothing to offer the woman'.[10] Harriet Tarlo goes further in reading the poem as 'a daring piece of lesbian eroticism' in which women express desire for the bride.[11]

'Hymen' expresses ambivalence about heterosexuality while celebrating the power of female sensuality. The poem is more focused on the act of consummation than on love, culminating in a description of penetration from a male perspective. 'Love' praises the bride's 'maiden kiss' and 'virginal' breath (H.D., *CP*, pp. 108–9) and describes how, like a bee in search of pollen, 'Quivering he sways and quivering clings / . . . One moment, then the plunderer slips / Between the purple flower-lips' (H.D., *CP*, p. 109). In contrast, the bride is silent throughout 'Hymen', discussed and described by others, seen through literal and metaphorical veils, highlighting the ways in which heteropatriarchy silences female desire. The poem also associates marriage with bereavement, since the loss of the bride's virginity reflects the end of her autonomy and place in a female community: the chorus of women lament, 'Like a light out of our heart, / You are gone' (H.D., *CP*, p. 104).

In its celebration of female auto-eroticism, 'Thetis' presents an alternative to 'Hymen'. The poem is suffused with organic, feminine shapes and elements, including the 'curved . . . moon crescent', the 'pool', 'wave-crest' and 'sea-flower' (H.D., *CP*, pp. 117–18), and the poem as a whole affirms the validity of a sensual female self outside a heterosexual context. H.D. resists the emphasis on sexual violation that conventionally defines Thetis, known in Greek myth as the woman who was raped by Peleus, by focusing on the pleasure of her experiences just before the attack.[12] The use of the future tense – 'You will step', 'You will pass', 'You will pause', 'your feet will tread' (H.D., *CP*, pp. 116–17) – keeps Thetis poised in the moment that precedes rape, thus saving her from this awful fate.

Like 'Thetis', the collection as a whole is characterised by female sensuality: many of the poems feature luscious colours, especially red, gold and purple, and revel in powerful physical sensations connoted by heat, sea (conventionally gendered feminine) and light. Women roam through wild places where different elements meet, such as shorelines, islands and cliff edges, or sites overgrown with flowers and trees, shimmering in the noon sun or swirled around by waves and storm winds. The colours and locations in these poems suggest female passion and are presented in a poetic form typical of H.D.'s rhythmic free verse with short lines, internal rhymes, assonance and repeated words, evoking waves of sensual delight: 'and the sea-stars / and the swirl of the sand / and the rock-tamarisk / and the wind resonance' (H.D., *CP*, p. 119).

Hymen not only expresses ambivalence about heterosexuality but also offers a direct critique of it. Several of the poems feature women made unhappy by romantic love for men, which is repeatedly associated with pain. Circe loves Odysseus and would sacrifice 'the whole region / of my power and magic' for his mere 'glance' (H.D., *CP*, p. 120) but finds him unattainable. Evadne wins but is then abandoned by her lover, Apollo: while she initially enjoys 'love sweetness' (H.D., *CP*, p. 132), happiness is soon usurped by heartbreak, leading her to abandon the child that results from their union. Women like Simaetha and Calypso (in 'Cuckoo') also lose their lovers; places themselves lose their meaning without the loved one – 'What are the islands to me / if you are lost' (H.D., *CP*, p. 127) – and unreciprocated love is communicated in a mournful list of all that the lover never did in 'At Baia'. The dangers of heterosexual desire are also indicated by the theme of sexual rivalry between women, which is expressed in the trio of poems, 'Phaedra', 'She Contrasts with Herself Hippolyta' and 'She Rebukes Hippolyta'.

Like 'Thetis' and the Hippolyta poems, 'Leda' draws attention to the sexual violence against women that is presented casually in Greek myth. While Hippolyta was raped by Theseus, Leda was raped by Zeus in the form of a swan. It may seem odd, in the context of *Hymen*, that 'Leda' focuses on the male figure and presents the rapist as attractive: the swan has a 'soft breast' of 'purple down' (H.D., *CP*, p. 120). However, the poem recognises female vulnerability and stresses the predatory nature of Leda's attacker, which is masked by his seductive appeal. The emphasis on 'red' signals that the swan is both desirable and dangerous: 'a red swan lifts red wings' (H.D., *CP*, p. 120). Further, the poem stresses the impact of rape on women by ending with an image of Leda as a 'gold day-lily' who lies 'beneath' the 'red swan wings' (H.D., *CP*, p. 121). Although beautiful, like the bride in 'Hymen', Leda is rendered invisible and powerless.

Same-sex desire between women is presented as an alternative to heterosexuality in certain poems. 'Fragment 113' invokes Sappho by using a line of her poetry as its epigraph: '*Neither honey nor bee for me*' (H.D., *CP*, p. 131).[13] Mirroring the quotation's emphasis on denial, the poem begins with 'not honey, / not the plunder of the bee', and goes on to use 'not' fourteen times, especially to reject 'honey . . . the sweet / stain on the lips and teeth' (H.D., *CP*, p. 131). Since the bee stands for the bridegroom in 'Hymen', this points to a rejection of heterosexuality, a reading that is endorsed by a refusal of the phallic 'tall stalk' (H.D., *CP*, p. 131). The poem suggests that the speaker's longing – the 'rapture' that 'blind[s] her eyes' and her 'hunger' (H.D., *CP*, p. 131) – cannot be satisfied by men. Nonetheless, the poem remains ambivalent about same-sex desire. In the third stanza the speaker's focus turns to the iris, a flower associated with the goddess of the same name, suggesting a female lover. In the final stanza, however, all flowers are dismissed, along with the 'old desire – old passion – / old forgetfulness – old pain' of the past (H.D., *CP*, p. 131). If flowers represent women, as they often do in H.D.'s poems, and 'honey' (and the bee) men, then the speaker seems to turn away from both: 'not this, nor any flower' (H.D., *CP*, p. 131). Ultimately, the poem imagines the possibility of passion with an unspecified former lover if he would change: if 'you' return and 'touch as the god', 'you shall feel, / . . . heat' (H.D., *CP*, p. 132). Thus, the poem implies that while the speaker does not reject men entirely, she demands that heterosexual relations be reconceived.

Other poems in the collection are less ambivalent about same-sex desire between women. 'White World' is an explicit celebration of lesbian union. Recognising that intimacy between women is invisible in heteronormative culture, H.D. recalled that, during her post-war travels with Bryher, 'We were always "two women alone" . . . but we were not alone' (H.D., *TF*, p. 50); 'White World' challenges this invisibility. Beginning 'The whole white world is ours' (H.D., *CP*, p. 134), the poem depicts a pastoral idyll of bay, olive and laurel trees, valleys of citron and snow-peaked hills, in which spirits never weary and 'joined is each to each / in happiness complete' (H.D., *CP*, p. 135), the strength of union emphasised by the rhythm and near-rhyme. Since Tarlo argues that white is a code for lesbian desire in *Hymen*, the sensual world of this poem may be read as emphatically female (Tarlo 1996, p. 96). Whereas the bee suggests plunder and loss in other poems in which male figures use sex to assert power over women, here 'the bee's soft belly' is 'ours' (H.D., *CP*, p. 135), suggesting mutuality and erotic union that lacks nothing offered by heterosexuality.

As a whole, then, *Hymen* is consistently focused on female experience, asserting that women are sexual, self-determining beings who have historically been silenced and inhibited by the norms of heteropatriarchy. Rather than writing about modern women, H.D. makes use of female figures renowned from the Classics, reimagining their experiences in ways that speak to a modern audience. The collection is particularly focused on the erotic potential of women, which is emphasised through the poems' sensual rhythms and their imagery of heat and intense colour as much as their content. Faced with the disaster of war, which brutally emphasised the divisions between men and women, H.D. devotes her poetic energies to recuperating lost and damaged women and, while she concentrates in *Hymen* on the capacities of women's bodies (as lovers, mothers and daughters), she extends this exploration of female power to include their spirituality in her next major poetic work, *Trilogy*.

After *Hymen*, H.D. fell into what she later described as 'a period of waiting, of marking time . . . of stagnation, of lethargy' (H.D., *TF*, p. 57). Despite this, she published steadily, producing novels, journalism and translations, and two further collections of poetry, *Heliodora* (1924) – which includes 'We Two', an affirmation of same-sex love – and *Red Roses for Bronze* (1931). The poems of this period remain invested in revising myths about women. For example, Helen of Troy was a longterm preoccupation for H.D. and in her translation of 'Chorus of the Women of Chalkis' (1915–16), she suggests that Helen did not – contrary to standard versions of the myth – consent to her abduction by Paris, but 'possessed, / Followed a stranger' (H.D., *CP*, p. 75). Likewise, 'Helen', included in *Heliodora*, offers a response to W.B. Yeats' representation of Helen as a *femme fatale* responsible for destruction in his poem 'No Second Troy' (1916). In contrast, by describing Helen as 'white', H.D. suggests that she is innocent: she has a 'white face' and 'white hands' and her 'still eyes' counter her image as a seductress (H.D., *CP*, p. 154). Later, in *Helen in Egypt* (1961), H.D. rescues Helen again by presenting a less common account of the Trojan wars, in which a ghost inhabits Troy in her place and she lives out the war in Egypt.

Trilogy, which H.D. began in 1942 and published in three annual parts from 1944 to 1946, is evidence of the poet's continued interest in celebrating and recuperating women. However, while *Hymen* focuses on women in Greek myth, in *Trilogy* H.D. turns her attention to the Bible, principally to Mary Magdalene. The persistence of a woman-centred perspective is reflected in the fact that the first book of *Trilogy*, 'The Walls Do Not Fall' (1944), is – like *Hymen* – dedicated to Bryher. However, shaped by the nightmare of war, *Trilogy* has little of the eroticism so evident in the earlier volume. Where *Hymen* celebrates women's sensuality, *Trilogy*, responding to this new social context, promotes female spirituality and 'points to a way out of war' (Taylor 2001, p. 175). Resurrection is the poem's central theme and it asserts the recuperative potential of women, whose power rivals that of male figures such as Christ and Ra. Just before the end of the war, H.D. wrote that 'we are here today in a city of ruin, a world ruined, it might seem, almost past redemption' (H.D., *TF*, p. 84). Nonetheless, reflecting her ambition to 'turn the whole tide of human thought', *Trilogy* suggests that redemption is possible through female figures and, further, that a woman writer can be the conduit for a new understanding of the world (H.D., *Notes*, p. 27).

'The Walls Do Not Fall', explores the role of the poet and the efficacy of poetry in the context of war. 'Walls' repeatedly invokes a hostile interlocutor who suggests that poetry is outmoded and misdirected, accusing the speaker, a poet, of being 'retrogressive' and attempting to 'scratch out / the indelible ink of the palimpsest of past misadventure', an allusion to H.D.'s revisionary project.[14] However, the role of the poet is presented as invaluable in connecting the diverse beliefs of other times and places, 'search[ing] the old highways / for the true-rune' (p. 5). Rather than being 'useless', the poet is like an oyster who produces 'self-out-of-self, / selfless, / that pearl of great price' (pp. 14, 9). Here, H.D. asserts the value of poetry by comparing it both to a pearl and, through an allusion to the 'pearl of great price' (Matthew 13), the Bible. The speaker's enemies may assert that poets are 'pathetic', but this disrespect of their art is 'heresy' because poets are needed to explain both 'what words say' and what they 'conceal' (p. 14): 'I know, I feel / the meaning that words hide' (p. 53), asserts the speaker in the face of her critics. Whatever damage war may do, truth endures in language: 'gods have been smashed before / . . . and their secret is stored / in man's very speech' (p. 15), speech that only poets understand.

Further, the speaker asserts that the importance of the poet is evidenced by her capacity to envisage union in the face of conflict.[15] The poem opens with an image of unity: 'An incident here and there, / and rails gone (for guns) / from your (and my) old town square' (p. 3), which acknowledges both the direct impact of the war on the domestic front and that this is a shared space, in which 'you' may be a single intimate or a wider community. In this poem, though, the principle of unification is expanded beyond the 'incidents' of the Blitz via a range of discourses from different historical moments, places and belief-systems, showing the 'power of primal symbols to endure ruin'.[16] The speaker's vision of Samuel and the Pythian, male and female prophets from the Bible and Ancient Greece respectively, on the streets of wartime London (pp. 3–4) is emblematic of a conviction that 'through our desolation, / thoughts stir, inspiration stalks us' (p. 3). Despite the misery of war, inspiration comes from an array of sources as a necessary counter to 'desolation'.

The speaker/poet envisages a composite saviour figure who encompasses Ra and Osiris (p. 25), archetypal fathers, and Christ the son. These figures appear to the speaker in revelations that make it clear 'that *Amen* is our Christos' (p. 27), connecting Ra (Amon) to Christ through the Hebrew word commonly used to end Christian prayers, 'Amen'. This strategy unites significant figures conventionally separated in different – sometimes even opposed – belief-systems. A multiplicity of faiths is encapsulated in the string of names, 'Amen-Ra, | *Amen*, Aries, the Ram' (p. 30), which combines Ancient Egypt, Hebrew, Christianity and astrology. The poem's vision also incorporates a significant female figure, Isis, whose 'secret' is that 'there was One / in the beginning, Creator, / Fosterer, Begetter, the Same-forever' (pp. 54–5), that is, a common origin not necessarily or only male. Isis, sister and lover of Osiris and emblem of motherhood and fertility, represents a female creator as powerful as father-figures such as Osiris, Christ and Ra. The presence of Isis in the poem thus prompts a reconsideration of the creation myth that is essential to all faiths, whether it is located in the Egyptian 'papyrus-swamp' or the biblical 'Judean meadow' (p. 55). Isis is associated with resurrection as well as birth because she was responsible for collecting all the body-parts of Osiris after his murder, making possible his rebirth. As DuPlessis notes, Isis is both mother and lover, 'an expression of H.D.'s desire for transcendent presence in *female* form' (DuPlessis 1986, p. 55). The capacity for birth and rebirth is an attribute of key female figures in *Trilogy* and a sign of their power.

Emphasising the theme of unity, the speaker asks, 'O, Sire, / is this union at last?' (H.D., *Trilogy*, p. 57), suggesting that recognising shared beginnings might foster harmony in the present and future, bringing an end to conflict, but it is significant that this is framed as a question, suggesting doubt. The final section, presented in italics, returns the poem's focus to London in the Blitz, contrasting the destruction of war with the possibility of renewal through '*zrr-hiss*' (p. 58), which evokes the sound of falling bombs but also echoes 'Isis'. Besieged by 'dust', 'powder' and 'fog' (p. 58), vision is literally and metaphorically obscured and the speaker concedes uncertainty at the last: '*we are voyagers, discoverers / of the not-known, / the unrecorded; / we have no map; / possibly we will reach haven, / heaven*' (p. 59). Madelyn Detloff criticises *Trilogy*'s 'redemptive logic' – that is, its vision of escape to 'haven' or 'heaven' – because it 'deflects our attention from [the] unpleasant reality' of the war.[17] However, while the poem ends with an affirmation of community ('we') and determination to continue the quest, there is no absolute conviction that salvation will result.

The second book of *Trilogy*, 'Tribute to the Angels' (1945), continues the visionary project established in 'Walls', opening with Hermes Trismegistus, a dual figure who combines the attributes of Hermes of Classical Greek myth and the Ancient Egyptian god Thoth. Connecting two cultures and associated with alchemy and learning, he embodies the unifying principle of 'melt down and integrate' that the poem promotes (p. 63). The role that language plays in rebirth is encapsulated in wordplay that combines *marah* ('bitter' in Hebrew) and *mar* ('sea' in Spanish) to make *marah-mar*, words that 'melted, fuse and join / and change and alter', moving through a transformative sequence: 'mer, mere, mère, mater, Maia, Mary' to become 'Star of the Sea, / Mother' (p. 71). As Aliki Barnstone makes clear (p. 187), these words are drawn from several different languages and traditions, and progress from water to the sea to the mother to arrive at the mothers of Hermes (Maia) and of Christ (Mary). This sequence encapsulates *Trilogy*'s movement from the female sensuality that also shapes *Hymen* ('mer, mere'), through the mother ('mère, mater') who appears in both collections, to arrive in the final book at a recuperated, multi-faceted female figure ('Mary'), associated as much with resurrection as birth, as much with the spiritual as the corporeal.

'Tribute' continues the theme of rebirth through two visions: one of a tree that is both burnt and flowering, and one of a 'Lady' carrying a book. The first is both an image from the Blitz and a reference to the Egyptian equivalent of the phoenix, the '*bennu* bird' that appears in 'Walls' (p. 35); the bennu is created from a fire in a holy tree, representing birth from destruction. Though 'burnt and stricken to the heart' (p. 82), 'we saw the tree flowering' (p. 83); this shared experience has enormous implications for the speaker. Even as she recognises that 'it is happening everywhere' (p. 84), as such trees are an everyday sight in bomb-damaged London, it symbolises the possibility of resurrection and so, although it was real, 'not a dream', it was also 'a vision, it was a sign' (p. 87), confirmation of her faith in the possibility of rebirth.

The theme of new possibilities is also communicated by the speaker's dream of a 'Lady' who appears when she is 'talking casually / with friends' (p. 89), again suggesting community.[18] When the dream ends, however, the figure is 'there more than ever' (p. 91), and it is here that the poem refocuses its interest from male to female figures: the speaker had been thinking of Gabriel, but 'the Lady herself' came instead (p. 92). Visions of the Lady – Mary, the mother – then proliferate in the poem, presenting the various ways in which she has been depicted and understood (pp. 93–4). Like the half-burnt tree, 'you find / her everywhere' (p. 94), but in contrast to these innumerable representations, the Lady in 'Tribute' has 'none of her usual attributes'; most importantly, 'the Child was not with her' (p. 97). Instead, the Lady carries 'a book' (p. 100), 'the unwritten volume of the new' (p. 103). This signifies that the future is yet to be written, and the Lady is transformative; like 'Psyche, the butterfly, / out of the cocoon' (p. 103), she is associated with the soul and rebirth, when '*we rise again from death and live*' (p. 110).

Across the first two parts of *Trilogy*, then, a hybrid male father/creator figure is gradually replaced by a female creator/saviour figure, who is emblematic not only of birth but of the possibility of resurrection. In the third section, 'The Flowering of the Rod' (1946), the focus narrows to specific women: Mary the Madonna and Mary Magdalene. Christ is associated with both of these Marys, one at the beginning and one at the end of his life; his mother is celebrated for her purity while Mary Magdalene is denigrated for her sexual sins. Mary Magdalene is one of the 'twisted and tortured individuals' (p. 129) who, like the thief at the Crucifixion, received Christ's blessing; considered 'an unbalanced, neurotic woman' (p. 129) she is 'the first actually to witness His life-after-death' (p. 129), signifying her importance and linking her to resurrection. 'Flowering' seeks to unite Mary Magdalene with the Madonna to create a female figure who, representing both birth and rebirth, will counteract destruction.

Much of 'Flowering' is preoccupied with Mary's acquisition of the precious ointment she is reported to have used on Christ's feet. This is told from the perspective of Kaspar, one of the Magi who visited the new-born Christ in Bethlehem bearing a gift of myrrh. Deborah Kelly Kloepfer reads Kaspar's jar of myrrh as comparable in its mystery and significance to H.D.'s poetry, suggesting that H.D. is a Kaspar-figure, since both link Mary Magdalene and the Virgin Mary.[19] The scenes in Kaspar's shop reconfigure the stereotypical representations of Mary Magdalene, presenting an articulate and self-possessed woman who 'knew how to detach herself, / another unforgivable sin' (p. 131) and is not intimidated by Kaspar, declaring 'I am Mary . . . of Magdala, / I am Mary, a great tower' (p. 135). The woman conventionally dismissed as a prostitute here asserts her strength and autonomy. The recuperated Mary Magdalene knows that 'there are Marys a-plenty' but asserts that she 'shall be Mary-myrrh' (p. 135), associated with the most precious balm on earth. While the poem redeems Mary for her so-called sexual sins, it does not imply that she is sexless. Kloepfer notes the eroticism in Kaspar's encounter with Mary when he is transfixed by the sight of her beautiful hair (Kloepfer 1989, pp. 136–8). Given the possibility that Kaspar reflects H.D.'s own longing to be connected to both Marys, the lesbian desire evident in *Hymen* may also be traced in *Trilogy*.

In 'Flowering', women facilitate visions that change male perceptions. Kaspar's encounter with Mary allows him to understand that the 'devils' cast from her include other disparaged women: '*Lilith born before Eve / and one born before Lilith, / and Eve*' (p. 157). Through the poem's reclamation of these three 'devils', H.D. extends the recuperation of female figures from Mary Magdalene to other women; although the identity of the one before her is uncertain, Lilith was cast from Eden for refusing to recognise Adam's authority, while Eve was castigated for attempting to acquire knowledge. In both cases women are punished for attempting to assert agency in a patriarchal order that deems them inferior. Like them, Mary Magdalene is repudiated for her supposed sins. However, while Kaspar wants to believe that Mary is 'unseemly' (p. 137), the vision she grants him contradicts this and demands reassessment of her and the women to whom she is connected.

Adalaide Morris argues that since Kaspar is himself a marginalised figure in the Bible, his centrality in 'Flowering' signifies that the male, too, may be redeemed by playing a part in the vision of unity with which the poem culminates.[20] Kaspar sees 'deeper' and 'apprehend[s] more / than anyone before or after him' (p. 165) in the vision that Mary provokes.[21] It takes him to 'a *point* in time' (p. 166): his memory of visiting the new-born Christ in Bethlehem, bearing a jar of myrrh that is twinned with the jar – 'there were always two jars' (p. 168) – that Mary Magdalene takes for the adult Christ's feet. The closing section of 'Flowering' describes the moment when Mary, mother of Christ, addresses Kaspar. Although she compliments him on the 'beautiful fragrance' of the myrrh (p. 172), he knows the jar is sealed and that 'the fragrance came from the bundle of myrrh / she held in her arms' (p. 172), the new-born Christ. The conventional focus of the Nativity scene is the Christ-child, but here he is a bundle of myrrh: not only precious, but inescapably connected to Mary, since 'Mary shall be myrrh . . . I shall be Mary-myrrh' (p. 135). 'Mary' not only stands for Christ's mother, who represents purity, but also Mary Magdalene and all the other 'fallen' women that she symbolises. At this archetypal birth scene, then, the 'allied or opposite vibration' (p. 166) – not death but rebirth – is invoked, signifying not only the resurrection of Christ that will come, but also the recuperation of the neglected and disparaged women of the Bible and of the ancient traditions of Greece and Egypt who have appeared in the poem. All are united in the figure of Mary, and redeemed.

In *Trilogy*, H.D. not only recuperates the disparaged women of the past but also positions herself in the revised Nativity, underscoring the centrality of the poet's role in the process of revision. Born in Bethlehem (in Pennsylvania), the connection between H.D., the spectrum of Marys that *Trilogy* invokes, and the Christ-child is implicit. This is confirmed by H.D.'s description of her most vivid dream during analysis by Freud in 1933. An unadorned Egyptian '*Princess*' descends steps (H.D., *TF*, p. 36), watched by H.D., 'the dreamer': 'There is no before or after, it is a perfect moment in time or out of time', she recalls (H.D., *TF*, p. 37). Freud argues that in this dream H.D. is represented either by the baby Moses that the Princess is about to find or by 'the child Miriam, half concealed in the rushes' (H.D., *TF*, p. 37). If the latter, H.D. is connected through Miriam, protector of the infant Moses, to Mary by casting herself as a mother. If she is the baby Moses, H.D. may be fulfilling a role, conventionally reserved for the male, to be 'the founder of a new religion' (H.D., *TF*, p. 37). Thus, the poet appears in the final scene of her poem as either Mary or Christ, taking a central place in a unified spiritual mythos that counters loss with resurrection and redemption through the female.

While *Trilogy* may be praised as a female-centred response to the wartime violence that patriarchy endorses, H.D.'s emphatic promotion of the poet as a gifted interpreter of a range of discourses may be criticised as the elitist view of a privileged artist protected from the deprivations of war. Lawrence Rainey takes issue with H.D.'s attempt to locate eternal truths in a visionary synthesis of past and present, which he regards as 'at once portentous and yet accommodatingly vague', typified by 'bland notions', 'vacuity' and 'intellectual limitations'.[22] Although Rainey criticises H.D.'s strategies, it may be argued that her work reflects the challenging position in which many modernist writers found themselves: Peter Nicholls argues that Modernist poetry is complex partly because it stems from a 'crossroads' between 'orthodox religious belief' and an 'aesthetic "religion"' that prioritises 'imagination and sensibility' over 'dogma and belief'.[23] Original yet conscious of the past, the themes and techniques of modernist poetry might offer consolation – or, at least, an alternative perspective – when religious belief falters in the face of conflict. H.D. is not the only poet of her era to respond to such difficult issues in an experimental, visionary mode: despite their differences, Ezra Pound's *Cantos* (1934–71), T.S. Eliot's *Four Quartets* (1936–42) and the work of Wallace Stevens all explore the relationship between world and perception in visionary terms. *Trilogy* prioritises 'imagination' over 'dogma', combining religion and myth in an innovative manner that reflects the interwoven nature of H.D.'s poetic concerns, revisionary impulse and response to war.

H.D. was in several respects a marginalised writer whose fame diminished across her career; indeed, she has now been resurrected as a writer in a manner comparable to the recuperation she offers women in her poetry. Despite the cushioning of her wealth, she was traumatised by the First World War and deeply preoccupied by the seemingly inevitable recurrence of conflict. Self-conscious and curious about her multi-faceted identity as a mother, daughter, lover and artist, H.D. consistently interrogates the ways in which spirituality might be expressed aesthetically in the face of oppression and destruction. Ultimately, while her poetry cannot create the redemption and renewal she craves, it unfailingly probes the ways in which the neglected and disparaged female – including the female poet – may play a central role in a society under threat.

Hymen and *Trilogy* are exemplary of H.D.'s poetic strategies and concerns because in both volumes she moves women from the margins to the centre, revises patriarchal narratives, and emphasises the importance of female experience. For these reasons, the two collections not only typify her work, but also establish that H.D., like her contemporary Virginia Woolf, deserves to be recognised both as a major modernist and as a founding mother of twentieth-century women's writing.

NOTES

1 H.D., *Notes on Thought and Vision* (London: Peter Owen, 1988), p. 27.
2 H.D., *End to Torment: A Memoir of Ezra Pound* (New York: New Directions, 1979), p. 18.
3 H.D., *Tribute to Freud* (New York: New Directions, [1972] 1984), p. 187. Abbreviated as *TF.*
4 E. Gregory, 'H.D.'s Heterodoxy: The Lyric as a Site of Resistance', in M. Camboni (ed.), *H.D.'s Poetry: "the meanings that words hide"* (New York: AMS Press, 2003), p. 25.
5 S.S. Friedman, *Penelope's Web: Gender, Modernity, and H.D.'s Fiction* (Cambridge and New York: Cambridge University Press, 1990), p. 66.
6 N.J. Christodoulides, 'Triangulation of Desire in H.D.'s *Hymen*', in C.C. Barfoot (ed.), *And Never Know the Joy: Sex and the Erotic in English Poetry* (Amsterdam and New York: Rodopi, 2006), p. 317.
7 H.D., in L.L. Martz (ed.), *Collected Poems 1912–1944* (New York: New Directions, 1983), p. 101. Abbreviated as *CP.*
8 R. Curry, *White Women Writing White: H.D., Elizabeth Bishop, Sylvia Plath, and Whiteness* (Westport, CT.: Greenwood Press, 2000), p. 33.
9 R.B. DuPlessis, *H.D. The Career of that Struggle* (Brighton: Harvester Press, 1986), p. 29.
10 S. Gubar, 'Sapphistries', *Signs*, 10.1 (1984), 55; G. Taylor, *H.D. and the Public Sphere of Modernist Women Writers* (Oxford University Press, 2001), p. 110.
11 Harriet Tarlo, '"Ah, could they know": The Place of the Erotic in H.D.'s *Hymen*', *Gramma*, 4 (1996), 92.
12 In *H.D. and Hellenism: Classic Lines* (Cambridge and New York: Cambridge University Press, 1997). Eileen Gregory identifies the poem with a section in Ovid's *Metamorphoses* which 'locates this descent immediately before the violent rape of Thetis by Peleus' (p. 117).
13 In *H.D. and Sapphic Modernism* (Cambridge University Press, 1999), Diana Collecott proposes that H.D.'s use of Sappho constitutes a 'lesbian poetics' (p. 10).
14 H.D., *Trilogy*, annotated by Aliki Barnstone (New York: New Directions, 1998), pp. 5–6.
15 For a reading that focuses on war trauma, see S. Graham, 'Falling Walls: Trauma and Testimony in H.D.'s *Trilogy*', *English*, 56 (2007), 299–319.
16 D. Chisholm, *H.D.'s Freudian Poetics: Psychoanalysis in Translation* (Ithaca, NY: Cornell University Press, 1992), p. 42.
17 M. Detloff, '"Father, Don't You See I'm Burning?": Identification and Remembering in H.D.'s World War II Writing', in E. Barnes (ed.), *Incest and the Literary Imagination* (Gainesville: University Press of Florida, 2002), p. 260.
18 As well as her war-time seances, the vision of the 'Lady' also evokes a dream H.D. describes to Freud: 'A figure is standing there, holding a lighted candle. It is my mother. I was overpowered with happiness and all trace of terror vanished' (H.D., *TF*, p. 175). In *Trilogy*, the Lady carries a book, but the optimistic vision of a woman bringing peace is consistent.
19 D.K. Kloepfer, *The Unspeakable Mother: Forbidden Discourse in Jean Rhys and H.D.* (Ithaca and London: Cornell University Press, 1989), pp. 134–5.

20 A. Morris, *How to Live/What to Do: H.D.'s Cultural Poetics* (Urbana and Chicago: University of Illinois Press, 2003), p. 114.

21 DuPlessis argues that Kaspar represents Freud (*Career*, pp. 96–7).

22 L. Rainey, *Institutions of Modernism: Literary Elites and Public Culture* (New Haven and London: Yale University Press, 1998), pp. 162–4. Rainey does not admire H.D.'s work and believes that Bryher's patronage meant that she had no need to engage with any audience beyond a limited coterie, to the detriment of her writing.

23 P. Nicholls, 'The Poetics of Modernism', in A. Davis and L.M. Jenkins (eds.), *The Cambridge Companion to Modernist Poetry* (Cambridge University Press, 2007), p. 52.

9

MATTE ROBINSON AND DEMETRIOS P. TRYPHONOPOULOS

HERmione and other prose

H.D. is best known as a poet: her imagist and long poems receive the most attention outside of a small circle of critics, and are usually the only parts of her oeuvre to be anthologised. Susan Stanford Friedman is the first critic to have written a book-length work on her prose: *Penelope's Web: Gender, Modernity, H.D.'s Fiction*[1] establishes that H.D. was not only a frequent prose writer, but also an experimental one, comparable with Gertrude Stein and Virginia Woolf. Despite H.D.'s efforts to publish some of them, many of her prose works remained unpublished during her lifetime, and some have taken more than half a century to see the light of day.[2] However, she wrote much more than she tried to publish, her prose being less vulnerable to the blocks and psychic breakdowns that halted her poetry. Like many modernists, H.D. worked over a lifetime at the same story, allowing it to evolve, mature and achieve a considerable depth, intricately and intimately bound up in her own life. Her poems, on the other hand, are more like offspring, separate, autonomous even in the post-imagist long poems, and inevitably breaking away from the life of their progenitor. Because of its distinct, intimate role in her writing, her prose is difficult, murky and opaque; but it is valuable not only as a significant experimental body of work but also as a rich source of companion material that informs her poetry in often unexpected ways.

Like her male modernist peers, H.D. saw all of art as part of a single esoteric endeavour; levels of initiation into the Eleusinian mysteries in her *Notes on Thought and Vision* correspond to the audience's ability to understand art: 'There is no trouble about the art, it is the appreciators we want',[3] she explains, betraying a kind of elitism that has less to do with an audience's education and more to do with a special kind of sensitivity. Her hierarchical categorisation of audiences – rather than art – places art at the apex not only of civilisation but of humanity's future. Emphasis is placed on the audience's ability to decode the work of art in general (whether it be poetry, prose, sculpture, paintings, etc.), the particular new work's goal being to help the audience access all great art. There has for ages been enough good art, 'enough in the fragments and the almost perfectly preserved charioteer at Delphi alone to remake the world' (H.D., *Notes*, p. 26), so the modern artist is to produce work that will help to train an audience in sensitivity, a transitive verb, energising the audience or object of the work. The fulfilment of this process will transmute civilisation: 'Two or three people, with healthy bodies and the right sort of receiving brains, could turn the whole tide of human thought, could direct lightning flashes of electric power to slash across and destroy the world of dead, murky thought' (H.D., *Notes*, p. 27). From this very early assertion through her entire career, H.D., whether she is using prose, poetry or film, makes art that is intended both for that mythical, rarefied audience and for those who are open to the experience of becoming more sensitive – of achieving a higher state of initiation – through the art.

H.D. actively (re)wrote the narrative of her own life in her many works that exist on the borderline between fiction and memoir, often with the names and a few details changed, sometimes even retaining real-life names in the early drafts. We will be focusing on an early work, *HERmione*, and a late work, *Majic Ring*, in order to discuss the way in which H.D. 'wrote' writers[4] into the narrative of history and culture. Like many modernists, H.D. lived through two World Wars, but she was not a war poet in the usual sense of the term: she did not write about war, but about the part poets play as active members of society, in war and peace. Through war, H.D. is able to expand the scope of her writing to the very vast and the very particular; the prose works provide a sense of the development and refining of the idea of the poet as a spiritual worker in a secular world, walking the earth and not the halls of an ivory tower.

There are several ways to divide H.D.'s fiction into time periods, the simplest of which is early (1920s), middle (1930s) and late (1940s–50s). Of these, the latest stage has the most yet to be written about because much of it is only now seeing publication. Thus, even Friedman's *Penelope's Web*, which first identifies the Six-novel Delia Alton cycle,[5] ends its roughly chronological Table of Contents with the Second World War. It may be better to think of it as H.D.'s life, rather than her prose, as a text that she was always reworking. In this important sense, all of her novels, even those taking place in remote places and times, are part of one work.[6]

The earlier novels (*HERmione*, *Asphodel*, *Paint It Today*) treat her childhood and adolescent days in Pennsylvania, focusing on her budding life as a writer and the forming of her first important relationships with men and women. In this period she begins weaving her notion of cyclical time and the way the same cast of characters lives through similar stories in different historical periods. Ancient Greece, Rome near the time of Christ and contemporary London are joined together in the three novellas of *Palimpsest*, anticipating the host of historical times treated in *The Sword Went Out To Sea* decades later. *Hedylus* further explores antiquity and the Classic poets, the name Hedylus being taken from a now-unknown poet mentioned in Meleager.[7] *Narthex*, another *roman-à-clef*, serves as a transition between the early work that focuses largely on events from the first decade of the twentieth century, to the middle work, which deals with matter from the 1920s.

The middle period includes *romans-à-clef* which deal with events of the previous decade, but this was also a time of experimentation, and of a writing block that largely kept her from writing poetry. Of particular interest is H.D.'s synthesis of her personal experiences with her readings in myth; while this tendency is common to all the high modernists, she looks beyond the mostly male-centred myths of her peers (of Odysseus, Dionysus, Zoroaster), incorporating Egyptian and occult cosmologies, all the while rewriting or correcting myths in order to include the feminine perspective, which had been worn away by centuries of patriarchy. *Nights*, based on an affair and a suicide in Switzerland, is contemporary and partly fictional. It is the closest H.D. comes to a blue novel, providing a rare personal glimpse into a piece of her complicated sex life, which she usually keeps heavily veiled. *Nights* was given a small private printing and distributed to friends, as was *Kora and Ka*, based on her time living in Switzerland with Bryher and Kenneth MacPherson. *Kora and Ka* is narrated by the Ka of Helforth, the MacPherson character: 'I am that sort of shadow they used to call a Ka, in Egypt. A Ka lives after the body is dead. I shall live after Helforth is dead.'[8] H.D. here draws on her wide reading in Egyptian mythology, particularly the work of E. Wallis Budge, to create a narrative device that rings oddly true in her belief system, which included reincarnation: allowing MacPherson's Ka to speak commits to paper a version of the story seen from an out-of-time dimension, that part which remains of the story when the physical bodies of the characters have died away.

Pilate's Wife[9] deals with the many layers of truth in the myth of the Christian tradition; though it has autobiographical parallels, it reads like a mystical short novel à la Hermann Hesse. Seen through the eyes of Pilate's wife, the Christ story makes incarnate the abstract ideas of the philosophers, transforming them into a real spirituality. Plato's love as two halves searching for each other is replaced by a love between two 'entire entit[ies]';[10] sin is not an abstraction connected to a specific act, but a failure to discern, to be sensitive to the reality of the situation, 'bungling the affair, missing the clue' (H.D., *Pilate's Wife*, p. 118).

The preoccupation with antiquity is further explored in the second phase of her writing; she returns to translation with two plays of Euripides, *Ion* and *Hippolytus Temporizes*, which, although in verse, contain significant prose notes. Early on, Robert Duncan identified these translations as the journeyman's final project before she became a master, 'initial to the major phase of her work that lasts from the inception of the War Trilogy with *The Walls Do Not Fall* in 1942 to the end of her life with *Hermetic Definitions* in 1960'.[11]

The third phase seems to be two: war and post-war, except that *Majic Ring* ties all the works together, serving as a key to the content, both of the poems and prose she was writing at the same time (1943–4) and to the later cycle of Delia Alton novels, all of which revisit the events described in journal entries and letters collected in *Majic Ring*. *The Gift* is spiritual autobiography, tracing her mystical and scientific heritage from, respectively, her Moravian mother and her scientist father. *Tribute to Freud* combines two texts, one a memoir and one a journal, concerning her analysis or apprenticeship with Freud and the spiritual awakening that accompanied it. *Bid Me To Live*, discussed below, though a late novel, is a *roman-à-clef* that completes what Friedman calls 'the Madrigal Cycle' (Friedman 1990, p. xi) of the early period (including *Paint It Today* and *Asphodel*), while *Magic Mirror* tells the very contemporary story of her stay at a sanatorium in Switzerland. The three late Delia Alton novels, *The Sword Went Out to Sea*, *The White Rose and the Red* and *The Mystery* tell and re-tell the historical 'romance' of the Hugh Dowding story in a dizzying array of historical periods.

HERmione: the unincarnated woman

H.D. had what she called major and minor 'initiators'[12] in her life (H.D., 'Compassionate', pp. 35, 72) all of whom are recurring characters in her fiction. Of those, and in this order, Ezra Pound, Sigmund Freud and Hugh Dowding are important in terms of their historical significance, their presence in her fiction and her need to assimilate and then overcome their influence. They also each correspond to a phase of her writing. There are other and valid ways of dividing up her work, and the association of each phase with a male figure in her life can lead to a number of dangers and distortions. Nevertheless, as a writer, a thinker and a 'religious' person, H.D. was forced into the position of confronting and overcoming male impositions. Pound was a dominating influence on her poetry, Freud on her intellect and Dowding on her connection with the spirit world. In H.D.'s life and writing, Bryher, particularly, was a much more important influence;

but the men were points of initiation, and their function in the fiction is as forces to be dealt with or even pitted against.

HERmione tells the story of her freeing herself from the first of these initiators, Ezra Pound, as well as Frances Gregg, who initiated H.D. into her bisexuality. *HERmione*'s biographical correspondence is to the time when H.D. still lived on American soil, and these two figures, Pound the male lover and poet returning from Europe, and Gregg the female lover and sophisticated woman-of-the-world, in some sense competed for her attention while forming their own bond with each other. H.D.'s family objected to her engagement to Pound, but became friendlier towards him when she instead began spending more time with the airy Gregg. This is a first major novel about the first major stage in her life as a writer, and it establishes a fluid, difficult prose style in sharp contrast to the chiselled imagist poetry she had been writing. The third-person narrator remains close to the protagonist's thought process. The melding of the narration with the character's mind is helped along and complicated by the character's name, Her, and by the hypnotic use of numerous mutating leitmotifs, including the character's constant (re)naming of herself.

The novel is set before H.D. was exposed to psychoanalysis, something the narrator mentions early and often. Though it existed in Europe, where Hermione/H.D. would end up, it had not reached her in her as-yet 'unincarnated'[13] state, still in America. This state was not simply to be outgrown, though: her family had come from Europe, and her trip to Europe would allow her to incarnate fully, while bringing along that which needed to be born in America. 'In Europe were races who had sent out their more energetic and more mystically-inclined offspring, their scourings and their scions to Pennsylvania' (H.D., *HER*, p. 9). H.D.'s Moravian immigrant heritage would become of more importance during the Second World War, post-Freud, with *The Gift* (discussed elsewhere in this volume) and the Delia Alton novels, particularly *The Mystery*, which refigures the late drama surrounding her 'romance' with Hugh Dowding in the story of Zinzendorf's founding of the Moravian church. For the time being, she/Her needed to leave Pennsylvania as well as the two figures, Pound and Frances Gregg,[14] who drew her in opposite directions towards dissatisfying, narrow fates. Friedman sees H.D. as Psyche,[15] to be reborn after passing through the psychoanalytic doorway; *HERmione* is the story of the butterfly's first attempt 'to break the wavering tenuous antennae' out of 'the husk of the thing called Her' (H.D., *HER*, p. 216). Pound (George Lowndes) is found to be 'inadequate' (H.D., *HER*, p. 216): 'He would have pulled back quivering antennae.'[16]

Pound as first initiator looms heavily in this work; though the late memoir *End to Torment* deals with him in much greater detail, his distinct voice is allowed to cut through the miasma of internal monologue and repetition, read in a letter: 'Hermione, I'm coming back to Gawd's own god-damn country' (H.D., *HER*, p. 28). The shock of this language (the rest of the paragraph drifts and eddies: 'It's too hot here. Gart is set like a bowl in this wood. It's too hot here. A canoe seemed rippling between weeds') is also the shock of mixed dimensions: it is a letter from Ezra Pound, delivered via George Lowndes and the post to Hermione as H.D. is writing her. One third of *Majic Ring* consists of carbons of letters H.D. had written to Dowding, with only the names changed, but here it is a single letter, woven into the prose and repeated throughout the text as leitmotif, in Pound's own voice. He was a poet as well and also an editor of other poets' work: Eliot's, Williams', H.D.'s. He shortened, refined: Hilda Doolittle becomes H.D., and the repetitious prose of *HERmione* is compressed here, made compact and paradoxical: 'Gawd's own god-damn country'.

Her's observation that 'it was incredible . . . and preposterous that George should say just that, "Gawd's own god-damn country"' (H.D., *HER*, p. 30) is never explained, but her constant repetition, as though to set the metaphorical parameters for her own identity, is not to be ignored. 'I am Hermione Gart' and 'I am Her',[17] she repeats, and this is an attempt to glue the parts of Her(self) together, the subject and object: 'Hermione Gart hugged HER to Hermione Gart. I am HER' (H.D., *HER*, p. 33). 'I am the word' ('the word was with God'), 'the word . . . Her', and 'the word AUM'. She is also 'a tree'.

'People are in things. Things are in people' (*HER*, p. 128) she repeats, and her being a tree refers at least in part to Pound's nickname for her, Dryad. 'Trees are in people. People are in trees' (p. 5). The problem is that 'she wanted to climb through walls of no visible dimension', but 'tree walls were visible' and 'in the end, walled one in' (p. 7). Pound nicknamed her H.D.; later, as she recounts in *End to Torment*, he would edit her writing ('Cut this out, shorten this line') and would 'scratch "H.D. Imagiste", in London, in the Museum tearoom, at the bottom of a typed sheet'.[18] Until she has left the land of her birth and found a new vocabulary with which she can understand and articulate her own experiences, Pound's influence is in danger of naming her, and so she repeats her names to herself. The repetition is like a mantra, and one of the words she repeats alongside 'I am' is 'AUM', the mystical syllable that she would have first encountered in the books Pound would bring her, 'Those little Wisdom of the East books' (H.D., *HER*, p. 68).

The word, both the sacred syllable and the word itself, associated with the oft-repeated 'I am' that is itself a name of God, is the business of both these poets; Pound/Lowndes' desire to name his fellow-poet on the one hand helps her refine and, on the other hand, limits and divides. She, too, must engage in the act of naming: 'you only have to address [Nurse Dennon, and any thing] by its name and it would do anything. Remove mountains. Its outer or world name is Amy Dennon. Its inner or occult name is Hamshem' (H.D., *HER*, p. 201). To learn to be a poet is to learn what poetry *does*, which is precisely a kind of naming of the as-yet unnamed. The act of poetry, the science of poetry is not scientific according to her father's and brother's definition, nor is it like the other arts. 'Science . . . failed her', 'she was no good for music'; the things she perceives might be portrayed in painting as 'green on green, one slice in a corner that made a triangle out of another different dimension' (p. 6), but 'people can not paint nor put such things to music, and science, as she saw it, had eluded her perception. Her Gart went on. "I must hurry with the letters"' (p. 6). Hurrying with the letters means getting on with the job of bringing in the letters, including the letter from George Lowndes, the man of letters; it also means that she must, herself, go on towards that science of letters that allows her to do what it is that poets do. The importance of naming, not only the *mot juste* but the occult name for things and people, for their many bodies and identities, is a central concern in all of H.D.'s prose and poetry; it is the science of magic words.

The story of Gregg, H.D., Pound, and the transition from Pennsylvania to Europe is continued in *Asphodel* and *Paint It Today*, the former picking up where *HERmione* leaves off, with the move to Europe, and the latter deeply exploring lesbian relationships in her life. 'A modern homoerotic novel of passage, *Paint It Today* focuses entirely on the young heroine's search for the "sister love" who would empower her spiritually, sexually, and creatively.'[19] In this final novel of the first trilogy, Gregg is lost and replaced with a life-companion, Winnifred Ellerman, known as Bryher. H.D. would later sum up these times thus:

> After that war, after a still-born child – and a baby, for years later, whose birth was a miracle and whose living was a wonder but who had all but taken my life – surely after a husband's subtle deflection and a friend's desertion and the falling away of an entire set of acquaintances, it seemed – surely, all this, this petty, small, provincial, already-stale war-story was excuse enough for any little after-war fling on the part of a disenchanted and frozen American woman who had been rescued from death by a last-minute friend, this strange little creature, who even then called herself Gareth [Bryher].[20]

HERmione is characteristic of H.D.'s early fiction, and contains all the elements to which she returns, and in some cases refines, in her later work. It is experimental prose, neither quite fiction nor autobiography, taking its structure from a psychological realism, delaying and distorting the narrative telling of sequential events with eddies created by fixed thoughts and instinctual or spiritual insights, conveyed in a language that flows, mutates and alters in the rolling psyche of the narrator. *HERmione* is part of a dialogue with other modernist prose works, but it also serves as a guide to her own later forays into memoir and long poetry. *Tribute to Freud*, *The Gift* and *End to Torment*, though presented as more 'true' than the fiction/memoir hybrids of which *HERmione* is representative, nevertheless use the same techniques, which must then be understood somehow to convey what to H.D. constitutes realism. In her long poems can also be found numerous examples of complete but nearly endlessly interrupted linear narratives, which convey the overall impression that the free play of the language, the lateral jumping from observation to recollection to dream to vision to narration to wordplay, *is* the experience of the work and of the life that it depicts. There is no central narrative to be interrupted, but rather, plot is one of a variety of interruptions interrupting each other, always to be encountered in pieces, and the larger structure is formed, like a web or tapestry, of the interweaving of these elements, none of which is more important or central than the other.

Majic Ring and the Delia Alton cycle

The name Delia Alton is associated with a few earlier novels, but is most closely associated with the late novels and a final, synthetic articulation of the poet's role in a warlike world. Friedman notes that Delia is 'almost an anagram for Hilda' (H.D., *Web*, p. 43), but it is also a true anagram of 'ideal', an adjective which resonates well with the concerns in this late fiction – to reconcile opposites and encounter the other. The name 'Alton' hints at that otherness, being an altered 'Aldington'. The other in all the Delia Alton novels is Hugh Dowding,[21] who only ever referred to H.D. as 'Mrs. Aldington'. H.D. frequently refers to Dowding as 'the Lone Eagle', and *Alton* is an anagram of *talon*, the claw of an eagle or bird of prey. Both the pen name and the novels are tied up in this late 'romance' with Dowding, the threads of which have not yet been disentangled. The final Delia Alton trilogy,[22] the complete story that she wrote over a lifetime, is finally available, and the consequent critical re-evaluation of her prose as it fits into her life and her life's work will be a major project for years to come.

Late in life, in large part due to the proddings of her literary executor Norman Holmes Pearson, H.D. began writing something like a true memoir and notes. Her 'H.D. by Delia Alton' is a clear summary of her own late view on her prose, while *End to Torment* is a lucid and highly readable summary of her time with Pound, especially when it is compared to the dense fictions in which he first appears like a twig in a tsunami. H.D.'s most widely read novel, *Bid Me To Live*, a memoir of the 'lost generation',[23] is a cleaned-up revision of an early unfinished work, and is in many ways her most accessible novel. It is a good starting point for those interested in her prose because it reads most like a conventional novel, the opacity and inward-gazing thrum muted, and in which the usual historical figures from her circle are easily recognisable. Though it was begun in the late 1930s (as *Madrigal*), it was finally finished in 1947, by which time she had achieved a clarity of thought about the events of thirty years earlier, being now focused on the Delia Alton cycle. Though *Bid Me To Live*'s manuscript once bore the name Delia Alton, the novel is perhaps best treated as a stand-alone, unique part of the oeuvre.

H.D. had written *The Gift*, *Tribute to Freud* and the first book of *Trilogy* by the time she began corresponding with her final initiator, Hugh Dowding. She was, more than ever, trying to 'catch something of the evanescent *light that never was* in this web, in these circles of time and these cycles of 4th dimensional myth and thought and vision' (*Majic Ring*, p. 156), and she had found another possible collaborator in Dowding. His presence would dominate the late fiction, but uniquely so in *Majic Ring*, because the disagreement that would cause their schism had not yet happened. *Majic Ring* is thus unique, in that it is highly intertextual with both the poetry and prose she was writing at the time, and at the same time it sets the template for future articulations of her mystical vision, which she felt needed modification after the failure in her communication with Dowding. As such, *Majic Ring* is the clearest, most direct articulation of H.D.'s philosophy, relatively free of self-doubt or of worry about personal affairs: it comes closest to the spirit of the final initiation that she sought all her adult life. Further, it represents the best articulation, according to her, of the story of the visionary events that had haunted her since 1920 (H.D., 'Compassionate', p. 54).

H.D. describes 'the final initiation, the integration, the final father-image that came miraculously into my life, in the person of the Air Chief Marshall Lord Howell who is the hero or *heros fatal* of the three novels, Sword, Rose, and Mystery' (H.D., 'Compassionate', p. 72); but as she writes this, she is only just rediscovering *Majic Ring* after having buried it for nearly a decade, and so only thinks of the later novels. Neither quite a memoir, a journal, a collection of correspondence, nor an occultist's dream-workbook (yet all these things, in part), *Majic Ring* ends up being the novel that she had been rewriting for over twenty years, and then forgot for a decade. 'The point is', she writes within its pages, 'I keep re-writing this book – and I can't finish it to my liking and I can't feel that I can conscientiously let the thing go altogether' (H.D., *Majic Ring*, p. 117). The story deals with visionary information she had received, in the manner of the 'overmind' messages discussed in *Notes on Thought and Vision*, the year after having written that early text (i.e. 1920): 'Actually, the pattern, the "writing" is there, I do not imagine or invent any of this' (H.D., *Majic Ring*, p. 218); but this story is only a part of *Majic Ring*, whose genre is more difficult to pinpoint than even such hybrid works as *The Gift* or *Tribute to Freud*.

Majic Ring is writing about writing. Most critical discourses on H.D. (nearly all of which unaccountably ignore *Majic Ring* in favour of other unpublished prose works) rather inappropriately describe her writing as 'palimpsestic', a somewhat awkward adjective taken from H.D.'s cue that her writing is something like a palimpsest. *Palimpsest* is an early collection of her fiction (1926), the subtitle of which defines the word as 'a parchment from which one writing has been erased to make room for another'. Usually, of course, the writings on palimpsests had little or no connection to one another, and without sophisticated technology, previous texts cannot be read, though they may fade back like ghosts over time. By the time of *Trilogy*, she speaks rather of a paradoxical 'indelible palimpsest',[24] and in *Majic Ring* she presents a set of alternative metaphors for the writing process which sees all writings coexisting in separate but linked dimensions, more like a network. The palimpsest or metaphor for writing as rewriting is itself rewritten in the later work to include all versions, all texts, as expressions aimed not at an external truth, but at the pattern through which the truth that has already been revealed in the experience can shine through, incarnate.

Writing is something akin to spiritualism for H.D., but it should not be supposed that spiritualism gave her the idea for receiving messages from other dimensions – she had come upon this idea on her own, long before any exposure to it. Spiritualism represented another step along the way, another new science, like psychoanalysis, that would help map out the invisible. H.D. presents an ever-changing set of metaphors for writing, mirroring her rewriting of events and experiences in her life, because writers have a role to play, and that role cannot be set down and codified in words because it comes straight from the invisible. The invisible gives rise to the vistas opened up by modern science – atomic processes, the subconscious – and to poetics in their original sense, as quasi-magical act that energises the reader, cleaning away layers of dead, murky thought.

The quest for 'spiritual realism' among writers/'initiates' is enacted in *Trilogy*, the last book of which tells the story of a personal illumination that rewrites an old biblical myth. This is *Pilate's Wife* remade in an ecstatic mode, free as the earlier novel is not of the *HERmione*-era preoccupation with asserting identity. With its consciousness in constant flux, from a mollusc to a worm (garden or silk) to a snake to a flock of geese, *Trilogy* sheds individual identity before it takes on the biblical story, seeking to tell it from an out-of-time perspective that makes room for alternative versions of the tale to coexist, not a palimpsest but a web or network of alternate versions.[25] *Majic Ring* comments on *Trilogy*, providing in-depth glosses of many of the images found in the poem as well as the source material, including the Book of Revelation, which is itself an account of spiritual information being recovered from a visionary experience and a commentary about the nature of texts.

If *Trilogy* is the enacting of a spell, then *Majic Ring* is the magician's workbook. The two texts support and are supported by *The Gift* and *Tribute to Freud*. *The Gift* provides H.D. with an origin myth, connecting her through mysterious circumstances to an esoteric tradition that links the spiritual secrets of Europe and the Americas. *Tribute* tells of H.D.'s transition to masterhood, thanks to the help of the Professor, whose only fear for H.D.'s health was that she wanted to 'found her own religion'.[26] H.D. knew coming out of this cleansing fire that she was not a priest or a prophet, but a writer: through writing and rewriting would she achieve her goal and find the poet's role again after its having been lost in the materialistic, positivistic cataclysm of war.

Majic Ring is an occult comedy, in that it paves the way for the final initiation enacted in *Trilogy*, while *Sword* is a spiritualistic tragedy, and the real-life failure associated with it caused H.D. to abandon largely her unique occult philosophy, replacing it with '[studying] mysticism or magic with the French writers, [Robert] Ambelain and [Augustin] Chaboseau' (H.D., 'Compassionate', p. 29). Serving at once as a collection of correspondence with Dowding, a complete catalogue of mystical visions she had received in 1920, and a journal-style real-time record of the events and research while the occult work after the 'final initiation' was at its fever-pitch, *Majic Ring* represents the philosophy that H.D. abandoned, preferring at last to be a Prospero rather than a Faust.

At the height of her faith, H.D. believed that she had been in contact with a master from the higher realms, probably the same multi-dimensional entity that had appeared one zodiac cycle ago as Jesus, who was making preparations to incarnate in order to bring about the new dispensation – the Age of Aquarius. Because of H.D.'s heritage (her 'Gift'), her profession (a writer) and her initiations (through the minor initiators, Freud, and Dowding), the entity had contacted *her*. 'His' first disguise was Peter Van Eck[27] aboard the *Borodino* in 1920. Though she had not yet been ready, years later as she was finally learning to write the definitive version of the story, the entity contacted her again in a dream as 'Amen' (who appears in both *Majic Ring* and *Trilogy*) and through the séance table as Z, who would send her coded messages. Because H.D. believed Dowding to be the final initiator, and because he, too, was in contact with Z, she believed that they were destined to work together to bring about the new dispensation, which would allow her, presumably through her writing, to help usher in a new global consciousness that would help, in turn, to usher in an era of peace.

Amen's 'presence' in *Trilogy* is a healing one; her old self becomes a 'shroud' that she wears, both a death-wrap and a cocoon (H.D., *Trilogy*, p. 20). 'I speak of myself individually / but I was surrounded by companions / in this mystery' (p. 20), she notes, suggesting the London séance circle, particularly Ben Manisi (Arthur Bhaduri), who in *Majic Ring* is shown to have also dreamed of Amen, and to recognise his Egyptian connections. She is also referring to the other writers engaged in bringing about this new dispensation out of the invisible realms; these 'companions / of the flame' (p. 21) serve the invisible, and are beyond 'your good and evil' (p. 20). The revelations come by way of the Dream, which is the avatar of the Holy Spirit in *The Gift*, *Majic Ring*, *Tribute to Freud* and *Trilogy*; it serves as the medium by which events distant in space and time are joined in a four-dimensional network: 'it merges the distant future / with most distant antiquity' (p. 29). When Amen first appears out of the Dream in *Trilogy*, he orders a rebirth, identifying himself first with Aries the ram, and with the young lamb (p. 30), and then at the end of 'The Walls Do Not Fall' with Christ and the fish (p. 39); the complicated web of astrological, alchemical and other esoteric symbolism in the poem is explained by the long passages in *Majic Ring* that reveal that Amen is one avatar of the same entity that appeared in the last astrological age as Jesus. At the point he last appeared he was closing the age of Aries the Ram as a sacrificial lamb, and opening the age of Pisces in the symbol of the fish. Now, in the new dispensation, the phoneme *nu* is hidden in the name Zakenuto, whose glyph in Egyptian hieroglyphs is identical to the symbol for the sign of Aquarius, the New Age. Such a reading of *Trilogy* would be inconceivable without a close reading of the material in *Majic Ring*, whose complex web of ideas only makes sense in action in the verse of *Trilogy*. This is only one of the many obscure passages in the poem that are surprisingly and specifically illuminated by a reading of *Majic Ring*; the lady, the triad of animals, the vision of the Kaspar as well as the fleck in the jewel in the crown, and H.D.'s idiosyncratic readings of seemingly familiar mythic references make up the bulk of the novel.

Majic Ring ends with a problem: 'Perhaps the woman on the boat going to Greece, in the early spring of 1920, did see God. Possibly, the girl and the woman did see projections of the white light that is final illumination'

(H.D., *Majic Ring*, p. 209), but 'there was separateness' in that, even though it was H.D. who had experienced all these things, some of them were experienced as a little girl, some of them as a younger woman, and some as an older woman. The problem of identity, wrapped up in the problem of the body, centres on the fact that even though it may be possible to achieve 'final illumination' while incarnated, it will still, paradoxically, be bound up in time. *HERmione* 'serves vividly as a microcosm of [a] larger pattern in her work', according to Friedman, because it is 'a narrative of awakening, transformation, birth' (Friedman 1990, p. 101); the novel's repetitive style, also, which repeats words and groups of words, arranging and rearranging them in similar patterns but with ever-changing content, serves as a microcosm for the larger patterns of writing and rewriting of the same story over time. It is the story of the awakening psyche – through the many levels of initiation and incarnation. The problem of incarnation, traced from the bodies in *Notes on Thought and Vision* to the not-yet-incarnated Her to the independent Ka in *Kora and Ka* to the Body of Christ in *Pilate's Wife* to the dream-bodies and avatars of *Majic Ring*, are acted out in the poetry, but *worked out* in the prose. There is a need for a great deal more scholarly attention to this and numerous not-yet-discovered themes in H.D.'s work: ultimately, the lines that divide H.D. the prose writer and H.D. the poet (not to mention her host of *noms de plume* and her birth name) need to be blurred or dissolved entirely, once all the components of the web are shown to operate as one organism.

NOTES

1 S.S. Friedman, *Penelope's Web: Gender, Modernity, H.D.'s Fiction* (Cambridge and New York: Cambridge University Press, 1990).

2 The University Press of Florida has lately published all of the late cycle that H.D. wrote under the pseudonym Delia Alton. *The Sword Went Out to Sea* was the first of these to be published, in 2007. *Majic Ring*, *The Mystery* and *The White Rose and the Red* all appeared in 2009.

3 H.D., *Notes on Thought and Vision* (San Francisco: City Lights Book, 1982), p. 26.

4 *HERmione* is representative of her earliest fiction cycle, which deals primarily with the coming of age of the poet self; *Majic Ring* is both the culmination of the 'Greek story' she tried to write for twenty-three years and the source material for the late Delia Alton cycle, as well as for much of the long poem *Trilogy*.

5 *Majic Ring*, *The Sword Went Out to Sea*, *White Rose and the Red* and *The Mystery* are variations on the same story; it should be noted, however, that H.D. seems to have crossed 'Delia Alton' off the proof of *The Mystery* and replaced it with 'H.D.' *Magic Mirror* and *Bid Me to Live* are also signed Delia Alton.

6 In her introduction to a collection of articles on H.D. recently published in *JCRT*, Colbey Reid offers a succinct summary of the nature of H.D.'s 'biographical'

literary productions and their reception by scholarly community which views authorial identity as an interpretive method with scepticism. See 'H.D. and the Archaeology of Religion', *Journal for Cultural and Religious Theory*, 10.2 (2010), 1–5 (2).

7 V. Quinn, *Hilda Doolittle (H.D.)* (New York: Twayne, 1967), p. 72.

8 H.D., *Kora and Ka and Ka with Mira-Mare* (New York: New Directions, 1996), p. 9.

9 This is a fictional study of the advent of the new world teacher, Jesus, as seen by a Roman noblewoman living in the sophisticated, syncretistic culture on the margins of the Roman Empire. An early grappling with the spiritual reality surrounding the many myths of Christ, *Pilate's Wife* reads well alongside the final third of *Trilogy*.

10 H.D., in J.A. Burke (ed.), *Pilate's Wife* (New York: New Directions, 2000), p. 118.

11 R. Duncan, *The H.D. Book* (Frontier Press, 1984), p. 132.

12 There are seven 'minor' initiators: Ezra Pound, Richard Aldington, John Cournos, D.H. Lawrence, Cecil Gray, Kenneth MacPherson and Walter Schmideberg. Erich Heydt might be an eighth, but may also be a 'charlatan'. These seven are seen as smaller stars around a central *etoile sacerdotale et royale*, representing 'the final initiation, the integration' (H.D., 'Compassionate Friendship', YCAL/ Beinecke, p. 72), which is identified with Hugh Dowding. Though not included in this list, Freud plays a major role as main gatekeeper at the portal or limen or propylaia, for without him 'I could never have faced this final stage of the initiation' (p. 31).

13 H.D., *HERmione* (New York: New Directions, 1981), p 10. Thereon abbreviated as *HER*.

14 Frances Gregg was H.D.'s first lesbian interest. The story of H.D., Gregg and Pound is continued, with the addition of other 'characters' in the sequel to *HERmione*, *Asphodel*, which sees them travel to Europe, 'where Fayne [Gregg] indeed continues to blight Hermione's artistic hopes and her emotional life, just as George Lowndes [Pound] had done'. See R. Spoo, 'Introduction', in *Asphodel* (Durham and London: Duke University Press, 1992), p. xiii.

15 Cf. her book *Psyche Reborn: The Emergence of H.D.* (Bloomington: Indiana University Press, 1981). The first half discusses H.D.'s unusual relationship with Freud, while the second is a detailed account of her lifelong involvement with the occult; unfortunately, it excludes *Majic Ring* from the discussion, thereby leaving her most detailed and explicit articulation of her occult philosophy untold.

16 It was Pound who famously called artists the 'antennae of the race'; see *ABC of Reading* (New York: New Directions), p. 73.

17 This formula repeats at another important stage of incarnation or initiation at the end of *Pilate's Wife*: 'I am Veronica' (p. 121), she states at the opening of the final chapter, and lists all the other things she is (just as one's Ka is only one of one's bodies): ultimately, in the story, she is the one who denies Jesus his wish to die, who instead saves him to keep on living. '"I am Veronica", said Veronica, realising at last, that she was that person' (p. 135) is the last sentence of the novel.

18 H.D., in N. Holmes Pearson and M. King (eds.), *End to Torment* (New York: New Directions, 1979), p. 40.

19 C. Laity, 'Introduction', in *Paint It Today* (New York and London: New York University Press, 1992), p. xvii.
20 H.D., in D.P. Tryphonopoulos (ed.), *Majic Ring* (Gainesville: University Press of Florida, 2009), p. 124.
21 Air Chief Marshal Hugh Caswell Tremenheere Dowding, First Baron Dowding, was the commander of 'the few', the Royal Air Force pilots who fought the Battle of Britain. After he retired, Dowding became increasingly interested in and involved with spiritualism. H.D. saw him speak on a couple of occasions, and began a correspondence with him on matters relating to the occult and spiritualism. Carbons of her letters to him form the first third of *Majic Ring*.
22 *The Sword Went Out to Sea*, *The White Rose and the Red* and *The Mystery*. The first of these three is a 'reassembled' version of much of the material from *Majic Ring*, but the earlier novel must not be treated as a draft of the later one, for H.D. did not refer to it when composing *Sword*; she had put *Majic Ring* away, not to be retrieved for a decade (see Tryphonopoulos, 'Introduction' in *Majic Ring*, p. xl). The later trilogy attempts to cope with the fact that Lord Dowding rejected her, whereas *Majic Ring* focuses on the occult philosophy she was constructing rather than on her personal relationship with Dowding.
23 H.D., *Bid Me to Live (A Madrigal)* (New York: Grove Press, 1960), p. 8.
24 H.D., Trilogy, in L.L. Martz (ed.), *Collected Poems 1912–1944* (New York: New Directions, 1983), p. 6.
25 'No one would know exactly how it came about' (p. 167); 'It had happened before / it would happen again' (p. 37); 'some say she slipped out and got away, / some say he followed her and found her' (p. 139); 'some say he was Abraham, / some say he was God' (p. 140).
26 H.D., *Tribute to Freud* (New York: New Directions, 1972), p. 51.
27 Pieter Rodeck was another passenger on the *Borodino*, and took H.D. and Bryher as far as the propylaea, but not into the temple of Artemis. In *Tribute to Freud*, *Majic Ring* and *The Sword Went Out to Sea*, H.D. tells the story of a seemingly hallucinated encounter with a physically altered Van Eck, who, in *Majic Ring*, is revealed to have actually been the Master disguising himself as van Eck.

10

EILEEN GREGORY

H.D. and translation

The idea and practice of translation is central to H.D.'s writing and self-conception throughout her career. Her first efforts as a poet were translations from Heine and Theocritus;[1] her first poems (1913) were translations from the Greek Anthology; her first published monograph was a translation, *Choruses from the Iphigeneia in Aulis of Euripides* (1916). This pamphlet and later 'choruses' from the *Hippolytus* (1919) were published in the Poets' Translation Series, which she helped her husband Richard Aldington to edit between 1915 and 1919. Early efforts culminated in *Collected Poems* (1925) with about ten lyric poems incorporating original translation,[2] translated 'choruses' from Euripides, and a translation of the opening lines of the *Odyssey*. Throughout the 1920s she wrote a series of essays on Greek writers and two historical narratives that incorporate translation from Greek. Her experiments continued with *Hippolytus Temporizes* (1927), an original play in close dialogue with Euripides' drama; with translations of other Euripidean choruses in *Red Roses for Bronze* (1931); and with her only translation of a complete play, *Euripides' Ion, Translated with Notes* (1937). Even at the very end of her career, after completion of *Helen in Egypt*, H.D. in a late diary (1955) was contemplating further translations of Euripides, which she apparently never initiated.[3]

Moreover, H.D. clearly imagined herself as translator, perhaps as much as poet. In autobiographical fictions – especially 'Hipparchia' in *Palimpsest* (1926) and *Bid Me to Live* (1960)[4] – she figures herself as a translator of classical poetry, an activity that in these narratives seems almost indistinguishable from original composition. Hipparchia in her translation is inspired, in an ecstatic state of 'intellectual sensuality', catching 'authentic metre [written] in the air' (pp. 77, 79); and the detailed reflection on the process of translation in *Bid Me to Live* (pp. 163–4) is perhaps the clearest statement of H.D.'s early poetics. Notably, too, H.D. takes her success as a translator of the *Ion* in 1935, after her analysis with Freud, as a sign of her recovered identity as a poet.[5]

However, if one accepts George Steiner's well-known definition – translation as 'the writing of a poem in which a poem in another language . . . is the vitalizing, shaping presence . . . its occasion, begetter, and in the literal sense, *raison d'être*'[6] – translation does not comprise a large portion of H.D.'s writing: a few lyrics (often with hidden relation to source poems), a few 'choruses', a play. Unlike Ezra Pound and Aldington, who embarked on comprehensive translation projects with didactic aims, she chose not to take on, for instance, translation of all poems of Anyte, as Aldington did – but, rather, *one* poem – or even (except in mid career) to translate a complete play. This anomaly – deliberately avoiding ordinary production in translation, and yet seeing translation as central to her work – reflects a habitual obliquity in her poetic activity. The peculiar status of translation in her writing suggests, paradoxically, the aesthetic, cultural and even religious seriousness with which she took up the task of the translator.

This last phrase alludes, of course, to the title of Walter Benjamin's 1923 essay on translation[7] and to the broader discussion of translation in the early twentieth century; and while we here focus on H.D.'s actual practice of translation, the recent flourishing of Translation Studies necessarily recasts the question. This new field – considering the work of translation in terms of its history, its theoretical paradigms and its religious and philosophical underpinnings – allows a way to bring into focus the character of H.D's investment in this activity.

The trope of translation as interpretation, as it is now approached in Translation Studies,[8] is resonant in H.D.'s career at many levels. In biographical terms, as one critic posits, 'H.D. has a natural affinity for the work of translation' in her earliest awareness of facing the 'language barrier' between male and female, father and mother, science and art. Thus her choice of expatriate status 'is a way of embracing foreignness', confirming a habitual sense of standing apart in a mode of translation.[9] Further, H.D.'s persistent fascination with signs needing decipherment points to a transferred sense of translation as hermetic clairvoyance or hermeneutics. Imagism for H.D. requires a reading and 'translating' of interiorised, occult signs; and many poems of *Sea Garden* (1916) consist in deciphering landscape for traces of presences.[10] This disposition comes to self-consciousness in her work with Freud. In *Tribute to Freud* her own habits of reading and her actual practice of literary translation are brought to bear upon the psychological work of translation, of reading dreams and symptoms so as to grasp latent content and make it manifest through telling and retelling.[11]

Moreover, H.D's efforts at classical translation expose her to many of the issues now explored in Translation Studies. In her early entry into the male domain of classicism and in the peculiarly vicious assessments of her efforts as translator,[12] she participates in the historically persistent 'metaphorics of translation' surrounding the trope of 'fidelity', which makes of the translator the betraying female, with illegitimate offspring, or else, in religious terms, the apostate, unfaithful to the spirit and the letter of the law.[13] Particularly in 'Hipparchia', set in Rome of 75 BC, H.D. shows her awareness of the hidden role of translation within the 'survival of the classics',[14] as the enslaved Greek poet here is translating Greek poems into Latin from manuscripts available through Rome's conquests. In this narrative, too, H.D. links the labour of translation with imperial appropriation, as well as with the historical experience of war and diaspora.[15] Moreover, her understanding of translation as hermetic and visionary, in the context of a religious sense of cultural regeneration, shares obliquely in gnostic traditions such as those articulated by Benjamin.[16]

In literary terms, critics have recently recognised the centrality of translation within modernism.[17] Translation of classical texts was especially important, in a modernist effort to return to western origins, to revitalise a sense of the literary past. However, it was especially charged, transpiring within an arena in which differing models of nineteenth-century romantic Hellenism confronted the stringent and ascetic classicism proposed by T.E. Hulme, T.S. Eliot and Pound. This modern revival of classicism, as a purification of style as well as a reversal of cultural decadence, set itself against the romanticism of most nineteenth-century predecessors. Moreover, as many have noted, it was a highly gendered debate, in which the old romanticism was figured as feminine, and the new classicism as masculine. H.D.'s early writing, and especially her efforts as a translator, entered this arena of debate, taking place in the pages of the *Egoist* and the other little magazines in which her poetry first appeared. Her status as a woman writer in these polemical terms was highly ambiguous, and her Hellenism manifest at once the new asceticism and the old strains of Shelley, Pater and Swinburne.[18]

Modernist writers saw translation as a literary mode in its own right, embracing it as part of an ambitious agenda of cultural renewal. They shared Benjamin's belief that a translator, in 'giv[ing] voice' to the intention of the original text, offers in the translation 'a supplement to the language in which it expresses itself'. He thereby serves the 'afterlife' of the text – the continuance of its accrued value in time – and enriches the present language (Benjamin 1923, pp. 21, 16). Steven G. Yao, in his recent study of translation within modernism, concludes: 'As both a compositional procedure and a conceptual structure . . . translation informs the entire range of modernist literary production.' Yao is the first to place H.D. firmly with other modernists in this regard, arguing that translation is formative of her poetics and that she pursues it 'as a uniquely generative literary mode', one that serves to contest masculinist biases in both modernism and the classical tradition (Yao 2002, p. 8).[19]

In these contexts, one may better assess the specific character of H.D.'s work as translator. Critics giving close attention to her translations have been relatively few,[20] and, as Yao points out (pp. 84–6), these follow a traditional antithesis, between 'fidelity' on the one hand and poetic originality on the other. I here bypass this question of fidelity and the various degrees of it ('strict' or 'loose' or 'creative' translation, 'adaptation', etc.). Rather, I attempt, more broadly, to define distinct aspects of H.D.'s translation and its implications in her other writing.

In her efforts as a translator, H.D. is distinct from both predecessors and contemporaries. In blunt terms, she is simply uninterested in translation in the ordinary sense, such as the smooth cribs in the Poets' Translation Series, Anyte and Meleager by Aldington, or Sappho by Edward Storer. Julia Ashton in *Bid Me to Live* 'brooded over each word, as if to hatch it. Then she tried to forget each word, for "translations" enough existed' (p. 163). H.D. here follows her own ways, just as in her insistently revisionary play with genre. As many have noted, her choice itself of texts and writers, in the context of modernist classicism, was politically resistant, focusing on Sappho, other Greek women poets, and male classical poets associated with a 'feminine' tradition, Euripides, Meleager and Theocritus.[21] She was an intelligent reader of her few chosen texts, in her early years engaging them at a minute lexical level, with acute awareness of sound and cadences. However, she intends neither 'faithful' reproduction nor pure originality, but some *tertium quid*. In her later Euripidean translation and interplay – *Euripides' Ion* and *Helen in Egypt* – she works less with the original Greek and more with intermediary bilingual translations in French, again, however, following her own purposes.

H.D. in her earliest translations discovers procedures that remain in play and further develop throughout her career. One of these might be called field translation. Though H.D.'s first poems published in *Poetry* were named as translations, strictly speaking they are poems that embed the translation of an epigram, and, even more accurately, they are amalgams of epigrams. In 'Hermes of the Ways', one may clearly discern the translation of a poem by Anyte; in 'Orchard', one by Dioscoros Zonas; and in 'Hermonax', one by Antipater of Sidon. However, for each of these poems, other epigrams from her source text, a dual-language edition edited by J.W. Mackail,[22] are suggested as well – for instance, another poem in Mackail entitled 'Hermes of the Ways'. More broadly, these poems reflect and condense a 'field' – the groupings in Mackail of epigrams, particularly under the headings, 'Prayers and Dedications', 'Religion' and 'Nature'. In effect, these poems establish an allusive, intertextual space, suggestive of much beyond the actual epigram translated. The topography of *Sea Garden* is to some degree a projection generated from Mackail's unified groupings – cliff temples, shoreline and sea-wash, cool brooks, shady trees, small homely things offered as tributes. This practice of establishing an allusive field holds true for the epithalamic lyrics of 'Hymen', which amalgamate fragments of Sappho's poems. On a larger scale, *Helen in Egypt* takes not primarily Homer but several Euripidean texts as an allusive field, not only the *Helen* but almost all the other plays treating the matter of Troy – *Andromache*, *Trojan Women*, *Iphigeneia at Aulis*, *Iphigeneia in Tauris*, *Hecuba*, *Electra* and *Orestes*.[23]

As another founding procedure, these early lyrics and choruses establish a spatiality far beyond the indications of the source text. This sharp concreteness, suggesting an active ritual of orientation, partly accounts for the power of these poems. Daniel Hooley, in his remarks on modernist translation, notes that in an era of increasing ignorance of classical languages and texts, modernists found that 'the literary heritage became less a burden and a curse than a terra incognita, an intellectual geography rendered strange and new' (Hooley 1988, p. 24). H.D. certainly understands this sense of estrangement, made more acute with a new sense, through anthropology, of archaic deities and rituals. These early translations seem to transpire within such a terra incognita.

The opening lines of the *Choruses from Iphigeneia* suggest not simply detached spectacle but sensory engagement and spatial orientation. Below is a literal translation of lines from the first chorus, followed by H.D.'s translation:

> I came to the sandy seashore of Aulis by the sea, pushing through the rushing strait of Euripos, forsaking my city Chalkis, nursed by the seaside waters of renowned Arethusa, that I might see the army of the noble Achaeans and the ship-speeding oars of the heroes . . .

I crossed sand-hills.
I stand among the sea-drift before Aulis.
I crossed Euripos' strait –
Foam hissed after my boat.

I left Chalkis,
My city and the rock-ledges.
Arethusa twists among the boulders,
Increases – cuts into the surf.

I come to see the battle-line
And the ships rowed here
By these spirits –
The Greeks are but half-man.[24]

Clear spatial features are indicated in the Greek text – sand, shore, sea, the hissing strait separating Aulis and Chalkis, Chalkis itself with its sea-cliffs and a river cutting into the sea-line. However, H.D. brings them to the fore, sharpening them, and, through abrupt syntax, short lines and anaphora, suggesting an incantatory summoning of place. Early lyric poems, such as 'Hermes of the Ways', are likewise cosmogonic. The physical location of the herm suggested in an epigram by Anyte – 'I Hermes, stand here by the windy orchard in the cross-ways nigh the grey sea-shore'[25] – becomes in 'Hermes of the Ways' 'the sensory, whirling, vectored space of part I (west, east, front) and the more static but differentiated space of part II (stream *below* ground, poplar-shaded hill *above*, sea foaming *around*)' (Gregory 1992, p. 169).

This cosmogonic feature of the early translations and poems remains an element within H.D.'s Hellenic fascination. It is not simply, as critics have suggested, an imagist focus on visualisation; rather, it is something like an archaic instinct to discover and orient oneself to sources of power – particularly powers within her imagined Hellenic cosmos. The orientation to the heights in early poems such as 'Shrine' and 'Cliff Temple' is reiterated in the opening of *Hippolytus Temporizes*, set where a wild ravine cuts down to the seashore; and in the opening of the *Ion*, with Ion's sky-seeking prayer to Apollo at the temple below Parnassus. The orientation to the sea and the liminal space of the shore, present throughout the early poems ('Helmsman', 'Wind Sleepers', the sea-flower poems and others) is ubiquitous within H.D.'s Hellenic writing. An unpublished essay on Euripides' *Helen*[26] opens with a vectored landscape identical to that of the first Iphigeneia chorus, the shoreline with intercepting river; *Hippolytus Temporizes* transpires on the shore; and *Helen in Egypt*, too, opens on a desolate beach.

A significant formal invention comes from H.D.'s early translation – what she repeatedly called the 'choros', 'choros-sequence' or 'choros-series' – and, along with it, experiments in lyric voice. Her early 'choruses' – an amalgam of the choral odes with some monologues in lyric metres – represent a lyric sequence. This form allows H.D. an oblique lyric rendering of dramatic action, one which, especially in Euripides, is highly imagistic and affective. Spatial and temporal dimensions are likewise complex, since the chorus shifts between a mythical past, a present witnessing, and an emotionally charged projection of the future.

Moreover, this form in H.D.'s practice allows her to explore lyric polyphony – the choral voice put beside monologues and dialogues, thus creating a persistent shift and reorientation of voice and consciousness. Another kind of polyphony is suggested in the choral voice itself, which is simultaneously 'I' – with a distinct set of emotions, perceptions and responses – and 'we'. This paradoxical collective voice is one of the richest of H.D.'s lyric discoveries, discernible in poems throughout *Sea Garden*; in the epithalamic songs of 'Hymen', presented as a ritual procession; and in poems such as 'The Helmsman' and 'Adonis', with their unsettling inclusion of the reader in their collective 'we'. Moreover, this collective voice can and does serve epic ventures, making possible in the longer poems a powerful public address and a spatial and temporal mobility. Arguably the magisterial command of collective voice in H.D.'s *Trilogy* finds its technical grounding in the choros-sequence, as does the shifting play of voices in *Helen in Egypt*.

The complexity of the choral 'I' is related to another element of voice in H.D.'s translations, and, more broadly, to a 'dialogic' quality, present in early and late writing. I use this word in several senses, but largely to suggest the way that H.D. establishes relationship with a text. Hooley proposes that the ancient texts, while distant from the modern world, are also constitutive of it, and thus they are 'continuously *proposing* themselves, requiring acknowledgement', and this reciprocation entails 'a concurrence and engagement of different sensibilities, an almost literal touching of minds past and present'. Thus, classical translation, Hooley says, is 'a fusion of interrogative and declarative modes' (p. 22). This formulation suggests the notion of translation as a dynamic, dialogic human activity.

The interchange not simply with a text but with a mind perhaps long since dead constitutes the excitement of what Kenneth Rexroth calls 'the living relationship of translation'.[27] This privileged imaginative experience – which H.D. knew from her earliest years – may explain why translation remained a precious activity to her, tied to deepest friendships and pivotal to her self-conception. Rexroth in his attempt to suggest this 'living relationship' cites the whole of H.D.'s poem 'Heliodora', which to him conveys the feeling of possession by the Greek words (p. 28). This poem, which takes the form of a narrated exchange between two classical poets (one of them the unnamed Meleager) vying to find the words for a tribute to Heliodora, ostensibly concerns original poetic composition; but it is simultaneously, as Rexroth sees, about the passion within the labour to translate, to find the phrase that will suffice as a true token of the original:

> He and I sought together,
> over the spattered table,
> rhymes and flowers,
> gifts for a name . . .

We strove for a name,
while the light of the lamps burnt thin
and the outer dawn came in,
a ghost, the last at the feast
or the first,
to sit within
with the two that remained
to quibble in flowers and verse
over a girl's name.

In this collaboration, with its absorbing urgency, the moment of illumination does come: 'I waited, even as he spoke, / to see the room filled with light, / as when in winter / the embers catch in a wind / when a room is dank' (H.D., *CP*, pp. 151–2). While in the poem's narrative, Meleager is possessed by the muse, at another level, H.D. as poet is here possessed with Meleager, and the poem concludes with her own translation of one of his most famous epigrams (*Palatine Anthology* 5.147), with its catalogue of epithets for flowers.

H.D. persistently seeks this dialogic relationship. She is bold in gestures that attempt to engage a classical text in an almost intimate way. Most notably, in almost all of her lyric translations, H.D. radically alters voice, most often from an impersonal voice to a lyric 'I'. This 'I', in effect, speaks back to the original text from the ground of its 'afterlife'. In 'Hermes of the Ways' and 'Orchard', H.D. shifts from the voice of the god (Hermes and Priapus) to a lyric 'I' that summons and propitiates it. Similarly dramatic reversals occur in other poems, such as in 'Epigram', when a lyric 'I' is shifted to an impersonal voice.

In another form of dialogic response, H.D. in both 'Evadne' and 'Thetis' (in *Hymen*) opens out a passage embedded in a classical narrative detailing a woman's rape. Here H.D. speaks back to Pindar (the source of 'Evadne') and Ovid (the source of 'Thetis') by creating, in a figure originally noted in passing, an interiority and presence. Where in Ovid a narrator notes a grotto to which 'Thetis used to come, naked, astride / Her bridled dolphin',[28] the voice in H.D.'s poem (H.D., *CP*, pp. 116–18) addresses Thetis in the intimate second person and in the present tense ('you will step carefully / from amber stones to onyx . . . You will pass / beneath the island disk'), imagining her descent into water, the power of the dolphin constrained by elegant artifice (the 'jewelled halter / and harness and bit') and its swaying movement beneath her. This intimacy is all the more powerful when put beside Ovid's text, in which this scene immediately precedes Thetis' violent rape by Peleus.

This 'living relationship of translation' occurred for H.D. with two writers pre-eminently – Sappho and Euripides. Her dialogic exchange with these poets was profound. In the case of Sappho, it was indeed too deep for words, because she translated not a single fragment, while her work with Euripides was publicly manifest from first to last.

H.D. responded to Sappho's poetry with acuteness and insight. Her essay 'The Wise Sappho' (written in 1920)[29] suggests, in my view, an understanding of Sappho's aesthetic and range far beyond the sometimes crude fantasies or arcane scholarship of her own day. Apart from Euripides, Sappho is the deepest classical presence in her writing, as Diana Collecott's work has shown.[30] H.D.'s poetic engagement with Sappho takes place at two very different registers. In her six 'fragment poems', she plays upon the words of a fragment cited in the subtitle, given in the translation of H.L. Wharton, her source text.[31] However, these poems – citing 'Sappho' as the mistress of erotic crisis – follow a conventional literary *topos*; and they are more in dialogue with nineteenth-century poets, pre-eminently Swinburne, than with Sappho's own poetry. One finds a different kind of textual engagement in the epithalamic poems of 'Hymen'. Here, H.D. arguably comes closest to 'translating' Sappho, in that she conveys something like the restraint, clarity, elegance and poignancy of the ancient poet. These lyrics synthesise countless Sapphic fragments about the loveliness and grace of girls and women, their distinct beauty signified by flowers. 'Hymen' as a whole – figured as a procession of women's choruses accompanying the bride to the nuptial chamber – acknowledges the ritualised, religious character of Sappho's writing.

The second of these songs, representing the voices of 'very little girls' gathering flowers, may serve as an example:

> Where the first crocus buds unfold
> We found these petals near the cold
>   Swift river-bed.
>
> Beneath the rocks where ivy-frond
> Puts forth new leaves to gleam beyond
>   Those lately dead:
>
> The very smallest two or three
> Of gold (gold pale as ivory)
>   We gatherèd.   (H.D., *CP*, pp. 102–3)

H.D. responds here to at least two fragments given in Wharton: 'A maiden [*pais*, child] full tender plucking flowers'; and 'I have a fair daughter [*pais*] with a form like a golden flower, Cleïs, the beloved.'[32] H.D. here returns delicacy with delicacy. She finds flowers for this first tenderness, the 'first crocus buds' unfolding in earliest, chilly spring. She comprehends the goldenness of first beauty, Cleïs like a golden flower, but responds with her own discrimination, gold that is almost white, 'pale as ivory'. She grasps Sappho's own implicit allusion – in the tender child gathering flowers – to Persephone at the threshold of death: 'new leaves to gleam beyond / Those lately dead'. The lyric's simplicity of form – a curtal Sapphic stanza, one might call it – is a metonym for the loveliness but also of the sharpness, crispness, of the first flowers and of the child. This poem, like many other early lyrics, shows a dialogue with Sappho in her own terms – affective discreteness, discrimination of beauty, elegance of language and form.

We have already suggested the importance of H.D.'s translations of Euripides. However, *Hippolytus Temporizes* is distinct in the intimacy of its textual dialogue with the *Hippolytus*, constituting a response that discerns and extrapolates its mappings of desire. However, this dialogue with the play is to some degree a 'translation' of a translation, her own 'choruses' from *Hippolytus* serving to mediate and to shape her later play. That early lyric sequence constitutes a kind of dream reflection of the drive of the plot, delineating the opposing daimonic powers that govern it and the mortals who suffer from possession by them. The chorus-sequence begins with Hippolytus' prayer to Artemis, but subsequently the selected passages follow the unfolding of Aphrodite's irresistible power, her possession of Phaedra and the subsequent destruction of Hippolytus. The choruses offer a clue to the trajectories that H.D. follows in *Hippolytus Temporizes*. Euripides' play seems to concern antithetical powers governing human desire – Artemis, withdrawn, natural and chaste, versus Aphrodite, intimate, refined, sensual. However, H.D.'s choruses point to the likeness of these goddesses – equally absolute, equally possessive, equally destructive in the compulsiveness they inspire. Thus, *Hippolytus Temporizes*, in H.D.'s dialogue with Euripides, sees an erotic confusion at the centre of the play, the fact that desire as it is suffered and as it transports one cannot be differentiated.

Hooley offers yet another clue to the peculiar place of translation in H.D.'s writing. It is insufficient, he says, to think of translation as a diachronic process – first, the original text, followed by a derivative one. In reality this process is synchronic: 'the translating poet must hold both texts in mind, in a kind of synthetic, creative present'. Moreover, 'the translator must balance his voice over against that of his precursor and in so doing gives both poems a degree of openness, a kinetic interconnectedness'. I take Hooley's notion of this 'composite intertextuality' and 'fluid interconnectedness' (p. 26) as a trope, in order to suggest that for H.D., translation is sometimes associated with a kind of textual symbiosis. H.D. imagines not simply living *with* texts, but – for certain fateful ones – living *in* them, as part of the fabric of one's temporality and one's horizons. This sense of textual symbiosis is, of course, especially true of H.D.'s lifelong work with Euripides. Chosen texts by him – especially the *Ion* and the *Helen* – were almost indistinguishable for her from actual memories and life-patterns. In most obvious terms, she lived through the wars with him, and he is consistently her cohort in her efforts to contend with and reflect upon war. More viscerally, the trauma of the war years is literally tied to him, as she was persistently translating his plays between 1915 and 1919, throughout her displacements, her suppressed grief, her husband's and her own infidelity, her pregnancies and her illness. H.D. might have been translating Euripides during the first months of the war and during her first pregnancy, issuing in a stillbirth in May 1915, and certainly during the summer after this death, when the first prospectus for the Poets' Translation Series appeared; *Choruses from the Iphigeneia in Aulis* was first published in November 1915. In the next year, H.D. was translating the *Ion* in Devon and Corfe Castle, during the time of Aldington's affair with Flo Fallas and during the displacement caused by his officer's training.[33] Both 'Hipparchia' and *Bid Me to Live*, referring to subsequent events in 1917 through 1919 – Aldington's affair with Dorothy Yorke, H.D.'s affair with Cecil Gray, her pregnancy and her illness from influenza – show the H.D. figure translating choruses while with her lover (Verrus and Vane, respectively) (H.D., *Palimpsest*, p. 73; *Bid Me to Live*, p. 162). Choruses from the *Hippolytus* appeared in 1919.

Perhaps because of this association, Euripides is profoundly implicated in H.D.'s psychological life – pivotally in the 'writing on the wall' episode in Corfu, Greece, 1920 – narrated in *Tribute to Freud*.[34] In a waking dream, she saw a series of images appear as though projected on the wall. This episode, in which Freud recognised dangerous symptoms, became one of the cruxes in her analysis with him. However, this 'writing' translates/displaces images of the *Ion* – young man, chalice, tripod, Nike and sun disk. She had been studying and translating this text for three or four years by this point in 1920, and a copy of it lay at that moment on her bedside table (H.D., *Tribute*, p. 167).[35] This oneiric intertextuality with the Euripidean poem determines a path which is stunningly fateful.

Thus, it is fitting that H.D. turns to a full translation of the *Ion* in 1934 and 1935 as a postlude to her Freudian analysis. Beyond its place in her psychological work, Aliki Caloyeras argues, the play may have fascinated H.D. for so long (almost two decades) because it suggests a trope for translation itself – translation as the illegitimate offspring of the paternal original: 'By translating the play, she could work through her complicated and ambivalent feelings toward being a woman poet/translator.' Moreover, Caloyeras points out that the plot is propelled by 'translations' in the Freudian sense – tellings and retellings of a central traumatic event, the rape of Kreousa (pp. 4, 6–24). Yet another layering of translation as interpretation takes place in H.D.'s version in the interspersed commentary that attempts to guide the reader's attention. In this sometimes strained effort, H.D. attests to the burden of her own long textual symbiosis with the play and the weight of meaning it has accrued for her.

H.D.'s lived association with Euripides' *Helen* is at least as long and as deep as that with the *Ion*,[36] and perhaps deeper, because, as with Sappho, it is to some degree hidden. She never made public her translation of a single line of it, destroying an early attempt and avoiding any translation in her early essay on the play. However, she clearly understood her *Helen in Egypt* as an effort to speak to Euripides' play and work out her relationship with it.[37] While that symbiotic importance is difficult to summarise briefly, it comprises the accrued significance of Hellas, associated with maternal nostalgia (her mother's name was Helen), and overlaid with a network of patterns tied to war and to erotic triangulation. One may justly consider *Helen in Egypt* as H.D.'s long-gestating translation of the *Helen* – but translation in the many transferred senses of her *Ion*. This poem is explicitly concerned with translation in complex ways,[38] as Helen – herself a text constantly subject to translation by others – becomes herself a reader and translator. Moreover, as in her *Ion*, H.D. here provides another layer of translation in the headnotes to the sections, in which a commentator mediates between the reader and the lyrics, deciphering their signs.

A poem from mid career, 'Chance Meeting', opens: 'Take from me something, / be it all too fine / and untranslatable and worthless / for your purpose' (H.D., *CP*, p. 231). This quotation suggests the centrality of translation for H.D., not simply as a poetic practice but as a guiding trope. It also raises the issue of translatability – what is or is not translatable – and of purpose – to what end one translates. These questions might serve to suggest the trajectory of translation in H.D.'s career. The early H.D. was exhilarated by the untranslatable – by the 'rose cut in rock' that cannot be broken (H.D., 'Garden', *CP*, pp. 24–5). Power belonged to a text to the degree that it resisted translation. Nevertheless, one 'strove for a name', laboured with the untranslatable, and with no purpose but to find what would suffice. However, the later H.D. – especially after Freud – has to a degree transcended the untranslatable, possessing a meta-language in which crucial mysteries can be decoded. Moreover, she translates with a purpose, a didactic aim that exceeds the text itself. This sense of assurance governs *Euripides' Ion* and *Helen in Egypt*, especially indicated in the authoritative voice of the commentator. Regardless of these distinctions, H.D.'s 'need to translate' (Caloyeras 2004, p. 4) remains central – a manifold need, at once artistic and epistemological, which governs her from beginning to end.

NOTES

1 'Autobiographical Notes', (p. 1), entry for 1910. Unpublished typescript in the Beinecke Rare Book and Manuscripts Library, Yale University.

2 These lyric poems incorporate translation of Greek or Latin texts: 'Orchard', 'Acon', 'Hermes of the Ways', 'Hermonax', 'Simaetha', 'Thetis' (in *Hymen*), 'Evadne', 'Lais', 'Heliodora', 'Nossis', 'Epigram' and 'Antipater of Sidon'.

3 In the unpublished 'Compassionate Friendship', H.D. refers to her desire to translate Euripides (pp. 23, 70). Typescript in the Beinecke Rare Book and Manuscript Library, Yale University.

4 M. Bruccoli (ed.), *Palimpsest* (Carbondale and Edwardsville: Southern Illinois University Press, 1968); and *Bid Me to Live: A Madrigal*, 2nd edn (Redding Ridge, CT: Black Swan Press, 1983). Subsequent citations of these editions will be given in parentheses in the body of the essay.

5 See her letter to Bryher, 17 August 1935, in S.S. Friedman (ed.) *Analyzing Freud: The Letters of H.D., Bryher, and Their Circle* (New York: New Directions, 2002), p. 528.

6 'Introduction', in G. Steiner (ed.), *Poem into Poem: World Poetry in Modern Verse Translation* (Harmondsworth: Penguin, 1970), p. 34.

7 'The Task of the Translator', trans. H. Zohn, in L.Venuti (ed.), *The Translation Studies Reader*, 2nd edn (London: Routledge, 2004), pp. 14–25.

8 See, especially, 'Understanding as Translation', in G. Steiner, *After Babel: Aspects of Language and Translation* (Oxford University Press, 1992), pp. 1–50.

9 A.S. Caloyeras, 'Translating Euripides: Repression, Repetition, and Transference in H.D.'s Ion', unpublished MA Thesis, New York University (2004), pp. 29–30.

10 L.S. Dembo, 'H.D. Imagiste and her Octopus Intelligence', in M. King (ed.), *H.D. Woman and Poet* (Orono, ME: The National Poetry Foundation, 1986), p. 223; A. Morris, *How to Live What to Do: H.D.'s Cultural Poetics* (Urbana: University of Illinois Press, 2003), p. 98.

11 On H.D.'s writing in terms of a Freudian notion of translation, see D. Chisholm, *H.D.'s Freudian Poetics: Psychoanalysis in Translation* (Ithaca, NY: Cornell University Press, 1992); and Caloyeros.

12 See Gregory, *H.D. and Hellenism: Classic Lines* (Cambridge and New York: Cambridge University Press, 1992), pp. 15–22 and 52–6ff., on H.D.'s place as a woman within 'classicism'. On the dismissal of her translations, see D. Bush, *Mythology and the Romantic Tradition in English Poetry* (1937), 2nd edn (Cambridge, MA: Harvard University Press, 1969), pp. 497–506.

13 L. Chamberlain outlines this paradigm in 'Gender and the Metaphorics of Translation', in L. Venuti (ed.), *The Translation Studies Reader*, 2nd edn (London: Routledge, 2004), pp. 306–18. Steiner summarises the religious paradigm underlying discussions of translation, pp. 251–6.

14 See 'Introduction' in A. Lianeri and V. Zaiko (eds.), *Translation and the Classics: Identity and Change in the History of Culture* (Oxford University Press, 2008).

15 For translation as colonisation, see Chamberlain, *Translation*, pp. 317–19; for H.D's depiction of translation within war and diaspora, see Gregory, *H.D. and Hellenism*, pp. 59–66.

16 See Steiner, *After Babel*, 62–8 ff., on Jewish mysticism in discussions of translation.
17 See, especially, D. Hooley, *The Classics in Paraphrase: Ezra Pound and Modern Translators of Latin Poetry* (London and Toronto: Associated University Presses, 1988); and S.G. Yao, *Translation and the Languages of Modernism: Gender, Politics, Language* (New York: Palgrave Macmillan, 2002).
18 On this modernist debate concerning Hellenism, see Gregory, *H.D. and Hellenism*, chapter 1.
19 For his discussion of H.D., see especially pp. 79–114.
20 See D. Carne-Ross, 'Translation and Transposition', in W. Arrowsmith and R. Shattuck (eds.), *The Craft and Context of Translation* (Austin: University of Texas Press, 1961), pp. 3–21; R.G. Babcock, 'Verses, Translations, and Reflections from "The Anthology": H.D., Ezra Pound, and the Greek Anthology', *Sagetrieb* 14 (Spring–Fall 1995), pp. 201–16; Gregory, *H.D. and Hellenism*, pp. 139–48, 158–9, 168–71, 209–11; and Yao, *Translation*, pp. 89–96, 102–5.
21 See R.B. DuPlessis, *H.D.: The Career of That Struggle* (Brighton: Harvester Press, 1986), pp. 17–30; Gregory, *H.D. and Hellenism*, pp. 139–72; and Yao, *Translation*, for a complex argument concerning H.D.'s choices of texts.
22 J.W. Mackail, *Select Epigrams from the Greek Anthology* (London: Longmans, Green, 1911).
23 See Gregory, *H.D. and Hellenism*, 218–19 ff.
24 H.D. in L.L. Martz (ed.), *Collected Poems 1912–1944* (New York: New Directions, 1983), p. 71. Subsequent citations of this edition will be given in the body of the essay as *CP*.
25 *Palatine Anthology* 9.314, trans. Mackail.
26 This essay is part of a collection entitled 'Notes on Euripides, Pausanias, and Greek Lyric Poets', located in the Beinecke Rare Book and Manuscript Library, Yale University.
27 K. Rexroth, 'The Poet as Translator', in Arrowsmith and Shattuck, *The Craft*, p. 24.
28 *Metamorphoses* 11.236–7, trans. A.D. Melville (Oxford University Press, 1986).
29 Published in *Notes on Thought and Vision and The Wise Sappho* (San Francisco: City Lights, 1982).
30 D. Collecott, *H.D. and Sapphic Modernism* (Cambridge University Press, 1999). See, especially, 'Appendix: Fragments of Sappho in H.D.'s Poetry and Prose', pp. 266–72.
31 Wharton's dual-language edition of Sappho (London: David Stott, 1885) was one of the 'Bibles' of H.D.'s generation.
32 Fragments 121 and 85, trans. Wharton; Wharton follows the numbering of Theodor Bergk (1835).
33 'Autobiographical Notes' (p. 6) indicates her work on the *Ion* in Devon, as does a letter from H.D. to J. Cournos (5 August 1916), from Corfe Castle (transcript in the Beinecke Rare Book and Manuscript Library, Yale University).
34 N.H. Pearson (ed.), *Tribute to Freud* (New York: New Directions, 1972), pp. 44–56.
35 I am indebted to Caloyeras (p. 61, n20) for calling my attention to this detail.

36 On the background of H.D.'s knowledge of the *Helen*, see Gregory, *H.D. and Hellenism*, p. 220.

37 H.D. refers to the destroyed manuscript in a letter to F. Wolle, dated 25 September 1954 (cited in Gregory *H.D. and Hellenism*, p. 282, n36), associating it with her new poem, the idea of which 'has been swimming for decades'.

38 Yao (pp. 112–14) offers a brief treatment of *Helen in Egypt* in terms of translation.

11

BRENDA S. HELT

Reading history in *The Gift* and *Tribute to Freud*

> Past, present, future, these three – but there is another time-element, popularly called the fourth-dimensional . . . This fourth dimension, though it appears variously disguised and under different subtitles, described and elaborately tabulated in the Professor's volumes . . . is yet very simple. It is as simple and inevitable in the building of time-sequence as the fourth wall to a room.[1]

By the end of the Second World War, H.D. had come to understand her writing – both poetry and prose – as prophetic. She was to mine her unconscious, her personal and family history, and Moravian American history generally, to point the way towards a future of peace built on a religious syncretism in which women's role was at least equal to that of men. The promise of that peaceful future was 'written' in history for those who knew how to read it – visionaries such as herself who had a divinely inspired 'Gift'. Psychoanalysis, H.D. believed, offered the tools she needed to access her gift for historical interpretation, but she also believed that her interpretive gift was a mystical inheritance passed down through her maternal Moravian ancestry.

In *The Gift* and *Tribute to Freud*, the relationship between history and psychoanalysis is a symbiotic one. In both works, H.D. uses psychoanalysis to 'read' history the way a fortune-teller reads cards – an analogy she uses several times in *Tribute to Freud* and a plot-sequence she invokes in the second chapter of *The Gift*, 'Fortune Teller'. H.D. derived from Freud's *The Interpretation of Dreams* her understanding of the 'fourth dimension' as a 'universal consciousness' outside time (*Tribute*, p. 71), with the precise form that consciousness might take at any given moment determined by particularities of time and place (or socio-historical space), and inflected with personal specificities.[2]

> [T]he dream came from an unexplored depth in man's consciousness . . . all nations and races met in the universal world of the dream . . . its language, its imagery were common to the whole race, not only of the living but of those ten thousand years dead . . . in the dream, man, as at the beginning of time, spoke a universal language, and man, meeting in the universal understanding of the

> unconscious or subconscious, would forgo barriers of time and space, and man, understanding man, would save mankind. (H.D., *Tribute*, pp. 70–1)

Authorised by Freud, H.D. both reads her personal history and reads history personally in search of that 'universal understanding of the unconscious', which she hopes to translate to 'save mankind'.

In her late works, H.D. recovers by reimagining lost histories (that of women like Helen of Troy in *Helen in Egypt*, for example, or the history of Moravian settlers in Pennsylvania in *The Gift*) and rethinks what constitutes 'history' by mining the universal consciousness via her personal unconscious. For H.D., history is not a fixed and knowable monolith that belongs to scholars, ethnic groups or nation states, but a multivalent and palimpsestic narrative that is communally shared but heavily imbued with the personal. Lest this seem too much like contemporary deconstructive ways of understanding history, it is important to note that, for H.D., history has a spiritual dimension discoverable through the divine inspiration of gifted artists, most of whom are not recognised as such by their contemporaries.

H.D.'s late works include those written from the time of the intensification of her interest in hermeticism (1939) and spiritualism (1941) to her death in 1961.[3] These are both challenging and fascinating because in many of them H.D. combines actual historical and autobiographical events with imaginary ones depicted as if they were verifiable facts. In *The Gift*, H.D. combines biography and autobiography with local Moravian American history and global history, mixing present and past, fiction and fact. History is further problematised in this genre-bending novel by H.D.'s inclusion of a notes section providing more information and primary source material seemingly authenticating both factual and fictional references. Similarly, in *Tribute to Freud*, past and present, fact and fiction merge in ways that expand what counts as history. Historical facts such as details about the Nazi occupation of Vienna merge with idiosyncratic remembered or reconstructed 'facts' about what happened in H.D.'s mind/psyche during and after her sessions with Freud. In this work, a look or remonstrance from Freud has as much significance and power to disturb as the swastikas chalked on the sidewalks and the rifles stacked on the street corners in Vienna (H.D., *Tribute*, pp. 16, 59). What happened and what is important are construed differently for H.D. than for practitioners of univocal, chronological, teleological, fact-based modernity – a tendency she shares with Virginia Woolf, Dorothy Richardson, Katherine Mansfield and James Joyce, not to mention Freud himself.[4] When what matters about what happened is understood in terms of events of lasting personal psychological importance (events like those Woolf called 'moments of being' or Joyce termed 'epiphanies'), what constitutes history must be rethought.[5] Unlike Woolf's or Joyce's lasting moments of psychological importance, though, H.D. understood some of her important psychological moments or episodes as revelatory not only for herself, but for all people of all times, and believed they could contain divinely inspired meanings legible to those with a special gift for reading them.[6] Such 'super-memories', as she called them, 'belong in the sense of quality and intensity, of clarity and authenticity' to 'a sort of halfway state between ordinary dream and the vision of . . . psychics or clairvoyants' (H.D., *Tribute*, p. 41). In the last twenty years of her life, H.D. came to believe that she possessed a gift for reading the collective global history inherent in her personal super-memories. *Tribute to Freud* and *The Gift* record H.D.'s attempt to understand herself as a visionary capable of conducting such readings while also demonstrating her gift for performing them.

Written in London during the Second World War, *The Gift* and *Tribute to Freud* give a sense of H.D.'s efforts to understand herself as a divinely inspired visionary or 'poet-seer' in the nineteenth-century Romantic sense traditionally reserved for male poets. In *The Gift*, H.D. reinterprets and reimagines both her childhood and her maternal ancestry, especially early eighteenth-century American Moravian history, to frame herself as a new rendition of that Romantic transcendentalist poet-seer: one who is female, American by birth and in ideology, and modern.[7] In *Tribute to Freud*, H.D. thinks through her training-analysis with Freud in Vienna in 1933 and '34, analysing her need to understand herself as a divinely inspired prophet-figure, but also disagreeing with Freud's pronouncements that such thinking is a 'dangerous symptom', a megalomaniacal tendency (H.D., *Tribute*, p. 51). For H.D., such readings or visions need not be understood as 'symptom'; they might be 'inspiration' (p. 51).

In the context of the Second World War, both *The Gift* and the epic poem *Trilogy*, also written at this time, respond to accusations of her contemporaries that art and artists serve no practical purpose during wartime.[8] In different ways, both works argue for the *increased* importance of the poet during wartime – especially the importance of the gifted female poet whose spiritually endowed vision serves as an essential corrective to the trauma of war and an opening towards eventual peace.

In November of 1939, hoping to activate or access that vision, H.D. returned from Switzerland to London, where she remained throughout the war, enduring the Blitz. Renegotiating her Moravian matrilineal ancestry and exposing her unconscious to the terrors of war, she mined both in the hope that she might prophesy a way forward into a peaceful future supported by a syncretist view of religion. Both *Tribute to Freud* and *The Gift* tell the story of a gifted poet coming to a full understanding and use of her powers to read and interpret history from an entirely new perspective.

Psycho-analytic readings: *Tribute to Freud*

In 1933, H.D. and Bryher convinced Freud to accept H.D. as an analysand and a student of psychoanalysis. H.D. hoped to overcome a writer's block and to enrich her work by exploring her unconscious. Freud was seventy-seven years old in 1933 and took on very few analysands, so to be accepted seemed to H.D. 'the high-water mark of achievement' (H.D., *Tribute*, p. 44), and she made much of the analysis – writing daily letters about it.[9] H.D.'s pride in being Freud's student and her strong affection for him as a person are clear in both the letters and the *Tribute*. Equally clear, however, is H.D.'s reluctance to grant Freud's omniscience in the realm of the unconscious; her memoir of these sessions alternates between praise for the 'intimate revelation' of the 'ironic Delphic oracle' and resistance to Freud's tenets: 'I was a student, working under the direction of the greatest mind of this and of perhaps many succeeding generations. But the Professor was not always right' (H.D., *Tribute*, pp. 72–3, 18).[10] H.D. believed that she, too, was a theorist of the human psyche, and that, as a poet, a woman, a Moravian American and a Christian, she had interpretive gifts equal to but different from those of Freud: 'my form of rightness, my intuition, sometimes functioned by the split-second . . . the quicker. I was swifter in some intuitive instances, and sometimes a small tendril of a root from that great common Tree of Knowledge went deeper into the sub-soil' (*Tribute*, p. 98). Freud, she understands,

> had brought the past into the present with his *the childhood of the individual is the childhood of the race* . . . prov[ing] that the traits and tendencies of obscure aboriginal tribes, as well as the shape and substance of the rituals of vanished civilizations, were still inherent in the human mind . . . But according to his theories the soul . . . showed its form and shape in and through the medium of the mind, and the body, as affected by the mind's ecstasies or disorders. (H.D., *Tribute*, pp. 12–13)

For H.D., however, the soul has a spiritual essence beyond the earthly: 'I had accepted as part of my racial, my religious inheritance, the abstract idea of immortality, of the personal soul's existence in some form or other, after it has shed the outworn or outgrown body.' She struggled with Freud's atheism: 'It worried me to feel that he had no idea . . . that he would "wake up" when he shed the frail locust-husk of his years, and find himself alive' (H.D., *Tribute*, p. 43). For H.D., 'there is another region of cause and effect, another region of question and answer' (p. 99). That region is spiritual, and so inaccessible by scientific method alone. Nevertheless, she needed Freud's insights, she felt, to fully develop her own:

> My own skinny hand would lay, as it were, the cards on the table . . . here with the old Professor. He was more than the world thought him – that I well knew. If he could not 'tell my fortune', nobody else could. He would not call it telling fortunes – heaven forbid! But we would lead up to the occult phenomena, we would show him how it happened. (p. 40)

Insightful though they often were, Freud's authoritative pronouncements must be handled with care, H.D. believed, for they sometimes contained within them the power to 'break something' in a person, as she put it, and she felt that 'something . . . would not, must not be broken' (H.D., *Tribute*, p. 16). Arguably, that 'something' H.D. felt she could not have broken was her faith in her ability to see differently as a *female* visionary – to read her personal and family history in terms both historical and spiritual, but against the grain of canonical patriarchal history and religion. Freud could help her, she believed, for 'the Professor himself is uncanonical enough' (p. 15); but in both the *Tribute* and the letters she wrote during the analysis, H.D. repeatedly juxtaposes Freud's insights with an insistence on the primacy of her own vision.

When H.D. writes of her 'vision' in the last twenty years of her life, that word must be understood to refer to her belief that she was *literally* a visionary – that she experienced divinely inspired visions she characterised as 'real': 'here and there a memory or a fragment of a dream-picture is actual, is real, is like a work of art or is a work of art' (H.D., *Tribute*, p. 35). H.D. adapts from Freud's theories a belief that, like works of art, certain personal experiences and perceptions draw their power to attract from the universal consciousness, so are socio-historically significant while also signifying outside of or beyond time.[11] Unlike Freud, though, H.D. understood the universal consciousness in supernatural and spiritual terms: 'For things had happened in my life, pictures, "real dreams", actual psychic or occult experiences that were superficially, at least, outside the province of established psychoanalysis' (H.D., *Tribute*, p. 39). Her work with Freud helped her interpret and distinguish between 'trivial' or 'confused' visions and those that are 'real', which contain both historical and 'healing' spiritual meaning: 'Those memories, visions, dreams, reveries – or what you will – are different. Their texture is different, the effect they have on mind and body is different. They are healing. They are real' (p. 35). They come, moreover, 'from the same source as the script or Scripture, the Holy Writ or Word' (p. 36). This insistence on both the reality and the divine source of certain visionary experiences should be understood not as metaphorical, but metaphysical – in light of H.D.'s late work and her burgeoning interest in mysticism and spiritualism.[12] In *Tribute*, H.D. is still working to understand herself as possessing psychic powers at the same time that she is analysing her psychological need for such a self-understanding.

In the *Tribute*, H.D. mediates Freudian theory to analyse her personal familial history in larger ahistorical terms, while simultaneously resisting the scientific atheism of Freud's methodology: 'We touched lightly on some of the more abstruse transcendental problems, it is true, but we related them to the familiar family-complex' (pp. 13–14).[13] H.D. understands 'super-memories' of her familial past as replicating classical historical 'patterns' that are also ahistorical or 'Heavenly' patterns. A memory of her older brother and herself sitting on a curb in Bethlehem, Pennsylvania, defying their mother, for example, forms 'a little group, design, an image at the cross-roads', and therefore links with a historicity that is beyond history in that it is a recurring pattern appearing in 'Greek tragedies', 'Grimm's tales' and even Egyptian myth (p. 29). Likewise, her memory of playing with a doll in her father's study is a super-memory with meaning both inside and outside history:

> A girl-child, a doll, an aloof and silent father form this triangle, this family romance, this trinity which follows the recognized religious pattern: *Father*, aloof, distant, the provider, the protector – but a little un-get-at-able, a little too far away and giant-like in proportion . . .; *Mother*, a virgin, the Virgin, that is, an untouched child, adoring, with faith, building a dream . . . symbolized by the third member of the trinity, the *Child*, the doll in her arms. (p. 38)

Such super-memories from childhood link not only to Freud's 'family romance', but also to the version of the Christian trinity celebrated by H.D.'s Moravian Christian maternal ancestors in the eighteenth century, for whom the Virgin Mary was symbolic of the Holy Spirit, and the Holy Spirit was female.

The two most significant examples of 'memories, visions, dreams, reveries – or what you will' that H.D. 'reads' or interprets in the *Tribute* are a vision she had in Greece in 1920 and what she calls 'the dream of the Princess' – a dream about the Pharaoh's daughter finding Moses in the bulrushes, which she had in Vienna in 1933, during her analysis (*Tribute*, p. 36). H.D.'s relation of these experiences shows her working to understand herself as a visionary in spite of Freud's disagreement with her belief in the occult or supernatural: 'He dismissed my suggestion of some connection with the old mysteries, magic or second-sight' (p. 173). In both cases, however, H.D. registers both Freud's reading and her own, carefully considering but sometimes rejecting Freud's interpretations. 'He said a dream sometimes showed a "corner", but I argued that this dream was a finality, an absolute, or a synthesis' (p. 119). Further, while H.D. understands Freud as the discoverer of the fourth dimension or universal consciousness, she implies throughout the *Tribute* that his conclusions require augmentation by someone who reads 'uncanonically' – someone like her (p. 15); so although Freud interpreted H.D.'s Princess dream to suggest that she wished to start a new religion, H.D. believed that it was Freud, not herself, who was symbolised by Moses in her dream: 'Obviously it was he, who was that light out of Egypt' (p. 119). Her role, she believed, was to further Freud's work in a way not yet clear: 'Is it possible that I (leaping over every sort of intellectual impediment and obstacle) not wished only, but *knew*, the Professor would be born again?' (p. 39). Having intimated early in the *Tribute* that she hoped to take the place of another student/analysand (killed in a plane crash) whom Freud had seen as the one who would 'carry on [his] ideas, but not in a stereotyped way' (p. 6), H.D. here implies that Freud's work might live again in her interpretations – a project she carried out in the *Tribute*, and less obviously in her epic poems *Trilogy* and *Helen in Egypt*.

The interpretation of super-memories and dreams may have occasioned interesting debates between the psychoanalyst and the poet, but when H.D. relayed the details of what she believed to have been a supernatural vision, Freud was disturbed; this, according to H.D., he considered a 'dangerous tendency or symptom' (H.D., *Tribute*, p. 41). H.D. occasionally alludes to what she called the 'writing-on-the-wall' vision in her work from the time of its occurrence in Corfu in 1920 and after, but only details the story fully in the *Tribute*.[14] She recalls feeling, while experiencing the vision, that she must 'drown' in her complete concentration on it and 'come out on the other side, or rise to the surface after the third time down, not dead to this life but with a new set of values, my treasure dredged from the depth' (p. 54). She remembers herself as then (in 1920) translating the writing to indicate that there would be another war, but that out of it would come a victory both global and personal: 'I, personally (I felt), would be free, I myself would go on in another, a winged dimension' (p. 56). Although this pronouncement might seem to foretell H.D.'s death and rebirth in a spiritual realm, by the time she wrote the *Tribute* in 1944, she had come to understand it to signify that she would be reborn as a prophetic poet-seer:

> Religion, art, and medicine . . . . working together, to form a new vehicle of expression or a new form of thinking or of living, might be symbolized by the tripod, the third of the images on the wall before me, the third of the 'cards'

> I threw down . . . for the benefit of the old Professor. The tripod, we know, was the symbol of prophecy, prophetic utterance or occult or hidden knowledge; the Priestess or Pythoness of Delphi sat on the tripod while she pronounced her verse couplets, the famous Delphic utterances which it was said could be read two ways. (pp. 50–1)

This 'third card', legible to Freud only as 'dangerous symptom', H.D. reads as a message 'from another world' signifying that she must combine Freudian psychoanalysis with her Moravian religious heritage and poetic gifts to achieve a personal victory with collective ramifications. She would use her psychoanalytic abilities to read the universal consciousness in her personal unconscious, together with her developing psychic gift for reading the timeless and the divine in the historically bound and the earthly. Just prior to writing the *Tribute*, she had been working out the autobiographical and historical logic she needed to support that quest in her writing of *The Gift*.[15]

Paradoxically, it was the experience of living through the bombing of London that gave H.D. that sense of rebirth, as she explained at the time in letters to Marianne Moore: 'I am glad you are spared all this, but sorry, too, as our fervor and intensity gives new life to the very bones', and

> every morning is a sort of special gift; a new day to be cherished and loved, a DAY that seems to love back in return . . . life should always have been like that, the wasted days, years! Every new morning is like a return from a bout of fever . . . and strangely I personally, and others who have been able to stick it, seem to feel more alive and physically stronger than for years.[16]

Having experienced during the First World War the sense of what she called 'my own pitiful inefficiency and powerlessness',[17] H.D. finally found with the Second World War what she felt to be her calling as a poet: to divine and impart to others a prophetic spiritual vision that she hoped might help to bring about world peace.

History and heresy in *The Gift*

The Gift can be understood as a turning point in H.D.'s oeuvre: using what she had gleaned during her work with Freud, H.D. here links her personal psychological history with what she understood as the universal spiritual unconscious of humanity in general and women in particular, the trend of most of her late work. Here, for the first time in H.D.'s prose, the gifted poet becomes a medium for the divine in the service of humankind; her poetic gift is viewed as a divine gift to humanity, not as a personal attribute setting the poet apart.

In this postmodern novel that its author termed an 'autobiographical fantasy', H.D. riffs on autobiography and history, blending fact and fantasy in ways that make attempts to distinguish between the two not only difficult, but also misguided.[18] *The Gift* is on one hand a semi-fictional account of key moments (or super-memories) in the artistic, spiritual and psychological development of the gifted child Hilda Wolle Doolittle who will become the poet-seer H.D., and on the other a feminist hermeneutic identifying the Second World War as the inevitable result of a long history of the political domination of the world by religious leaders who continuously ignore and even violently suppress (as heresy) the divinely inspired spiritual insights of gifted artistic prophets or visionaries in their midst. Here, H.D. fictionalises 'memories' from her childhood, completely invents other events (those of Chapters 2 and 5, especially), then skips in the final chapter to the Nazi bombing of London, where the mature poet is readying herself psychologically to fulfil the potential of her gift as the poet-seer. Complex motifs together with historical and biographical fiction-facts provided by the novel's multiple narrators render H.D.'s gifted difference in a familial, religio-historical and global context.

The feminist hermeneutics of *The Gift* revolves around three (fictional) doctrinal concepts of the early Moravian *Unitas Fratrum* or United Brethren: the Promise, the Secret and the Gift. H.D. alludes to these concepts throughout the novel, fleshing them out fully in Chapter 5, 'The Secret', when Hilda's grandmother Mamalie falls into a trance and tells Hilda the story of her and her first husband's discovery and mystical translation of original documents recording an early Moravian Brethren ceremony. Through the relation of this story, both the child and the reader learn of the peace-loving, syncretist tenets of the early *Unitas Fratrum* and their violent suppression by the patriarchs of the canonical Moravian Church, who deemed such beliefs heretical.

Mamalie's story – again, an invention of H.D.'s – begins with the 'Promise', a pact made between a syncretist God, the Moravian Brethren, and the Shawanese people on Wunden Eiland in the mid 1700s.[19] In a ceremony presided over by the Shawanese chief Paxnous and the Moravian Cammerhof, Mamalie tells Hilda, the Brethren promised to recognise spiritual truths that unify all religions as one religion, all gods as one God, and to work together with the Shawanese to bring this understanding of one harmonious religio-spiritual unity to the world at large. That God, in exchange, agreed to bring peace to the world. From a Christian viewpoint, it was heresy to imagine that the Judaeo-Christian God was also the Great Spirit of the Shawanese and other Native American peoples. That Promise was broken a few years later when the Brethren and the Shawanese initiates were massacred at

Gnadenhuetten – a massacre instigated by the Moravian patriarchs and executed by an unfriendly tribe of Native Americans who were incensed against the Shawanese for their peaceful collaboration with the white intruders. Following the massacre and burning of Gnadenhuetten, all that was left to document the Promise ceremony on Wunden Eiland was a box of documents written in a lost runic language – half language, half music – that Mamalie tells Hilda she and her first husband found and deciphered, but that were subsequently lost in a fire. In relaying the story to Hilda, Mamalie passes to the child the responsibility of restoring the Promise.

A second heresy inheres in the concept of the 'Secret', the mystic Moravian Count Zinzendorf's belief that God, in the form of the Holy Spirit, is always with us, literally, physically, as the female *Spiritus Sanctus*: 'an eternal creative feminine spirit continually manifesting as the living bearer of peace to the world' (Augustine 1998, p. 1). The Moravian 'Gift', then, is the divine gift of that manifestation in a particular individual of either sex. The gift can take any artistic form, but the purpose and responsibility of gifted individuals is to help to fulfil the Promise. Both the understanding of the gifted artist as the literal human bearer of the Holy Spirit and the understanding of the Holy Spirit as female and equal to God the Father are heretical in canonical Christian doctrine.

In *The Gift*, it becomes clear that not only is the child Hilda's uncle Fred, a musician, gifted in the Moravian sense, but so was her grandmother and her mother, though both abandoned their gifts as young women when discouraged by male family members; and though Hilda's mother cannot perceive her daughter's gift because of her own unwillingness to embrace the uncontrollable passion that seems to accompany the gift – because, more precisely, of her acceptance of the more puritanical strain in Moravianism that came with the forceful (and fictional) suppression of the early *Unitas Fratrum* – Hilda has inherited her mother and grandmother's gifts: 'I seemed to have inherited that. I was the inheritor' (H.D., *Gift*, p. 37). For Hilda, that gift is both a personal promise enabling the fulfilment of H.D.'s individual spiritual/artistic gift and a hope for the fulfilment of a divine promise of eventual world peace and spiritual unity for all – the Promise originally (and, again, fictionally) imparted on Wunden Eiland to the early Moravians of H.D.'s matrilineal heritage.

Being born in Bethlehem might cause one to imagine one might be Christ-like in some way, and the child Hilda considers that possibility quite early in life. Not only is her birthplace repeatedly stressed by the child, but she also relays in the second chapter, 'Fortune Teller', the story of the prediction of her own birth by a fortune teller her mother visits before her marriage – a prediction that 'the Gift would come to a child who would be born under a

Star' (H.D., *Gift*, p. 79). Hilda's mother, Helen, dismisses the notion that she might bear a gifted child, just as she previously dismissed her own early hopes that she herself might be gifted and gave up singing when her father discouraged her. To consider that the prediction might be true, Helen reasons, would be 'superstitious, irreligious', and yet she feels that

> there was some sort of hidden meaning in all this . . . This woman belonged to the superstitions and magic of the old Indian legends. She belonged, did she, to the old, old wisdom, that had led the very Magi to a star? Star? That is what she had said, there was a black patch, a rose, there was a star. (p. 77)

But all children are born under a star, reasons Helen later, 'Hadn't Bishop Leibert said at little Fred's christening . . . that every child was born under the Star of our Redemption' (p. 79); so Helen continues at once dismissing and encouraging by relaying the prediction to her children throughout their lives: '"It's funny, the fortune-teller told me, I would have a child who was in some way especially gifted." It was that that stuck. We were not any of us "gifted", as if we had failed them somehow' (p. 51). The reader is meant to perceive that Helen is wrong; that, like Christ's own, Hilda's gifted difference is not recognised among her own people.

Throughout the novel, Hilda's gifted difference is repeatedly juxtaposed to rationality and literal-mindedness and causally connected to her ability to lose herself in art, in family stories, in words themselves, and in the products of her own imagination. In the third chapter, the reader witnesses Hilda's deep emotional loss when she finds her mother has given away her copy of Grimm's fairy tales, a book Helen believes to be too morbid for a child, but which Hilda found darkly beautiful and with which she strongly identified:

> There was the princess with the brothers, she had long hair and lilies in her arms, there were ravens and the little hut in the forest. All that had been given away – it was not possible – you can not give away yourself with a star on your forehead and your brothers flying over a tower above a forest and a hut in the woods. (H.D., *Gift*, p. 101)

The child's conflation of her self and her experiences with the princess and her story exemplifies the narrative technique of the novel as a whole, which elides differences between autobiographical and imagined selves, and between factual and fictional histories in an attempt to access the universal consciousness H.D. believed was inherent in myths and fairy tales. Examples of Hilda's ability to perceive differently, artistically, abound throughout the novel, so by the time Hilda encourages her grandmother Mamalie's trance in order to glean the story of the early Moravian pact with the Shawanese at Wunden Eiland, the reader is prepared to understand her as the inheritor of the Gift in her family, the one to whom Mamalie must relay the story of the Secret and the Promise so that Hilda might 'do the work' and 'follow the music' to fulfil the divine Promise (p. 172). Hilda's early willingness to embrace and explore the dark passages of history – the forbidden, the perverse, the heretical – enables the development of her gift over time.

Hilda's childhood fears of fire and a shooting star foretell the adult poet H.D.'s very legitimate fear of a bomb falling on the house in London in the final chapter, and because the narrative intermittently flashes ahead to that time, the reader is well aware of the symbolic nature of this childhood fear when it is first expressed. This symbol is associated with Hilda's father's and brother's astrological assurances that a shooting star cannot possibly fall on the house in Pennsylvania; such scientific assurances are repeatedly held up to the reader as the empty and unconvincing masculinist bravado representing the anti-spiritual, individualistic scientific modernity that, H.D. implies, necessarily culminates in war. Against such scientific-mindedness, H.D. asserts in this novel the intuitive 'dark' knowledge of the gifted child Hilda, poet-seer to be, with her Moravian maternal background of religious syncretism, and her endowment with the feminine *Spiritus Sanctus*.[20]

In the final chapter, the falling bombs – the fact of violence, terror and war – force these fictionalised memories to surface, providing the adult poet hope, meaning for her life, and a purpose for her poetry at a time when others find optimism impossible and claims for the poet irrational. Paradoxically, in *The Gift* the Nazi bombings initiate the possibility of a redemption at once personal, global and historical, all enabled through the spiritual mediation of the gifted female poet-seer endowed with the *Spiritus Sanctus*. Such a poet must be able to access the 'inner sanctum' of her gifted psyche, and H.D. believed that the combination of her psychoanalysis with Freud and the catharsis that the Second World War occasioned for her enabled her full access to her visionary and prophetic gift as poet-seer. Thus, she finally realises, as the bombs fall around her in London, that her poetic gift is also the divine spiritual Gift of her Moravian ancestors: 'Now it was perfectly clear that I had been conditioned, as it were, to something of this sort' (H.D., *Gift*, p. 213).[21]

Early in *Tribute*, H.D. writes of Freud, 'there was an argument implicit in our very bones' (p. 13). This 'argument' pits scientist against poet, atheism against spirituality, rationalism against mysticism, secularism against religion – even, one might say, modernity against romanticism. The reading of history H.D. performs in *The Gift* – a religio-historical hermeneutic that endows her with the Moravian *Spiritus Sanctus* that renders her poetry divinely inspired – is not one Freud could endorse, especially at the time he was working with H.D., as the Nazis were taking power in Vienna and asserting the divine supremacy of the Aryan race as an argument to justify the worst atrocities. H.D. had peaceful altruistic intentions behind her mediation of Romantic transcendentalist notions of the divine inspiration of the poet-seer. H.D.'s work aims to reclaim the role of women in history – especially in religious history – and to forge power for women in matters religious and spiritual specifically for the purposes of achieving lasting peace. Her work takes its place within its socio-historical contexts – as part of first-wave feminism in the western tradition, as part of women's religious history, and as consistent with the early twentieth-century interest in spiritualism and in the possibilities for peace implicit in various religious teachings. Nevertheless, claims to speak with and for a supreme being flirt dangerously with megalomaniacal authority, and invite careful critical assessment. This, too, is part of reading history in H.D.'s late work.

NOTES

1 H.D., *Tribute to Freud* (New York: New Directions, [1972] 1974), p. 23.

2 Although H.D.'s understanding of the 'universal consciousness' appears similar to Jung's theory of the 'collective unconscious', as late as 1955 H.D. claimed not to have read much of Jung's work. See S.S. Friedman, *Psyche Reborn: The Emergence of H.D.* (Bloomington: Indiana University Press, 1981), p. 192. John Walsh persuasively argues that what retrospectively appears Jungian in H.D.'s work is the result of her having read many of the same sources that Jung read ('H.D., C.G. Jung & Küsnacht: Fantasia on a Theme' in Michael King (ed.), *H.D.: Woman and Poet* (Orono, ME: National Poetry Foundation, 1986), pp. 59–66).

3 These include *The Gift*, *Trilogy*, *Majic Ring*, *Tribute to Freud*, *By Avon River*, *The Sword Went Out to Sea*, *White Rose and the Red*, *H.D. by Delia Alton*, *The Mystery*, *Helen in Egypt*, *Magic Mirror*, *Bid Me to Live*, *End to Torment*, and numerous shorter works.

4 On what Merrill Cole calls 'the insistence on multiple meanings that Freud and H.D. share' (95), see 'Symptom or Inspiration? H.D., Freud, and the Question of Vision', *Journal for Cultural and Religious Theory*, 10.2 (Spring 2010), 83–98.

5 On her narrative disruption of chronological history, H.D. comments: 'I do not want to become involved in the strictly historical sequence. I wish to recall the impressions, or rather I wish the impressions to recall me. Let the impressions come in their own way, make their own sequence' (H.D., *Tribute*, p. 14).

6 As Adalaide Morris points out, H.D.'s technique 'sets off alarms for a reader schooled in post-colonial theory', since it 'conflates individual and cultural memory', obscuring important socio-historical and personal differences. For its time, though, H.D.'s approach was an innovative literary use of accepted contemporary scholarship in the social sciences: 'this swift transit from the personal to the universal was a familiar habit in early twentieth-century

archaeology, anthropology, ethnology and psychology. The work of Sir James Frazer, Jane Harrison and the Cambridge Ritualists, Mauss, Durkheim, Freud and Jung relied on the assumption of correspondences across cultures that enabled H.D. and others to imagine autobiography as a kind of research into culture' (*How to Live/What to Do: H.D.'s Cultural Poetics* (Urbana: University of Illinois Press, 2003), p. 139).

7 Cassandra Laity demonstrates how H.D. adapted late Romantic (or Victorian) Decadent Aesthetic subversive tropes of the powerful femme fatale and the homoerotic male androgyne/aesthete, especially in her poetry. See *H.D. and the Victorian Fin de Siècle: Gender, Modernism, Decadence* (Cambridge and New York: Cambridge University Press, 1996).

8 See N. Holmes Pearson's foreword to *Trilogy* (New York: New Directions, 1973), pp. v–xii.

9 H.D.'s letters during and about her psychoanalysis with Freud are in S.S. Friedman's *Analyzing Freud: The Letters of H.D., Bryher, and Their Circle* (New York: New Directions, 2002).

10 H.D. also explores her ambivalence about Freud's insights in her 1935 poem, 'The Master' (L.L. Martz (ed.), *Collected Poems 1912–1944* (New York: New Directions, 1983), pp. 451–61).

11 See also H.D.'s theorisation in *The Gift* of the creative role of the 'dream, the memory, the unexpected related memories' that make up the 'province of the fourth-dimensional', the sudden emergence into consciousness of which might signify either 'madness' or 'inspiration' (pp. 83–4).

12 In her later novels *The Sword Went Out to Sea* and *Majic Ring*, which H.D. always insisted were actually written by her psychic medium, Delia Alton, she fictionalised her supernatural experiences with spiritualism and occultism: psychic readings, table-tipping, seances, visionary experiences, communications with spirit guides and dead RAF pilots.

13 For a detailed analysis of H.D.'s mediations of Freudian theory, see D. Chisholm, *H.D.'s Freudian Poetics: Psychoanalysis in Translation* (Ithaca, NY: Cornell University Press, 1992).

14 See sections 32 to 41 of the first part of *Tribute to Freud*, 'Writing on the Wall', pp. 44–56.

15 H.D. wrote *The Gift* in 1941–4. She wrote most of *Tribute to Freud* in November of 1944, using notes she had written in Vienna during the analysis in 1933 and 1934.

16 'Letters from H.D. to Marianne Moore, the first undated but probably written in June 1940, the second dated 24 September 1941, the Rosenbach Foundation' (Zilboorg 1992, p. 250). The letters are quoted in C. Zilboorg (ed.), *Richard Aldington and H.D.: Their Lives in Letters, 1918–61* (Manchester University Press, 2003), p. 249, n. 11.

17 H.D. to John Cournos, Letter of 14 September 1916, cited in D. Krolik Hollenberg, 'Art and Ardor in World War One: Selected Letters from H.D. to John Cournos', *The Iowa Review: H.D. Centennial Issue*, 16.3 (Fall 1986), 126–55 (138).

18 H.D., *H.D. by Delia Alton, The Iowa Review: H.D. Centennial Issue*, 16.3 (Autumn 1986), 180–221 (189). For an interpretation of 'H.D.'s autobiographical fantasy as a critical and occult supplement to Freud's *Autobiographical Study*', see Chisholm *H.D., Freudian Poetics*, pp. 68–120. For a constructive

discussion of *The Gift*'s 'mixed genre' (p. 3), see Augustine's introduction in J. Augustine (ed.), *The Gift by H.D., The Complete Text* (Gainesville: University Press of Florida, 1998), pp. 1–28. All further references to *The Gift* will be to this edition.

19 For a careful consideration of the historical accuracy of H.D.'s historical narrative of the relations between the eighteenth-century Moravian settlers of Pennsylvania and the Shawanese, see Augustine's introduction to *The Gift* and her notes to H.D.'s notes, pp. 1–28, 279–88. See also C. Gavaler, '"I Mend A Break in Time": An Historical Reconstruction of H.D.'s Wunden Eiland Ceremony in *The Gift* and *Trilogy*', *Sagetrieb*, 15.1–2 (1996), 94–120.

20 In *Tribute to Freud*, H.D. understands herself as combining her two heritages through psychoanalysis: 'I am on the fringes or in the penumbra of the light of my father's science and my mother's art – the psychology or philosophy of Sigmund Freud' (p. 145).

21 In *Tribute to Freud*, too, H.D. repeatedly attributes her gift or vision to her maternal ancestry: 'Obviously, this is my inheritance. I derive my imaginative faculties through my musician-artist mother, through her part-Celtic mother, through the grandfather of English and middle-European extraction' (p. 121).

FURTHER READING

Primary works

Doolittle, Hilda. *Asphodel*. Edited with an introduction by Robert Spoo. New York: New Directions, 1992.

Bid Me to Live (A Madrigal). New York: Grove Press, 1960.

By Avon River. New York: The Macmillan Company, 1949.

Collected Poems 1912–1944, edited by Louis Martz. New York: New Directions, 1983.

End to Torment: A Memoir of Ezra Pound. New York: New Directions, 1979.

The Gift, edited and annotated by Jane Augustine. Gainesville: University Press of Florida, 1998.

'H.D. by Delia Alton', edited by Adalaide Morris, in *Iowa Review* 16, no. 3 (1986): 174–221.

The Hedgehog. New York: New Directions, 1988.

Hedylus. Redding Ridge, Connecticut: Black Swann Books, 1986.

Helen in Egypt. New York: New Directions, 1974.

Hermetic Definition. New York: New Directions, 1972.

HERmione. New York: New Directions, 1981.

Hirslanden Notebooks. MS. H.D. Papers. Beinecke Library, Yale University, New Haven Connecticut, Box 43, Folders 1106–9.

Hippolytus Temporizes and Ion, with an introduction by Carol Camper. New York: New Directions, 2003.

Kora and Ka and Ka with Mira-Male, with an Introduction by Robert Spoo. New York: New Directions, 1996.

Majic Ring, edited with an introduction by Demetres P. Tryphonopoulos. Gainesville: University Press of Florida, 2009.

The Mystery, edited with an introduction by Jane Augustine. Gainesville: University Press of Florida, 2009.

Nights by H.D. [John Helforth], with an introduction by Perdita Schaffner. New York: New Directions, 1986.

Notes on Thought and Vision. San Francisco: City Lights Books, 1982.

Paint It Today, edited with an introduction by Cassandra Laity. New York and London: New York University Press, 1992.

Palimpsest. Carbondale: Southern Illinois University Press, 1968.

Pilate's Wife, with an introduction by Joan A. Burke. New York: New Directions, 2000.
'Sagesse', in *Hermetic Definition*, pp. 57–84.
Sea Garden, London: Constable & Co., 1916.
Selected Poems of H.D., edited by Norman Pearson. New York: Grove Press, 1957.
The Sword Went Out to Sea. By Delia Alton, edited with an introduction by Cynthia Hogue and Julie Vandivere. Gainesville: University Press of Florida, 2007.
Tribute to Freud. New York: New Directions, 1972.
Trilogy, annotated by Aliki Barnstone. New York: New Directions, 1998.
Trilogy, edited with an introduction by Norman Holmes Pearson. Manchester: Carcanet, 1997.
White Rose and the Red, edited with an introduction by Alison Halsall. Gainesville: University Press of Florida, 2009.
'Winter Love', in *Hermetic Definition*, pp. 85–117.

Secondary works

Anderson Linda and Trev. L. Broughton. *Women's Lives/Women's Times: New Essays on Auto/Biography*. Albany: State University of New York, 1997.
Bloom, Harold (ed.) *H.D. Bloom's Major Poets Series*. Broomall, Penn.: Chelsea House Publishers, 2002.
Bornstein, George. *Material Modernism: The Politics of the Page*. Cambridge University Press, 2006.
Boughn, Michael. *H.D.: A Bibliography, 1905–1990*. Charlottesville, VA: University Press of Virginia, 1993.
Bryher. *The Heart to Artemis*. Ashfield, MA.: Paris Press, 2006.
Buck, Claire. *H.D. and Freud: Bisexuality and a Feminine Discourse*. Hemel Hampstead: Harvester Wheatsheaf, 1991.
Camboni, Marina (ed.) *H.D.'s Poetry: The Meanings that Words Hide*. New York: AMS Press, 2003.
Castle, Terry. *The Apparitional Lesbian: Female Homosexuality and Modern Culture*. New York: Columbia University Press, 1993.
Chisholm, Diane. *H.D.'s Freudian Poetics: Psychoanalysis in Translation*. Ithaca, NY: Cornell University Press, 1992.
Christodoulides, Nephie, J. 'Triangulation of Desire in H.D.'s Hymen', in C.C. Barfoot (ed.), *And Never Know the Joy: Sex and the Erotic in English Poetry*. Amsterdam and New York: Rodopi, 2006.
Collecott, Diana. *H.D. and Sapphic Modernism 1910–1950*. Cambridge University Press, 1999.
Connor, Rachel. *H.D. and the Image*. Manchester and New York: Manchester University Press, 2004.
Curry, Renée R. *White Women Writing White. H.D., Elizabeth Bishop, Sylvia Plath, and Whiteness*. Westport, Conn: Greenwood Press, 2000.
Dekoven, Marianne. 'Modernism and Gender', in *The Cambridge Companion to Modernism*, edited with an introduction by Michael Levenson. Cambridge University Press, 1999.
DuPlessis, Rachel Blau. *H.D.: The Career of That Struggle*. Brighton: Harvester Press, 1986.

Writing Beyond the Ending: Narrative Strategies of Twentieth-century Women Writers. Bloomington: Indiana University Press, 1985.

Edmunds, Susan. *Out of Line: History, Psychoanalysis, & Montage in H.D.'s Long Poems*. Stanford University Press, 1994.

Ellis, Havelock. *Sexual Inversion. Studies in the Psychology of Sex*, 3rd edn, Philadelphia: F.A. Davis, 1915.

Friedman, Susan Stanford (ed.) *Analyzing Freud. The Letters of H.D., Bryher, and Their Circle*. New York: New Directions, 2002.

'"I Go Where I Love": An Intertextual Study of H.D. and Adrienne Rich'. *Signs: Journal of Women in Culture and Society*, 9.2 (1983), 228–45.

Mappings: Feminism and the Cultural Geographies of Encounter. Princeton University Press, 1998.

Penelope's Web: Gender, Modernity, H.D.'s Fiction. Cambridge and New York: Cambridge University Press, 1990.

Psyche Reborn: The Emergence of H.D. Bloomington: Indiana University Press, 1981.

'Women's Autobiographical Selves: Theory and Practice', in Sidonie Smith and Janet Watson (eds.), *Women, Autobiography, Theory: A Reader*. Madison: University of Wisconsin Press, 1998.

Friedman, Susan Stanford, and Rachel Blau DuPlessis (eds.) *Signets: Reading H.D.* Madison: University of Wisconsin Press, 1990.

Freud, Sigmund. 'The Psychogenesis of a Case of Homosexuality' in J. Stratchey (ed. and trans.), *Case Histories II*. London: Penguin Books, 1979.

An Outline of Psychoanalysis. London: Penguin Books, 2003.

Gill, Jo. *Women's Poetry*. Edinburgh University Press, 2007.

Gregory, Eileen. *H.D. and Hellenism: Classic Lines*. Cambridge and New York: Cambridge University Press, 1997.

Grosskurth, Phyllis. *Havelock Ellis: A Biography*. New York: Alfred A. Knopf, 1980.

Gubar, Susan. 'The Echoing Spell of H.D.'s *Trilogy*', in S.M. Gilbert and S. Gubar (eds.), *Shakespeare's Sisters: Feminist Essays on Women Poets*. Bloomington: Indiana University Press, 1979.

Guest, Barbara. *Herself Defined: The Poet H.D. and Her World*. New York: Doubleday, 1984.

Hanscombe Gillian and Virginia L. Smyers. *Writing for Their Lives: The Modernist Women 1910–1940*. Boston: Northeastern University Press, 1987.

Hickman Miranda, B. *The Geometry of Modernism. The Vorticist Idiom in Lewis, Pound, H.D. and Yeats*. Austin: University of Texas Press, 2005.

Hollenberg, Donna Krolik (ed.) *Between History and Poetry: The Letters of H.D. and Norman Holmes Pearson*. University of Iowa Press, 1997.

H.D. and Poets After. University of Iowa Press, 2000.

Johnston, Georgia. *The Formation of 20th Century Queer Autobiography. Reading Vita Sackville-West, Virginia Woolf, Hilda Doolittle, and Gertrude Stein*. London and New York: Palgrave Macmillan, 2007.

Jung, C. G. *Psychology and Alchemy*. Translated by R.F.C. Hull. London: Routledge, 1993.

King, Michael (ed.) *H.D. Woman and Poet*. Orono: The National Poetry Foundation, 1986.

Korg, Jacob. *Winter Love*. Madison: University of Wisconsin Press, 2003.
Kristeva Julia. *Powers of Horror*, translated by Leon S. Roudiez. Columbia University Press, 1982.
Black Sun, translated by Leon S. Roudiez. New York: Columbia University Press, 1987.
Tales of Love, translated by Leon S. Roudiez. Columbia University Press, 1983.
Laity, Cassandra. *H.D. and the Victorian Fin de Siècle: Gender, Modernism, Decadence*. Cambridge and New York: Cambridge University Press, 1996.
Marcus, Laura. *The Tenth Muse: Writing about the Cinema and the Modernist Period*. Oxford University Press, 2007.
Materer, Timothy. *Modernist Alchemy: Poetry and the Occult*. Ithaca and London: Cornell University Press, 1999.
Milner, Marion. *On Not Being Able to Paint*, with an introduction by Anna Freud. Los Angeles: J.P. Tarcher, Inc., 1957.
Montefiore, Jan. *Feminism and Poetry: Language, Experience, Identity in Women's Writing*. London: Pandora, 2004.
Morris, Adalaide. *How to Live/What to Do: H.D.'s Cultural Poetics*. Urbana: University of Illinois Press, 2003.
Plath, Sylvia. *Collected Poems*. Edited by Ted Hughes. London: Faber & Faber, 1989.
Rainey, Lawrence. *Institutions of Modernism: Literary Elites and Public Culture*. New Haven: Yale University Press, 1998.
'Canon, Gender, and Text: The Case of H.D.', in G. Bornstein (ed.), *Representing Modernist Texts: Editing as Interpretation*. Ann Arbor: University of Michigan Press, 1991.
Robinson, Janice. *H.D. The Life and Work of an American Poet*. Boston: Houghton Mifflin Company, 1982.
Scott, Bonnie Kime and Mary Lynn Broe (eds.) *The Gender of Modernism: A Critical Anthology*. Bloomington: Indiana University Press, 1990.
Seward, Barbara. *The Symbolic Rose*. New York: Columbia University Press, 1960.
Sword, Helen. *Engendering Inspiration: Visionary Strategies in Rilke, Lawrence and H.D.* Ann Arbor: University of Michigan Press, 1995.
Ghostwriting Modernism. Ithaca, NY and London: Cornell University Press, 2002.
Taylor, Georgina. *H.D. and the Public Sphere of Modernist Women Writers 1913–1946. Talking Women*. Oxford University Press, 2001.
Tryphonopoulos, Demetres P. 'Introduction' to *Literary Modernism and the Occult Tradition*, edited by Leon Surette and Demetres P. Tryphonopoulos, Orono, Maine: National Poetry Foundation, 1996, pp. 19–49.
Zilboorg, Caroline (ed.) *Richard Aldington and H.D.: The Later Years in Letters*. Manchester, England, and New York: Manchester University Press, 1992.

INDEX

Cambridge Companions to. . .

AUTHORS

Edward Albee edited by Stephen J. Bottoms

Margaret Atwood edited by Coral Ann Howells

W.H. Auden edited by Stan Smith

Jane Austen edited by Edward Copeland and Juliet McMaster (*second edition*)

Beckett edited by John Pilling

Bede edited by Scott DeGregorio

Aphra Behn edited by Derek Hughes and Janet Todd

Walter Benjamin edited by David S. Ferris

William Blake edited by Morris Eaves

Brecht edited by Peter Thomson and Glendyr Sacks (*second edition*)

The Brontës edited by Heather Glen

Bunyan edited by Anne Dunan-Page

Frances Burney edited by Peter Sabor

Byron edited by Drummond Bone

Albert Camus edited by Edward J. Hughes

Willa Cather edited by Marilee Lindemann

Cervantes edited by Anthony J. Cascardi

Chaucer edited by Piero Boitani and Jill Mann (*second edition*)

Chekhov edited by Vera Gottlieb and Paul Allain

Kate Chopin edited by Janet Beer

Caryl Churchill edited by Elaine Aston and Elin Diamond

Coleridge edited by Lucy Newlyn

Wilkie Collins edited by Jenny Bourne Taylor

Joseph Conrad edited by J.H. Stape

H.D. edited by Nephie J. Christodoulides and Polina Mackay

Dante edited by Rachel Jacoff (*second edition*)

Daniel Defoe edited by John Richetti

Don DeLillo edited by John N. Duvall

Charles Dickens edited by John O. Jordan

Emily Dickinson edited by Wendy Martin

John Donne edited by Achsah Guibbory

Dostoevskii edited by W.J. Leatherbarrow

Theodore Dreiser edited by Leonard Cassuto and Claire Virginia Eby

John Dryden edited by Steven N. Zwicker

W.E.B. Du Bois edited by Shamoon Zamir

George Eliot edited by George Levine

T.S. Eliot edited by A. David Moody

Ralph Ellison edited by Ross Posnock

Ralph Waldo Emerson edited by Joel Porte and Saundra Morris

William Faulkner edited by Philip M. Weinstein

Henry Fielding edited by Claude Rawson

F. Scott Fitzgerald edited by Ruth Prigozy

Flaubert edited by Timothy Unwin

E.M. Forster edited by David Bradshaw

Benjamin Franklin edited by Carla Mulford

Brian Friel edited by Anthony Roche

Robert Frost edited by Robert Faggen

Gabriel García Márquez edited by Philip Swanson

Elizabeth Gaskell edited by Jill L. Matus

Goethe edited by Lesley Sharpe

Günter Grass edited by Stuart Taberner

Thomas Hardy edited by Dale Kramer

David Hare edited by Richard Boon

Nathaniel Hawthorne edited by Richard Millington

Seamus Heaney edited by Bernard O'Donoghue

Ernest Hemingway edited by Scott Donaldson

Homer edited by Robert Fowler

Horace edited by Stephen Harrison

Ted Hughes edited by Terry Gifford

Ibsen edited by James McFarlane

Henry James edited by Jonathan Freedman

Samuel Johnson edited by Greg Clingham

Ben Jonson edited by Richard Harp and Stanley Stewart

James Joyce edited by Derek Attridge (*second edition*)

Kafka edited by Julian Preece

Keats edited by Susan J. Wolfson

Rudyard Kipling edited by Howard J. Booth

Lacan edited by Jean-Michel Rabaté

D.H. Lawrence edited by Anne Fernihough

Primo Levi edited by Robert Gordon

Lucretius edited by Stuart Gillespie and Philip Hardie

Machiavelli edited by John M. Najemy

David Mamet edited by Christopher Bigsby

Thomas Mann edited by Ritchie Robertson

Christopher Marlowe edited by Patrick Cheney

Andrew Marvell edited by Derek Hirst and Steven N. Zwicker

Herman Melville edited by Robert S. Levine

Arthur Miller edited by Christopher Bigsby (*second edition*)

Milton edited by Dennis Danielson (*second edition*)

Molière edited by David Bradby and Andrew Calder

Toni Morrison edited by Justine Tally

Nabokov edited by Julian W. Connolly

Eugene O'Neill edited by Michael Manheim

George Orwell edited by John Rodden

Ovid edited by Philip Hardie

Harold Pinter edited by Peter Raby (*second edition*)

Sylvia Plath edited by Jo Gill

Edgar Allan Poe edited by Kevin J. Hayes

Alexander Pope edited by Pat Rogers

Ezra Pound edited by Ira B. Nadel

Proust edited by Richard Bales

Pushkin edited by Andrew Kahn

Rabelais edited by John O'Brien

Rilke edited by Karen Leeder and Robert Vilain

Philip Roth edited by Timothy Parrish

Salman Rushdie edited by Abdulrazak Gurnah

Shakespeare edited by Margareta de Grazia and Stanley Wells (*second edition*)

Shakespearean Comedy edited by Alexander Leggatt

Shakespeare on Film edited by Russell Jackson (*second edition*)

Shakespeare's History Plays edited by Michael Hattaway

Shakespeare's Last Plays edited by Catherine M.S. Alexander

Shakespeare's Poetry edited by Patrick Cheney

Shakespeare and Popular Culture edited by Robert Shaughnessy

Shakespeare on Stage edited by Stanley Wells and Sarah Stanton

Shakespearean Tragedy edited by Claire McEachern

George Bernard Shaw edited by Christopher Innes

Shelley edited by Timothy Morton

Mary Shelley edited by Esther Schor

Sam Shepard edited by Matthew C. Roudané

Spenser edited by Andrew Hadfield

Laurence Sterne edited by Thomas Keymer

Wallace Stevens edited by John N. Serio

Tom Stoppard edited by Katherine E. Kelly

Harriet Beecher Stowe edited by Cindy Weinstein

August Strindberg edited by Michael Robinson

Jonathan Swift edited by Christopher Fox

J.M. Synge edited by P.J. Mathews

Tacitus edited by A.J. Woodman

Henry David Thoreau edited by Joel Myerson

Tolstoy edited by Donna Tussing Orwin

Anthony Trollope edited by Carolyn Dever and Lisa Niles

Mark Twain edited by Forrest G. Robinson

John Updike edited by Stacey Olster

Virgil edited by Charles Martindale

Voltaire edited by Nicholas Cronk

Edith Wharton edited by Millicent Bell

Walt Whitman edited by Ezra Greenspan

Oscar Wilde edited by Peter Raby

Tennessee Williams edited by Matthew C. Roudané

August Wilson edited by Christopher Bigsby

Mary Wollstonecraft edited by Claudia L. Johnson

Virginia Woolf edited by Susan Sellers (*second edition*)

Wordsworth edited by Stephen Gill

W.B. Yeats edited by Marjorie Howes and John Kelly

Zola edited by Brian Nelson

TOPICS

The Actress edited by Maggie B. Gale and John Stokes

The African American Novel edited by Maryemma Graham

The African American Slave Narrative edited by Audrey A. Fisch

Allegory edited by Rita Copeland and Peter Struck

American Crime Fiction edited by Catherine Ross Nickerson

American Modernism edited by Walter Kalaidjian

American Realism and Naturalism edited by Donald Pizer

American Travel Writing edited by Alfred Bendixen and Judith Hamera

American Women Playwrights edited by Brenda Murphy

Ancient Rhetoric edited by Erik Gunderson

Arthurian Legend edited by Elizabeth Archibald and Ad Putter

Australian Literature edited by Elizabeth Webby

British Literature of the French Revolution edited by Pamela Clemit

British Romanticism edited by Stuart Curran (*second edition*)

British Romantic Poetry edited by James Chandler and Maureen N. McLane

British Theatre, 1730–1830, edited by Jane Moody and Daniel O'Quinn

Canadian Literature edited by Eva-Marie Kröller

Children's Literature edited by M.O. Grenby and Andrea Immel

The Classic Russian Novel edited by Malcolm V. Jones and Robin Feuer Miller

Contemporary Irish Poetry edited by Matthew Campbell

Crime Fiction edited by Martin Priestman

Early Modern Women's Writing edited by Laura Lunger Knoppers

The Eighteenth-century Novel edited by John Richetti

Eighteenth-century Poetry edited by John Sitter

English Literature, 1500–1600 edited by Arthur F. Kinney

English Literature, 1650–1740 edited by Steven N. Zwicker

English Literature, 1740–1830 edited by Thomas Keymer and Jon Mee

English Literature, 1830–1914 edited by Joanne Shattock

English Novelists edited by Adrian Poole

English Poetry, Donne to Marvell edited by Thomas N. Corns

English Poets edited by Claude Rawson

English Renaissance Drama, second edition edited by A.R. Braunmuller and Michael Hattaway

English Renaissance Tragedy edited by Emma Smith and Garrett A. Sullivan Jr.

English Restoration Theatre edited by Deborah C. Payne Fisk

The Epic edited by Catherine Bates

European Modernism edited by Pericles Lewis

Fantasy Literature edited by Edward James and Farah Mendlesohn

Feminist Literary Theory edited by Ellen Rooney

Fiction in the Romantic Period edited by Richard Maxwell and Katie Trumpener

The Fin de Siècle edited by Gail Marshall

The French Novel: from 1800 to the Present edited by Timothy Unwin

Gay and Lesbian Writing edited by Hugh Stevens

German Romanticism edited by Nicholas Saul

Gothic Fiction edited by Jerrold E. Hogle

The Greek and Roman Novel edited by Tim Whitmarsh

Greek and Roman Theatre edited by Marianne McDonald and J. Michael Walton

Greek Lyric edited by Felix Budelmann

Greek Mythology edited by Roger D. Woodard

Greek Tragedy edited by P.E. Easterling

The Harlem Renaissance edited by George Hutchinson

The Irish Novel edited by John Wilson Foster

The Italian Novel edited by Peter Bondanella and Andrea Ciccarelli

Jewish American Literature edited by Hana Wirth-Nesher and Michael P. Kramer

The Latin American Novel edited by Efraín Kristal

The Literature of London edited by Lawrence Manley

The Literature of Los Angeles edited by Kevin R. McNamara

The Literature of New York edited by Cyrus Patell and Bryan Waterman

The Literature of the First World War edited by Vincent Sherry

The Literature of World War II edited by Marina MacKay

Literature on Screen edited by Deborah Cartmell and Imelda Whelehan

Medieval English Culture edited by Andrew Galloway

Medieval English Literature edited by Larry Scanlon

Medieval English Mysticism edited by Samuel Fanous and Vincent Gillespie